MW00694729

Lorelou Desjardins

# A FROG IN THE FJORD

## ONE YEAR IN NORWAY

NORTH**PRESS**

© North Press 2022

ISBN: 978-82-303-4919-9

3rd edition 2022

Book cover illustration: Rejenne Pavon
Layout and copy editing: Ionuț Burchi
Author portrait picture: Anna-Julia Grandberg, Blunderbuss
Section Illustrations: Freepik.com

Author's blog: www.afroginthefjord.com

This book is a work of non-fiction based on the experiences and recollections of the author. Except for the author, all names of people and identifying details have been changed to protect the privacy of others.

www.northpress.no

*To my grandmother Arlette,*
*whose love brought me all the way to Norway*

# CONTENTS

## SUMMER

## FALL AND WINTER AGAIN

# PREFACE

Over the years, I have met many people who dream of discovering Norway. Some are from the United States, with their Norwegian names telling of their ancestry. They often carry pieces of Norwegian culture and language with them, 150 years after their family crossed the Atlantic Ocean. They dream of this land they have heard about but never set foot on.

Others are foreigners from Europe and beyond. They have seen pictures of the breathtaking Norwegian nature. The fjords, the northern lights or the Lofoten Islands make them want to travel here, if not move to Norway. When so many of us are caught up in our busy city lives, those pictures of red wooden huts by a lake, surrounded by snowy forests are just too hard to resist. Why can't I live there just for a few years and take a break from everything? Wouldn't my life be so much better?

United Nations reports and media articles show, year

after year, that Norway has the happiest people in the world. High standard of living, low unemployment rate, high gender equality. Best country to be a mother. Recently the trend of so-called Scandi-living concepts, IKEA-sounding names like *hygge*, *friluftsliv*, and *lagom* have come to international fame. According to newspapers and glossy magazines, Scandinavians have all the tools we need to survive everything from winter depression to a pandemic. It seems too good to be true. Is Norway as beautiful as the travel magazines say, and as wonderful a society as the United Nations reports write?

This book shares my personal experience of moving to Norway and traveling all around the country: how I cycled alone across fjords and Sami festivals, learned the Norwegian language, cracked the unwritten codes of Norwegian working culture, navigated the dating scene to find a local partner, and adapted to everything Norwegian from skiing to Taco Friday. This book will not give you an answer as to whether Norway is perfect, because every person needs to live their experience and find out their own truth. All I can say is that I discovered a country with much more diversity than I expected, in terms of dialects, social codes, and eating habits. I will take you on my journey throughout Norway, and hope that you will laugh at all my mistakes, as well as learn from them. I hope to avoid stereotypes but cannot promise not to reflect on a few of them.

The people who end up living here are not just foreigners who have dreamed of moving to Norway. Sometimes life brings you here by coincidence. This is what happened to me. I had no intention of living here — I knew almost nothing of Norway but found a very interesting short-term job. My plan was to stay for a short period of time and move on with my life somewhere else. Maybe a tropical island, maybe a European capital? Certainly not a country where the winter lasts for 6 months.

Many Norwegians are studying abroad, often bringing "home" a partner who is yet to discover all the quirkiness of the Norwegian way of life. I have met many of those partners, who fell in love with an extroverted Norwegian in Nairobi, Bangkok, or Caracas, and after some years decided to settle down and have kids. The Norwegian convinces their partner to move back to Norway – often to the most conservative or the rainiest village in the whole of Norway – just across the street from their Norwegian parents "because it will be so much more practical this way. We'll have a free babysitter" (and sometimes free land to build a house on, a cabin nearby etc.).

Whatever your charming partner says about Norway, and whatever the travel magazines show you of fjords and northern lights, neither show the full picture: Norway is a much more complex country. At the beginning of my Norwegian journey, somebody told me, "Norwegians are like a Thermos bottle. Hard and cold on the outside, and soft and warm on the inside. The key is to manage to open the lid!"

I was born in France but my father is from Québec in Canada. My mother is born in Morocco and I was partly raised in Australia and on beaches in Indonesia. You would think that I am used to adapting to different cultures. Yet I have never experienced such unbelievable culture shock as when I moved to Norway. I have lived in six different countries as an adult, including in the Philippines, Indonesia, Canada and the United Kingdom, and I never could have imagined that a small nation of five million souls stuck between Europe and the North Pole would be the toughest cultural nut to crack. It is to be expected that even for Western Europeans, understanding and adapting to Norwegian culture will be something totally new.

This book has a strange name. I am a frog in the fjord. Fjords are not a natural habitat for frogs. They should not be there, yet here I am, trying to hop from rock to rock and make it

8

to a Norwegian life. Frogs are also a cliché representation of French people, and even though I don't eat frog legs, I did feel like I was swimming against the current very often. *A Frog in the Fjord* is also the name of my blog about Norway, which I started in 2013 and which became widely read by foreigners and Norwegians. It landed me a column in Norway's most read newspaper Verdens Gang where I still write regularly.

This book is for non-Norwegians who have an interest in Norway or Scandinavia in general: those who want to travel here, move here or just learn about Norwegian culture because of a friend, a Norwegian partner, boss, colleague, or family member. It is also a book for Norwegians to learn about how foreigners see their culture, and to gift their foreign friends, colleagues or partner to explain what Norway is all about.

Finally, it is also a book for those looking for a change of scenery, those seeking to travel without leaving their living room, wherever that might be.

It is a condensed tale of my first 5 years in Norway, scrambled into one (because let's face it, my life is not that intense that all these adventures happened to me over the course of 12 months).

In this new edition I showcase the trust Forbes has had in me when claiming this book is one of the 5 most revealing books about Scandinavia. The French version is coming out later this year, and I cannot wait!

*Bonne lecture!*

Oslo, June 2022
Lorelou Desjardins

I

# WINTER

# MOVING NORTH

There was nothing I could do. I just gave up. No matter how hard I tried to sit on my suitcase, it would not close. Just when I was about to open it again to take some things out, my grandmother came with three bottles of wine (one red, one white, one rosé), five different types of cheese and my favorite homemade jam: the minimum requirements for a French person to survive abroad.

"I'm sure they have food there too," I told my grandmother in her Paris apartment.

"You never know," she answered, full of doubt. "It's cold up there. What can grow there, besides snow and tuberculosis?"

"Potatoes?" I answered. A wild guess: potatoes grow in the most hostile climates. To be fair I didn't know much about what Norway grows. I didn't know much about Norway full stop. And yet I was moving there.

I accepted her presents. There was no point in fighting my

grandmother as she is a very stubborn lady. Now, all I had to do was manage to get all my luggage in the taxi to the airport. As I was at the door with approximately 50 kilos shared between a backpack, a suitcase, and a big plastic tube with my favorite posters, she gave me a glass jar wrapped in a kitchen cloth.

"*Mamie*, I cannot take anything else. Look how much I'm carrying already," I told her.

"It's honey. You have to take it. It will keep you warm and strong in the winter, and it will make sure your life there is as sweet as honey," she answered.

She hugged me tight as if I were leaving for a polar expedition, not sure whether I would be eaten by a polar bear or contract scurvy. Maybe I would never survive this flight from Paris to Oslo? So far. So dangerous. An adventure into the unknown.

My Norwegian journey began a few weeks earlier, in a room without windows, on a gray and snowy day in the city center of Oslo, where I was interviewed for my dream job.

I had been working in Copenhagen for one year, as a lawyer in international human rights law at the Danish Institute for Human Rights. I had a fascinating job, giving legal advice to multinational corporations on their environmental and human rights responsibilities. But I was on a short contract and uncertain it would get renewed. I needed a job, ideally in Denmark since my boyfriend and I lived there. I looked for a job in Denmark, but after sending more than 60 CVs I landed a total of zero job interviews. Three (!) recruiters called me to say that I was highly qualified for the job, but because I didn't speak Danish, I was an irrelevant candidate.

"You need to look outside our borders," the third recruiter said. That is when I decided to expand my job search to Sweden, especially jobs in commuting distance to Copenhagen such as Malmö and Lund, and when this job in Oslo came up, I thought, "Why not?"

I got on a fifty-minute flight from Copenhagen for the job interview. It took me a while to find the building where I was supposed to have the job interview. The address I was given was on "*Grensen*" which means "the border". The interview was on a border, which one? This made no sense, until I realized Grensen is a street. It was close to the Parliament which the Norwegians call *Stortinget*, which my translation app translated to "the big thing." Jeez, these Norwegians are very informal, I thought, to call their Parliament "the big thing."

It was November in Norway, so my Danish boyfriend Aske had advised me to put on my warmest clothes: thermal leggings, a woolen jumper and the thickest winter coat I owned, as well as hiking shoes with those socks one uses to go skiing. Unfortunately, I could not possibly show up like that to the interview, so I changed into a suit, which was getting wetter by the second. I was freezing, despite the hiking shoes I had on, but excited about this interview. The Norwegians around me in the street seemed to have a much higher tolerance to cold as some were walking around in T-shirts and sneakers with bare ankles.

The job description involved managing projects led by indigenous peoples living in Indonesia, and fighting for their land rights in order to save the rainforests of Southeast Asia. The funding was Norwegian, so the office was Oslo-based, but the job would involve traveling to Indonesia. This was a country I knew well since I lived there for several years and spoke the language. The environmental organization I had applied to, Rainforest Foundation Norway, offered me a three-year contract, attractive benefits in addition to a steady and decent salary. Something scarce since I was young and in a very competitive field, working for democracy and human rights. There was high competition in the business of saving the world.

I found the office, changed my hiking shoes in the lobby, and started the interview with three Norwegians, colleagues and managers at the organization. They were wearing very casual clothes. None wore suits or ties. I even saw someone passing by the meeting room wearing socks without shoes. After many questions about my qualifications, Bjørn, the director of the organization, asked me, "If you were offered this job, would you be willing to move to Oslo and learn Norwegian? It is the working language in our office, and we will not change it for you." He was a tall man in his 60s with curly blond hair and a warm smile.

"Sure, I've learned Indonesian before. And English. And some Spanish. How hard can it be to learn Norwegian after that?" I answered confidently.

I wondered whether Norwegian was hard to learn. I was just hoping it wasn't like Danish, I had tried to learn that language while living in Copenhagen and had failed miserably. When Danes said *køkkenet* (the kitchen) I still heard "coconut." I took intensive Danish classes for two months to make things better. We were a bunch of foreigners repeating sounds that do not exist in any other language, like glottal stops and soft Ds.

After all this I could pronounce Danish words but still did not understand what people talked about. So I didn't exactly have a good track record at learning Scandinavian languages. I was not going to tell Bjørn that. At this stage, I was ready to tell them I would learn to juggle with fireballs if that could get me the job. This was a once-in-a-lifetime opportunity to work on what I had been passionate about during many years.

"I would learn your language, but only if you pay for the courses," I added.

"Sure, we will," answered Bjørn, with a smile. "Great, we'll get back to you as soon as possible about this position."

After four and a half hours of interviewing, I walked out

feeling exhausted. First the questions, then a tough language test, where I had to analyze a budget in Indonesian language. I was pretty sure I had failed. When I walked outside, I had no idea what time it was, but it was dark. It was even colder than earlier, and a freezing icy rain was whipping my face and my suit. Of course, I had forgotten to change back to my winter gear.

Ane was waiting for me outside the office. She was the only Norwegian person I knew. We worked together at the Danish Institute for Human Rights and became friends. She was the person who had sent me this job offer. We chatted and drank coffee in a very nice café called Bare Jazz. I imagined it meant The Bar of Jazz in Norwegian, but I later realized that it actually meant Only Jazz. We talked about the interview and said how cool it would be if I got the job.

The same night I flew back to Copenhagen. Aske and I had met at the office since we were both working at the same institute but in different departments. He was doing research for his Master's thesis. We went out several times and somehow naturally got together. After a few months, I eventually lost my room in the flat I was sharing with two students in Østerbro and Aske suggested that I move in with him in Nørrebro.

We had a very cozy life. He was finishing his studies. I was finishing my contract. We lived by a cemetery, which may sound horrifying, but it was actually a popular picnic location. The philosopher Søren Kierkegaard is buried there. All I needed was a job so that we could settle down for good. The one-bedroom apartment he bought several years earlier as a single guy was small, but we were in love and did not need much more for now.

A few days later, I heard the singing tone of the Norwegian-tinted English accent of Bjørn greet me on the phone.

"We had a total of 60 candidates, and we're offering you the job. What do you say?" he asked.

I thought about it for half a second. "I accept the job! When am I starting?" I asked.

"You will be starting in January, if that is okay for you. But we would really like for you to come to our annual office Christmas party mid-December, so make sure you are in Oslo. It will be a great opportunity for you to meet all your colleagues informally."

Aske was speechless. "Did you just accept the job?" he asked, as he watched me hang up the phone from our living room in Jægersborggade in Copenhagen.

"Yes. This is what we wanted, right?" I asked.

"Ha, I guess. Norway is far. It is a completely different culture from Denmark, you know."

"Really? Isn't Scandinavia a lot of the same? You guys were all Vikings once, right?" I said in a laugh.

We talked about it later that night. He understood that this move was important to me. The job would be amazing. I would travel to the Indonesian jungle and learn so much.

"Okay," he concluded that night. "I will finish my Master's thesis and stay in Copenhagen until May next year and join you in Oslo in the Spring. It will only be a few months of long distance. But you must promise me we will move back to Copenhagen in two years, maximum. I have all my friends here, and my parents. I want to live here," he said.

"Two years. It's a deal," I answered with a smile. This was all going to work out just fine. We had a plan. What I later learned was that plans are completely useless. The clearer the plan for your life, the less your life is interested in following that plan.

In my case, my plan was to stay in Norway for one to two years and then live a peaceful life with Aske. Since I was used to living in one place for far less than two years, I decided to bring all my books and clothes in boxes packed in Paris at my grandmother's house.

The immediate plan was to go to Oslo for the office Christmas party Bjørn invited me to, spend Christmas holidays with my family, and move to Oslo for good in the new year. Bjørn warned me that Oslo would be totally empty during Christmas holidays, or *roumyula* as he seemed to call it, so it was best for me to go home. But I would have time to meet my colleagues and maybe register with immigration in those few days I would spend in Oslo.

I had absolutely no idea what Norway had to offer, and very little idea of how life would be in Oslo. Before moving from Paris to Copenhagen, I remembered thinking that it was a huge sacrifice to move so far up North. I imagined Copenhagen as extremely cold, filled with unwelcoming people following obscure social rules.

The job at the Danish Institute for Human Rights was a short-term contract, but extremely interesting. Denmark is a wonderful country, don't get me wrong. I even started making Danish friends. But the language was hard to learn, and the country was so flat. It is the only country I ever visited where I passed by the country's highest peak without even noticing it. The "Mountain of the Sky" is only 170 meters above the sea. My commitment to this country was more a commitment to my boyfriend. And despite the rain and the flatness, I was ready to move back here. Learning Norwegian would help me to get a job in Denmark afterwards, I thought. I would at least speak one Scandinavian language that recruiters would be interested in.

I had to tell my parents I would be moving. Again. And not anywhere closer to home. I had left Marseille, France's second biggest city and the capital of Provence, at the age of 18 to study South-East Asian languages in Paris. My parents thought I would come home as soon as I finished my degree, but I caught the travel bug and never moved back to Marseille. After a few years in Paris, I studied law in Québec in Canada, which is where my father comes from. I then moved to Indonesia and later the Philippines to work in local human rights organizations.

To pay for my travels and studies, I worked in corn fields in the South West of France, sold croissants in Paris, and later sold goat cheese on the French Riviera. Cheap or free higher education definitely made everything doable. Eventually I studied for a Masters of Laws in International Human Rights Laws in Essex in the United Kingdom. It is this experience and education that landed me the legal job in Denmark.

By then I spoke a few languages, none of them being Norwegian. I had lived in five countries as an adult, and I moved to each one alone. I wanted to go to Norway not because of its landscapes I knew nothing of, or because of its food I had never tasted. It was because I was ambitious and this job was very interesting, and it was close to Denmark. The fact that the job was in Norway was secondary. It could have been Sweden, Jutland, Northern Germany, or Holland for that matter, as long as there was a direct plane less than an hour away from Nørrebro.

I knew nothing of Norway, but it did not scare me. If I could live with 12 people of nine different nationalities in a single flat for a year as a student in the United Kingdom, I could certainly adapt to Norway, no matter how cold and unwelcoming I imagined it would be. There had to be nice people there too. I just had to find them.

My parents, on the other hand, had hoped I would come home after Copenhagen. I had traveled and seen the world enough, right?

"Maximum two years. Enough time for me to get enough work experience," I tried to convince them via Skype.

The silence on the other side of the line was not due to a bad connection: my parents had no idea I could move to a place that is even further North than Denmark.

"But where will you go next?" asked my mum. "Siberia? Norway is very far away from France."

Why did my parents think Norway was so far away? They would go to Thailand or Bali on holiday without thinking twice, and Norway was much closer than that.

"Mum, Norway is not that far from France. There are flights from Paris to Oslo several times a week and the flight takes only two to three hours."

"Out of all the places in the world you can move to, why choose Norway?" she asked.

After moving around in their youth, my parents settled down in Marseille for a reason: it is sunny and warm almost all year around. Even then, they find winters cold. Anything below 15 °C (59 °F) requires gloves and a warm hat. And I was moving to Norway. The chances of me drinking from a coconut on the beach there were very slim. Later, I found out that there were beautiful beaches in the Lofoten Islands, and I did drink Løiten Aquavit on one of them once. But sadly, when I made that call to my parents, I didn't know enough about Norway to convince them.

I managed to fit the pot of honey into one of my suitcases and took the taxi to Roissy Charles de Gaulle-Paris airport. Arriving at the airport I started looking around for the boarding gate to Oslo. That was quite easy to find; there aren't that many queues where only tall blond people line up neatly, not yelling or trying to cut in line, all of them wearing clothes from the same two brands: Norrøna and Bergans of Norway.

We boarded the plane in silence. I really wanted to tell the woman in front of me in the queue that I was moving to her country and ask if she had any tips for me. But because she didn't hold the door for me when we passed the numerous doors to the plane, and instead banged it into my face, I assumed she was not in the mood to chat with a stranger.

As I tried to put my luggage in the overhead compartment, it turned out I was way too short to reach it. I was on the tip of my toes, trying to get it in, and all these tall Norwegians were looking at me without giving me a hand. What is wrong with these people? In France, a woman in need of help does not need to ask; hands naturally come to help. There was a man and a woman standing at both my sides, both about 30 centimeters taller than me and both looking at me while I was struggling.

Eventually I asked one of them to help me and he smiled and said "Yes, of course," and lightly took my luggage and put it where it belonged with no effort: the compartment was at the level of his head. Mine was at the level of his elbows. Same for doors and stuff: don't ever expect anyone to hold it for you, it's like these people don't have manners or something. But I hadn't even arrived in Norway yet, let's not be too negative about the whole country and its people, I thought. Maybe only the ones on the plane were like that, or maybe they have their own reason for behaving like this.

The man next to me on the plane kept on playing with a little black ball of something and putting it in his mouth. The lady on the other side was knitting like a maniac. Neither of them talked to me, but I did not either as I was too busy reading a book in French on learning Norwegian.

As we landed in Oslo, everyone left the plane in more silence and order than I've ever seen in my life. I imagined getting off a plane in France just before the beginning of the

Christmas holidays. On one such flight, the flight attendant announced, "We ask all our passengers not to turn on their cell phones until we have stopped and reached the terminal. For all of those who already turned it on, give Christmas greetings to your families!"

Well, they were calm, until we reached the luggage area in Oslo Gardermoen. Then they all disappeared somewhere, and I stood there alone with an Indian woman in crutches waiting for my luggage.

Where have they gone? I wondered. It was 11:30 at night and the last train was about to leave for Oslo central station. I wondered what was so important they would rather miss the last train. They all came back at some point with Oslo airport bags filled with alcohol in bottles and cardboard boxes and bags of candy. Wine and candy — that is what is worth missing the last train home for? Strange, I thought. Can't they just buy those things in regular shops in Norway?

I arrived in the city on the darkest night I had ever seen and checked into the hotel my company had booked for me until I found a place to stay. Alone in an overpriced and undersized hotel room, I stared at the snow falling in the night.

Oh God, what did I just sign up for? I could be anywhere else right now, a place where the sun actually shines for a few hours during the day. Instead of that I was waiting for tomorrow to come while eating the only Norwegian food the hotel receptionist could point me to: something called *pølse i lompe* from a place called Narvesen, a local 7/11. As I ate this sausage wrapped in a cold pancake that tasted like potato, I wondered how high the suicide rate was in this country, not to mention the use of various drugs.

# MY FIRST *JULEBORD*

The next day was the day of my new workplace's Christmas party. I decided to drop by the office to say "hi" and confirm that I had arrived in Oslo and would be coming to the party. On my way there, heavy snow swirled around with the wind. I had lived in Canada, so snow did not scare me. Neither did the cold. But the difference is that in Montreal, everything is designed to protect pedestrians from the cold, with underground tunnels created between shopping centers, universities, and metro stations. In Oslo, on the other hand, it is as if the weather was not an issue. Here it seemed like people wanted to be outside, even when it was -15 °C (or 5 °F) on this Thursday morning in December. They even seemed to enjoy it.

The bus eventually arrived, and as I got on I saw that every person was sitting alone with their bags on the seat beside them. And this was before the coronavirus pandemic! There were also empty pairs of seats, but as I wanted to be friendly, I sat next to a lady who did not have her bag on the seat next to hers. I smiled at her and said "Hi."

As she did not answer, I assumed she had not heard me. So I touched her arm and smiled at her again, saying, "I just moved to Norway, do you come from here?"

She looked at me as if I were harassing her. By the time I had finished my second sentence she had gone to sit at another seat with no one next to her. Did she not like immigrants? Maybe I had bad breath? Maybe she was in a bad mood and did want to talk? It must be such a lonely trip to work if one cannot talk to fellow passengers on the bus. In Marseilles, we can laugh with a neighbor and chat for a whole trip and then say "Au revoir, bonne continuation!" by the end of our trip together. This bus in Oslo was no fun at all. No one talked to anyone; they all looked ahead or scrolled on their iPhones. Newcomers on the bus always tried to sit alone. If such a spot was not available, and only then, would they sit next to someone and have to ask them whether they could move their bags to the floor. Norwegians don't seem friendly on a Friday morning, I thought. Maybe it was because of the weather.

I got to work and entered the lift. I was going to the fifth floor. A man entered the lift on the second floor. Trying to be polite and welcoming, I said "Hello, good morning!" to him. He mumbled "*hei*" and looked at me with a look of great surprise on his face. Then he looked at his shoes. I suddenly remembered something Aske had told me about Norwegians. There are two types of Norwegians: the introverts and the extroverts. How do you tell the difference between an introverted Norwegian and an extroverted Norwegian? When talking to you the introvert looks at their shoes, while the extrovert looks at your shoes. Maybe the man from the lift was an introverted Norwegian?

The organization's receptionist and human resource manager was there, her name sounded like Owse.

"No, Å-s-e," she said, showing me how it was written. So this lady's name was something a non-Scandinavian person would read as "ass?". Great. What was it with Norwegian names that made them so strange to the rest of the world?

She showed me around the office. She gave me some papers to read, and then informed me about the fire escapes in the building. She also pointed to my desk, and two friendly faces waved at me. Turban and Uva would be my closest colleagues, said Åse.

They both worked in the organization's Asia team , where I would also work.

Uva — or was it Uve she was called? These Norwegian names sounded so foreign to my French ears — was a tall woman with red hair and beautiful green eyes. Then again, everyone in Norway is tall compared to me.

"I come from a place called Voss, on the West Coast of Norway," she said in English. "I have to warn you my dialect in Norwegian is hard to understand and I write in the other Norwegian language: New Norwegian or *nynorsk*."

What? Wait a minute, when Bjørn told me I would have to learn Norwegian, he never mentioned two languages, let alone dialects. How was I going to pull this off? I just smiled.

"Great! Looking forward to learning your dialect!" I said.

Turban was a bald bearded man who gave me a warm handshake. "*Selamat datang!*" he said. That means "Welcome" in Indonesian. He would be working with me with Indonesian rainforest projects. I saw a pair of skis behind his desk, and he seemed to be wearing skiing gear. He was the guy walking around in his socks when I had my interview here.

"My dialect is from around here so it should be easier for you to understand me. Do you like skiing?" he asked, as he had followed my eyes looking at his skis.

"Ha well, I haven't skied much in my life. I come from the South of France where it snows once every 15 years and they shut the city when that happens."

He laughed. "Okay, we can teach you. I just bought new skis for my daughters. We are going skiing this weekend if the weather allows. We can teach you one day!" Sure, that would be great, I thought. Such friendly people were a very good start for this new job.

Suddenly Åse said, "Oh look, it's already dark outside!"

"What do you mean by 'dark outside?' Like *night*?" I looked at my watch, then at the window, then at my watch again. This was not an error: it was only 2:30pm and the pitch-dark night covered Oslo.

"Don't worry. The sun turns in two weeks. It will only get better from there," she said.

"The sun turns? What do you mean?" I asked.

"Winter solstice. You know, days get longer after the 21st of December," she added, as if it was something anyone in the world knew. Except most of us live in places where longer or shorter days are not something we look forward to that much.

"How much time of daylight do we gain every day from then?" I asked.

"A few minutes, I think," she replied.

Fantastic. By the time I am 45 it will be light outside again.

Half an hour later, Åse said "*Gouyul!*" with her backpack on her shoulder.

"Wait a second, are you leaving? It's 3pm!" I asked.

"Yes," said Åse, laughing. I have to pick up my kids from kindergarten," she replied, putting on her winter coat and boots.

"But aren't you joining us at the Christmas party?" I asked. But she had gone already. Maybe she was organizing things for the party and that was the reason she left so early? What did *Gouyul* mean? Must be the Norwegian word for goodbye.

"*Gouyoul*," I replied, waving at a closed door. Luckily Uva and Turban were still there, and they were going directly to the office Christmas party. The dinner started at 5pm, if you can imagine that. In France, only toddlers get to have dinner that early.

Before we left the office all my colleagues going straight to the party changed to much more formal clothes. We walked to the King's castle, to a flat behind a place called *Litteraturhuset*, the House of Literature. I had also changed to a nice black dress and the highest heels I had in my cupboard: three centimeters. When we got there Bjørn opened the door and said, "*Gouyul!*" and hugged me.

"Goodbye?" I replied to his hug.

He laughed. "'*Jul*' means 'Christmas' in Norwegian," said Bjørn. "'*God jul*' means 'Merry Christmas,' and this party is a *julebord*, or 'Christmas table' in literal Norwegian. This is your first Norwegian lesson," Bjørn added.

All the men were wearing suits and women looked beautiful in dresses and makeup. It was hard to believe these were the same people who wore such informal clothes at the office or during a job interview.

We were in Bjørn's home, and he had set huge tables turning around the flat like a giant caterpillar, with all the chairs looking like legs. There were almost 30 plates there, and a lot of food on the tables. We all sat down and Bjørn made a speech. It reminded me of Danes. Those people love their speeches, and the drunker they get the more speeches they make. I got Uva, the colleague sitting next to me, to translate. Bjørn was saying that he was welcoming us to the office's *julebord* and then he said this would be a typical Norwegian Christmas feast, and then he welcomed the new employees including myself. When he said something sounding like my name, I waved at the people looking at me with welcoming smiles.

There was a lot of food on the table, including smoked salmon, gravlaks, something that smelled like rotten feet but was very good: *rakfisk*. There was also potato salad, potato pancakes called *lefse*, pickled beetroot, more potatoes, dried lamb, other kinds of salted or dried meat and many other things I had not yet identified. I tasted a bit of everything, but although it was a lot of food, everything was cold. So I assumed it was the first course and did not eat too much. And waited for the main course to come. Maybe lamb, maybe warm fish. In the meantime, a very silent man with orange hair was pouring a very strong alcohol in our glasses every time they were half empty.

And I waited more. Until I understood that everyone was getting drunk and nobody was eating that much anymore. So I whispered in Uva's ear: "Is there more food coming?"

"No, this is the whole dinner. There will be dessert and coffee. And more alcohol," she said. "If you are still hungry you should eat now." She showed me how to put *rakfisk* in the *lefse* and mix it with cream and leek sauce. Then we were served ice cream with warm berries on top, and lots of coffee. And then they took the tables and chairs away. That is when I understood why we were all in light dresses despite the cold outside: we would be dancing all night. The serious and shy people who had been waving discreetly at the beginning of the dinner were now losing it on the dance floor.

I took this opportunity to talk to people, including a very tall bald man who made very funny jokes, a tall woman with dark hair who spoke very good French, and the two French guys who were already working there: Marc and Roger. Marc had been in Norway for almost 12 years, and Roger had just arrived. They were both working on land rights in Africa. I was also introduced to a man named Erik who made everyone laugh every time he spoke. He was one of the guys at my interview.

By the end of the night, I could hardly believe my eyes. Marc had fallen asleep on the sofa. Erik had fallen asleep under the sofa. All that while the music was still very loud. Other colleagues were in the kitchen putting their hands in the pot of warm berries, taking them with their hands. Roger did not stay long at the party because he ate too much *rakfisk* and suddenly felt very sick. People were dancing a lot, and some were dancing very close to each other, as if they were going to make out. Then I saw two people who looked like they should both be retired kiss each other passionately like teenagers. "What on Earth is happening here?" I thought. All these very polite and reserved people were suddenly loosening up and becoming someone else. At some point I figured I had only two choices: get drunk or leave. So I decided to accept more of the strong drink from the silent man who always had the bottle in his hand, and asked him what it was.

"*Aquavit*. This one is warm and Norwegian, the other is cold and Swedish. If you are a real Norwegian, you should not take the cold one. That one is for sissies," he said very seriously. Well, off we go with the warm one!

At the end of the night, it felt like I had made 30 new friends. I did not remember half of their names. It seemed like half of the women were called Tine, Trine, or Katrine and the other half were called Ane, Anne, or Hanne. Men had names filled with sounds that were hard to pronounce: Eustaïn, Aoudoun, Goat, and Tourchiell. They laughed and danced and went home with their ties on their heads, but I must admit I did not feel completely at ease yet. There seemed to be invisible social codes I did not quite manage to see yet, and they were friendly in a distant manner. As I left the building to walk back to the hotel, I saw a man in a very expensive suit peeing in the street with what looked like a piece of cream cake on his head. People get really crazy in this country when given alcohol, I thought.

Good thing I didn't go to bed early, as the sun had just risen when I woke up the next day at 10am. Although it was cold, I decided to leave the hotel room until I found a place to myself. I wanted to discover the city on my day off. I walked a few meters down the hotel's street and saw a man with skis on his shoulders and a very tight costume in latex. He was waiting for the bus, just there in the middle of the city. Where is this guy going? Isn't it Saturday? I wondered. We are in the center of a European capital city. Can there be skiing slopes just a bus ride from here?.

Then I saw about ten more people with skis, so I assumed there were nearby skiing slopes. Others were running in the snow, wearing very bright yellow and green tights and jackets that hurt my eyes. Did I have a hangover, or was the fashion in Oslo to make sportswear in colors that gave epileptic seizures to people they crossed? Probably a bit of both.

It was a Saturday, the temperature was at -12 °C (or 10 °F), and they were running or skiing before noon. What is wrong with these people, I thought. Why aren't they in their homes by the fireplace instead of working out in the blizzard?

I walked around, trying to get a feel of the city. My first impression was that people here really like building stuff. There was construction work literally everywhere, especially on the seafront next to the Oslo Opera House. I went to the harbor called Aker Brygge and to the big ski jump in Holmenkollen from where one can see the whole city and the fjord. It was so nice. And so cold. I really wondered how Norwegians managed to walk around and even run with this temperature.

That evening I met Ane in a bar in town. It had been dark for more than six hours now, and I felt like sleeping, but things seemed to be moving in the streets of the city center. Ane was waiting for me at the bar.

"How is Oslo treating you?" she asked.

"Well, my colleagues spent two hours with me before leaving, and it's dark all the time. People I meet don't want to talk to me" I replied. "I am so glad I know you here, I am really starting from scratch in Norway," I added.

"That's fine, I can introduce you to my friends. I won't be in town all the time as my new job requires a lot of traveling, but I will be around. I am actually having a party soon, so you can hopefully meet people there," she said. She had just started working for the Norwegian Refugee Council.

We spent the rest of the evening drinking very expensive half-filled glasses of wine and talking about what our former colleagues were doing. I walked back to the hotel around midnight. Extremely jolly people were walking around, and there seemed to be much more people in the streets than in the morning. To my great surprise, a group of people started talking to me, being extremely friendly. This guy put his hand on my shoulder and his friend offered me a sip from her beer. Wow, Norwegian people were actually touching me. Unheard of in my two days in this country. My personal conclusion that night: Norwegians are much friendlier in the evening than in the morning. It seems it has to do with liquids: lack of coffee in the morning and loads of alcohol in their blood in the evening.

*Note to self:* Norwegians might seem like cold people when talked to on a bus, sober and before going to work. But they are much warmer when talked to in the evening and under the influence of liquor. Norwegians do not seem able to make that extra small talk that other nations love.

There is very little light in this country, and it's cold in winter, but that does not stop people from going skiing at 10am on a day when they don't work instead of staying in bed and watching television.

Wine is very expensive in Norwegian bars, but not of very good quality. When I see that one glass of wine in Norway costs approximately twice the price of a bottle of wine in France I want to cry.

# A NORWEGIAN OFFICE

That first week was filled with administrative tasks. The usual when moving to a new country. I had no identity here yet. I had to register with Norwegian immigration and tax authorities, get a social security number, apply to open a bank account to receive my salary, register in Norwegian classes and find a place to live. And I had to work, of course. I started with the immigration, which took me a whole morning of waiting in line. They promised they would send me a personal number soon, which would allow me to create a bank account, receive my salary, and pay taxes. That process turned out to take two months, during which I lived on pasta and tomato sauce. No bank account meant a salary on wait. Life was so expensive in Norway without a local salary.

The first days at work were quite calm. I was reading extensively to get to know the organization, learning about its history. I was also observing my colleagues to figure out how to fit in, and avoid cultural missteps. I could already notice that things were different here: colleagues would not kiss on both cheeks when they met. They shook my hand the first time we'd met and after that they just said "Hei" from a distance. Some mornings they did not even say "Hei". People barely touched each other, not even a tap on a shoulder. Also, people seemed very focused and rarely took coffee breaks. But they would leave work very early, around 4pm or as earlier as 2.30pm when they had kids to pick up. With Christmas coming up, people worked even shorter days.

Also, somehow everything that had happened during the *julebord* had been erased from their memories. Every time I tried to bring it up to show some kind of connection between us, they kept silent and walked away. I learned that those who had been kissing were married to other people, and they didn't even seem to like each other that much at work. Was I day-dreaming? All these things happened, right?

"What happens at *julebord* stays at *julebord*," said Uva when I asked. I had so much to learn about Norwegian social codes at work.

The pace sped up after the holidays, and I was invited to my first Norwegian work meeting. It was a staff meeting, with all 30 staff members present around the table. The whole meeting was in Norwegian, so I understood nothing. I tried to read body language and intonations to guess what was going on. It was difficult to follow what was being said in the meeting because of strange sounds coming out of the people sitting at the table. Some were making humming sounds, without opening their mouths.

It seemed the humming people were expressing an opinion: either agreeing or disagreeing with what was being said. Hard to tell, they were all looking at their hands laying on the table, not looking at each other. And then some others were making aspiration sounds, like a "ha!" as if they just learned something shocking and needed to stop and breathe. Maybe they had asthma? Maybe they were conveying an opinion too? I was just hoping they wouldn't all faint at once.

Another enigma was a knitting lady. I had never in my entire life seen people knit during office hours. There is a first for everything, I guess.

*Note to self:* get the knitting colleague to knit me gloves, those with little Norwegian patterns in wool. They seem much warmer than the ones I had brought from Denmark.

During the break, I asked her whether she had problems following the content of the meeting. She said knitting made her focus better. I thought of what made me focus better: listening to jazz music, drinking red wine. Could I do that too during a Norwegian meeting? I should ask my boss, Bjørn, about that. She also said she was not working in this office but was doing some kind of survey on working conditions in hand-picked companies. Damn it, I was not going to meet her again, I would have to find someone else to knit me those gloves. Sadly I never saw any knitting ladies in my office after that.

I was so disturbed by all this that I had a second cup of coffee. I checked my watch; we weren't even halfway through the meeting. Luckily, there was a lot of coffee on the table to help me get through the rest with an alert brain.

Another surprise: our boss was not speaking much. But every other person around the table had something to say and said it. The tone of people was leveled all along, and all-in-all they were very polite and measured. There were usually long pauses between each person. The boss was listening, taking notes, and at the end of the meeting it did not seem anyone was happy or sad. Then he said something in an equally gentle voice. If all meetings are as peaceful as this one, working in

Norway is going to be like a dream come true, I thought.

When we got out of the meeting Bjørn asked me: "So, what did you think of your first Norwegian meeting?"

"I did not understand the words, but it seemed like this meeting went really well!" I said.

He laughed. "Really? Why do you think that?" he asked.

"Everyone was so calm, no conflict, no anger, no irritation. No one was speaking louder, interrupting one another or being aggressive like one would hear in French offices," I answered.

"Well," said Bjørn, still smiling. "The meeting did not go well. People were very irritated, they disagreed with most of the propositions, and we did not pass item two on the agenda. We had to schedule several other meetings to reach a compromise and agree on solutions."

"Okay, I'm not that good at reading Norwegian people yet." I said. "But why did you not just decide in the end instead of scheduling another meeting? You're the boss, right?" I asked.

"Yes, I am, but in Norway bosses cannot just decide without taking into account what their employees want. Norway's workplaces have a much less hierarchical structure than most countries. We all need to talk about things before we make decisions. I have to go now — new meeting. Good luck, Lorelou!" he said, giving me an encouraging smile.

I went back to my desk completely puzzled. How could I have been so wrong at reading body language and tones of voices? Can Norwegian and French ways of showing irritation, conflict, and disagreement be so different that I interpreted everything upside down? If this is how they disagree, how do they show they agree then? French people can speak loud and be aggressive and arrogant, but it is really clear when someone disagrees with you.

After the meeting we went to have lunch. At 11:30 am. In a French setting, this would be a late breakfast. My colleagues were walking around the office kitchen with pieces of hard bread they called *knekkebrød*, a rectangular bread that made the sound "knekk" when one broke it, also known as crispbread in English. They added things on the bread, which seemed very different from each other (fish, vegetables, pastes coming out of tubes) but all had the same name in Norwegian: *pålegg*. Not many words for food in this language, I thought. Not much warm food either. The whole thing was over in less than 30 minutes.

Over the weeks, I tried to integrate by eating *knekkebrød* with the white cheese Norwegians like. Although it was way too mild for me, I was trying to blend in. Despite my efforts I received many comments on things I was doing wrong. In Norway one's lunch shouldn't be too expensive. I was told that any cheese more expensive than the cheapest *gulost* or *hvitost* (yellow or white hard cheese sold in blocks) was too fancy to eat on an everyday basis.

"You eat that for lunch? It is only for parties usually" said Erik one day at lunch. Any Norwegian cheese that had some kind of interesting taste to me such as Østavind, was not suited for a Norwegian lunch.

"This is tapas cheese," said Torbjørn. "We eat it on Friday evenings or for special occasions."

So there was nice Norwegian cheese but they had rules about when I could eat it? How could there be so many social codes around a simple lunch made of bread and toppings?

Another issue: there was social control as to how much cheese one should have on one's bread.

"Wow, that is a lot of cheese. When I was a kid, we could only have a very thin slice," Åse once said. So not only do I have to eat tasteless cheese, but on top of that I cannot eat much of it? Why are they submitting me to war rationing when they live in the richest country in the world?

*Pålegg* was 30 different things. I did not understand how so many different things could be covered by a single Norwegian word. I knew that *på* was a preposition which could be broadly translated by *on* and *legg* came from the verb *to lie*. Norwegians love to stick words together. Sometimes that new word has a whole new meaning.

*Pålegg* seemed to be a Norwegian concept which defines all the things Norwegians came up with to lie on a piece of bread or crispbread. It can be ham, cheese, red pepper, avocado, smoked salmon or smoked trout. They also had *Svolværpostei* a.k.a "the paté from Svolvær," a village in the Lofoten Islands. It is a paté made from fish eggs and cod liver. Or *leverpostei*, a pork liver paté mixed with spices. Norwegians like to have combinations: cheese and red pepper. Or the luxury avocado and salmon. Or only jam. Very important: the cheese needs to be mild. As a French person, I was surprised that cheese producers in Norway advertise their cheese as "mild". "If it has no taste, why would anyone buy it?" I asked myself.

They made me taste something called *brunost*, or brown cheese which tastes very sweet. To take a slice of that brown cheese sold in bricks, they handed me an *ostehøvel* or cheese slicer which everyone was very proud to tell me was a Norwegian invention. Some are proud their nation invented the alphabet or electricity, but I guess a cheese slicer is also great.

The brown cheese tasted like caramelized condensed milk. I had to admit it had great properties, such as the advantage of being stored in a fridge for months without rotting and being great as fuel. In January 2013, a truck full of 27 tons of *brunost* caught fire in Nordland and the combination of sugar and fat burnt so well that it took four long days for firefighters to put the fire out. It took three years and over eight million Norwegian kroner for the tunnel to be re-opened. Who knew *brunost* could also be a weapon of mass destruction? Norwegian media called it *Brunostbrannen* (the Brown Cheese Fire). It was even picked up by international media, with the headline: "Meanwhile in Norway…"

They made another *pålegg* out of brown cheese, called Prim, which was made of brown cheese, cream, and more sugar. "Don't worry, that is a *pålegg* for kids," said Uva at lunch once when I asked what that was from the office's fridge. How many diabetics were there in Norway, I wondered, if this is food for children?

But the strangest *pålegg* is not white cheese or even brown cheese. It is *pålegg* in tubes. In Norway one can find many kinds of food in a tube: *makrell i tomat,* i.e. mackerel in tomato sauce. Or my worst nightmare: *rekeost.*

You have to be Norwegian to think of making a semi-liquid paste of shrimps and cheese to spread on a slice of bread. Other strange mixes such as a liquid paste of bacon and cheese, locally called *baconost.* And another one called *kaviar.* You would think that it's caviar (those big eggs that cost a lot of money, usually sold by Russians) but Norwegian caviar tastes a bit like something my grandmother makes that we call *tarama,* a recipe she got from her best friend from Bulgaria. She makes it from scratch with a mix of fish eggs, oil and bread. And a lot of salt. It was a kind of fish egg mayonnaise. I managed to taste *kaviar,* but *rekeost* and *baconost* were too much to ask from me at this stage. I was ready to learn Norwegian and adapt to this culture but eating food from tubes every day was a commitment I was not ready to make for the Norwegian integration process.

Strangely enough, they did not import the Danish thin layers of chocolate which are exactly the size of the bread. That would be a great *pålegg* to have in Norway.

*Note to self:* It is okay to knit woolen things in a Norwegian meeting, if it helps you concentrate. Whatever you say in a Norwegian meeting must be said in a very calm voice. If Norwegians want to show aggression, they will raise their eyes to the sky or have a light change of tone, sending subtle passive-aggressive messages to their fellow Norwegians who will automatically understand how annoyed or how much they disagree. All of it is undetectable to foreigners like me. Disturbing noises are allowed during Norwegian meetings as long as they are 1) slurps of coffee drinking, 2) asthma-like inhales, or 3) humming sounds. These sounds are not passive aggressive (I know, it's getting kind of complicated). It is an accepted conclusion to a meeting that we need another meeting. One can also ask for a meeting to complain about the meeting culture. One can also ask for a meeting to decide on meeting-free days.

About language, Norwegians have words for things that nobody else in the world seems to feel the need to find words for. One of them is *pålegg*. I think I covered the meaning of that one, lunch after lunch at my Norwegian office. Another one was still a mystery. Something called *kousheli*, a word Norwegians were saying all the time and which I didn't yet understand.

# SAY MY NAME

At work, I was getting to know Turban and Uva more and more, as we shared an office space. At least that is how I understood their names. Turban was very helpful and patient in explaining Norwegian words, so I started with his name.

"Is Turban a common Norwegian name for a man?" I asked.

"I am called Torbjørn," he said, writing it down so I could see how it was spelled. "*Tor* comes from the god Thor and *bjørn* means bear," he added. He made me pronounce it many times until I got it right.

"Does it mean our boss' name is actually 'bear'?" I asked.

"Yes, exactly," he answered. "Norwegian names are often inspired by old Norse names, gods, and natural elements such as islands, wind, the sun, and animals. Ylva is actually derived from *ulv* which means *wolf*," he added, pointing at our other colleague. So she was not called Uva as I had believed all this time. I repeated Ylva's name, but they said I had it wrong.

"Here," said Marc at lunch that day. "To make the Y sound in Norwegian you need to place a pen under your nose and squeeze between your upper lip and your nose." I did that and repeated "Ylva."

"Yessss!" Torbjørn and Ylva said in unison.

I wasn't the only one having trouble pronouncing names. Norwegians also had trouble with mine. "What did you say your name was?" is the question Norwegians would ask me every single time I introduced myself. "Loulou? Is that your real name?" they asked, holding and shaking my hand just a little longer. Note that in Norwegian the letter O is pronounced like a French OU.

"Lorelou, in one word. You spell it L-O-R-E-L-O-U," I always added.

Somehow, Norwegians often believe it is a name coming from a fairytale. At my office, people started howling "lorlorlo" and I assumed that was just another Norwegian sound. It took me several weeks to understand they were calling my name. Or just saying my name because it amused them. Eventually I got used to the strange way Norwegians pronounced my name and started answering when they were making gurgling sounds. I should have started spelling my name *"Lårølo"* for Norwegians to pronounce it right.

To be fair, my name is also uncommon in France. It comes from a song by Gilles Vigneault, a famous singer from Québec. The song is called *"Gros Pierre"*, which literally means "Fat Peter." The story of a boy who is in love with a beautiful girl whom he longs for for years, while she is living her life in the city, until he dies of sadness in their village. Somehow this song from my father's childhood inspired him to give me the name of this woman, condemning me to a life of explanations and, I must say, originality. So if someone says my name in the street, I'm pretty sure it's me they are calling.

My Norwegian language skills were better. I could pronounce my colleagues' names. It was time to learn other words
in Norwegian, for me to follow meetings and have actual
conversations. My office enrolled me in a Norwegian course
I would be attending until I reached a proficient level to work
in Norwegian.

My class was learning from a book called "*Ny i Norge*" or "New
in Norway" and the first chapter was about a Thai girl called
Urai who had moved to Norway because she was married to
a Norwegian. This text and its questions were all about how
Urai would fill in the papers to get support from the Norwegian social security system called NAV. The whole chapter was
about how to get benefits from the social security system when
one is pregnant and a foreigner.

After reading this all of us students were puzzled. There were a
variety of profiles in the course. An Indian IT engineer called
Ramu, a female Lithuanian finance analyst, two Filipino au-
pairs, an Italian cook married to a Norwegian woman and a
Polish kindergarten teacher.
   None of us ticked any of the boxes of the story the book
was telling us about immigrants in Norway. None of us were
interested in knowing how to fill in a NAV form.
   I wanted to know what "*kousheli*" meant. I wanted to know
why Norwegian language is so close to Danish in its written
form but so far from its oral pronunciation. And why do
people say "*ikke sant*" all the time?

Our teacher was as helpful as a cotton hat in January in
Finnmark. I developed techniques to appear more fluent than
I really was. Before anything, I tried to master Norwegian pronunciation and melody. I found out later that there are as many
melodies to Norwegian language as fjords in Western Norway.

The melody I was learning was the one of the Oslo dialect. It was all about pretending one is very happy at the end of each word and sentence: the pitch would go up. "*Sier du DET?*" which means "Do you say SO?" (capital letters = happy ending). "GlasmagasinET" (a shopping center in Oslo), etc. This trick helped me hide my lack of vocabulary for a while.

I believe thirty words well-pronounced will make one appear more fluent than 500 words pronounced so badly that no one understands even after repeating three times. I tried to forget about the advice I had gotten from my Danish teacher, which was to swallow all the vowels. It turned out Norwegians like to pronounce every sound distinctively.

One can only answer "*Ja*" (yes) or "*Nei*" (no) to so many sentences, and that wasn't enough for me to make friends. To hide the fact that I did not understand what people said when they talked directly to me, I learned small words and sentences that made others believe that I understood.

For example, if I met a person I knew in the street, and they told me in some obscure dialect from a place called Molde that they are going on holiday to Greece or re-doing their bathroom, I just answered "*så spennENDE!*" when they were done telling their little story, with a smile. It means "so exciting!" and Norwegians use it a lot. I was saying "*så spennende*" to just about anything anybody said, until one day my colleague Torbjørn said to me in English, "This is not *spennende*. I just told you my dog died. Do you even understand what I'm saying?" Oh no. I was caught red handed.

"Well, no, I don't always understand what you say. But I like listening to you, it makes me learn Norwegian. What does one say to something sad? Like to keep the conversation going?" I asked.

"Well, maybe "*så trist*" (so sad!) or "*uff, da!*" Got it. When I did not understand what people were saying I read their body language, if they looked happy, I would say "*så spennende*", otherwise, if they looked sad or annoyed with a shaking of the head for example, I would say "*uff, da*" (sad ending). "Uff, da" is a Norwegian expression which is very difficult to translate, as it is used when people feel for you when you are telling them something negative happened. Imagine the following conversation:

"I was sick for three days and then on the day I went back to work there was a train strike." "*Uff, da*" would then be an appropriate Norwegian answer to that. Do not make the mistake I made once. "*Uff, da*" is kind of trivial, i.e. not for really important sad news such as the death of a family member.

When someone appeared to be trying to get my approval or tell me a long story, I understood maybe 30 percent. I wanted to make sure I blended in, so I tried to adopt all the expressions one uses to passively show that one is following a conversation. All that without giving any feedback or asking any questions to the person talking. I call them "conversation fillers" or "Norwegians' way of surviving small talk."

One example is the "*MmmmMMhh*" humming sound some make when wanting to show they agree with what someone is saying or encouraging them. "Keep talking, I am listening." The expression "*ikke sant*" (hard to translate, it literally means "not true" or "isn't it" but is used in a completely different context) actually has the same purpose as the humming sound. Another one that has the same purpose is the inhaling "ha" sound which I mistook for asthma during my first Norwegian meeting. I have found all of these very useful for encouraging Norwegians to continue talking so I could get more time to figure out what on Earth they were talking about.

Other conversation fillers are very convenient to pretend one understands what a Norwegian person is saying. "*Såpass*" for example. I use it exclusively when a Norwegian is expressing something that they felt was outrageous. For example, if they say "My parents-in-law bought their apartment for one million kroner above appraised value," I would say *"såpass!"* ("That much!"). It's only to be used when one needs to show how impressed one is by something completely out of proportion. Norwegians (who obviously understand everything other Norwegians are saying) also use them, but to pretend they are interested in whatever other people are saying.

Then most of them are just using this time of passive approbation to make up a creative excuse to get out of uninteresting small talk wasting 10 minutes of their life. That excuse often starts with the word *"oj"* as if they suddenly remembered something very important that needed their attention. They pronounce it OY. *"Oj,* I need to pick up my kid at kindergarten," *"Oj,* it is already 5.30pm. I need to get to the shop to buy beer" (beer sales stop at 6pm most days in Norway), *"Oj,* I need to catch my train," and so on.

**Note to self:** Pretending to be fluent in Norwegian is an art almost as hard to master as speaking the language. Norwegian has an infinity of words and expressions which aren't really found in Norwegian textbooks, but which are absolutely crucial to understand Norwegian conversations and social cues.

# NORWEGIAN STEREOTYPES

I was still enrolled in the Norwegian course, but it wasn't very interesting because it didn't give me any of those strategies to become fluent fast or differentiate dialects. All we were doing was repeat words and grammar rules. In other words, I was bored.

I was reading a comic book called *Pondus* that Torbjørn had recommended. Every time I came with questions about new words from *Pondus*, the teacher wouldn't answer them as they were not from the textbook. What was more interesting was that the others in the course had lived in Norway for longer than I had and could teach me some things about Norwegians. There was a clear contrast between what the teacher was telling us about Norwegian culture and society and what the other students were saying.

The Italian guy, Mario, had cycled from the North Cape to Rome one summer. That is when he met his future wife who lived in what he said was "a Christian village with not a single beer in sight." He told me that he had cycled in many different countries: Macedonia, Turkey, even Iran. He had never been so badly welcomed on the road as in Norway. When he had knocked on peoples' doors in Northern Norway, Trøndelag, and on the West Coast to borrow a piece of their garden or land to plant his tent he had mostly been rejected. Apparently not by everyone, as he met his wife on the way! In any case, he could not believe how hard the ice was to break, and how reserved some Norwegians could be.

"You will never make a Norwegian friend," he warned me. "It's almost impossible."

Gerda, the Lithuanian finance analyst, had another view: "No," she said, "the biggest problem here is that men don't talk to women. Whatever we do, however we dress, they just never try to seduce us," she said, looking helpless.

"And they are extremely nationalistic. Have you seen what happens on the 17th of May?" she asked. I had no idea what she was talking about. Ramu, the Indian IT engineer, had an opinion about relationships with Norwegians.

"But Gerda, Norwegian women are unchaste. That's what we learn in India. That is probably why their men don't need to make an effort to seduce them."

I had to admit I had heard that one before, that Scandinavian women are very beautiful, but also very unchaste.

"No, listen. It's not like that," said Marte, the Polish kindergarten teacher who was also a biology student at the University of Oslo. "Norway is a fantastic place to be a woman. Women can be bosses here. They have it all, the career and the kids! Norway has one of the best working cultures in the world, because it enables people to have a private life outside of work. And salaries are much better here."

47

The teacher was not happy about these stereotypes, especially the one about women. She told us not to forget that Norway has the highest gender equality in the world and is the best place to be a mother.

"And women are not easy, they are free. It is different" added the teacher.

She seemed very proud to be a Norwegian, and any criticism coming from any of us was taken as a personal offence. She asked us to stick to the book, which said that Norway is the richest country in the world, with the best standard of living. She praised the Norwegian system of welfare, redistribution to all, and the equality principle. It gave everyone in society a chance. She added that the Norwegian nation is one, and very uniform, and that the country was exposed to immigrants as late as the 1970s. She added:

"Norway is actually the best country in the world."

I had heard that before, but where? Ah, I remember! In every single country I have been to. Ever. Australia, Canada, Denmark, the United States of America. It turns out many people believe that their country is the absolute best in the world.

"Yes, but in the case of Norway, it is true," she answered.

The funny thing is that even Danes have stereotypes about Norwegians. I remember their reactions when I told them I was going to live in Norway.

"We call them *fjellaper*, mountain monkeys," said Aske's friend at a party. I had believed until then that Scandinavians were close-knit and that there was a true solidarity between them.

"Norwegians are very irritating. They are so rich. All that wealth should have been ours," said another guy at the same party. Probably because Norway was once under Danish rule, many seem to think the Norwegian oil is in fact Danish.

Let's talk about a few more misconceptions about Norway. For many people living outside of Scandinavia, Norway is hard to pin on a map. It is a place somewhere hidden in the North Pole, covered by ice all the time. I was asked a few times whether penguins and polar bears run free in Oslo.

Many also struggle to figure out what its capital city is, and whether Norway is in fact or a country. Or a region, or maybe a city? Some believe it is part of a big country called Scandinavia, which has a very unstable capital city. I have been asked by a hairdresser in France whether everything was fine for me in Stockholm, the capital of Norway. Or Norway, the capital of Sweden. Or Copenhagen, the capital of Scandinavia (Norway isn't an actual country, is it?).

All in all, those living outside of Norway seem to have a very approximate idea of what is really going on in this country. Those living here on the other hand, have very definite ideas of what Norwegian life is like.

*Note to self:* there seemed to be many conceptions and potentially misconceptions about Norway and Norwegians. Norwegians are unfriendly and unwelcoming, they are nationalistic, that Norwegian women are easy to sleep with, and that this country is the best to work in, especially as a woman. I also heard many times from Norwegians, sometimes joking, sometimes seriously, that Norway is the best country in the world.

I saw these stereotypes as a personal challenge. I would try to find out whether they were true, and my own conclusions would be based on my observations. Some obviously weren't - I had not seen any wild penguins in Oslo, so I could check that one off the list. But others seemed to be more plausible.

But first I had to find a place to live.

# OSLO APARTMENT HUNT

After work, I visited places to live which would be big enough for both Aske and I to live, and affordable. My colleagues advised me to look for a flat on www.finn.no ("*finn*" means "find"), the Norwegian website where people sell and buy just about anything except their souls.

At first, I looked for whole flats to rent in the city center, but the prices were so high it was insane. It was around 15,000 NOK for an apartment with one bedroom. That is around 1,800 USD or 1500 EUR. Aske planned to move a few months later. He would need time to find a job to contribute towards the rent. That meant probably a year where I would need to pay the rent on my own, with my salary which after all was not as high as I had initially thought considering prices here. Ane advised me to look on the outskirts of the city center, still accessible by metro. More importantly to put up an ad myself, in order to get access to flats that were not even advertised on the website. The ad said we were a French-Danish couple wanting to rent a whole flat or house with the maximum rent of 10,000 NOK. When I visited places in the outskirts of Oslo, I discovered how close nature is to the city center. In which other capital city can one live in the forest, 10 minutes' walk from a lake, and still be 20 minutes by metro from the city center? Norwegians living in Oslo didn't seem to realize the luxury that is in itself. Parisians would kill to have access to such beautiful nature so close to the city center.

We received emails from many owners who had homes to rent. They were empty homes which were just waiting to be lived in, maybe by me. Most of the owners were wealthy people who had one or two extra houses on their property. We were the only ones visiting them. Aske came back and forth on weekends to visit flats with me and see what he liked.

The places we were visiting were out of this world. Or maybe out of our social class? Every single flat or house we were offered to visit were in areas with names ending in "*kollen*": Grefsenkollen, Voksenkollen, Holmenkollen. All were in the Western part of Oslo, which, as I learned later, is the richer part of town. All houses had a beautiful view on the Oslo fjord, only the angle changed.

The first place I visited was a 65-square-meter apartment, totally furnished. I went alone because Aske could not make it that weekend. The rent was very low, 7000 NOK per month, and I was really tempted. The first issue was that the kitchen smelled like someone died in there and had stayed in the heat for two weeks.

"What is this smell?" I asked the old lady who showed me the place.

"Oh, the previous tenant forgot the fridge and freezer open for several weeks and everything has been rotting in here, including meat." she answered.

I wondered how one could get rid of that smell. The second issue was that the whole place was furnished with stuff that even my 84 years old grandmother would not have wanted.

"Can I bring in my own furniture?" I asked. I didn't own any but thought I could buy things that would be nicer than all of the things here.

"No, everything must stay this way," she answered.

"Even the bed?" I asked. The bedroom had enough space for a double bed but there was a single bed there.

"No, I don't want anyone getting a double bed in this home. Anyway, what would be the use of a double bed to you? You are not married, right?" Right. But the ad said I have a boyfriend. I looked around. Crosses everywhere.

"I come from the Smith's Friends community," she said as if that explained everything. Smith's friends? Who was Smith? What was this lady talking about?

On the metro back to the hotel, I Googled Smith's Friends and found out that it's a Christian community with over 8000 members in Norway and that some say it might be a cult. This was not going to work out after all, despite the low rent.

The next home we visited was a basement flat with about as many windows as a prison cell. This time, Aske was there. The place was 37-square-meter, had little daylight coming in and rented out at 10,000 NOK. The bedroom had no window, and she explained that this was a wonderful place. It must be, for a person who doesn't need to breathe or see the sun, I thought.

"The couple who lived here before were very much in love, so the lack of windows was not an issue," the landlady said to us. Aske and I looked at each other and rolled our eyes to the roof at the same time.

The last flat we visited was another basement flat. As we entered this last place, in the Holmenkollen area, we wondered how anyone would ever want to live here. There were no windows in the kitchen or in the bathroom. No lights either in the first room, so I had to stand there to get used to the dark before continuing to see the rest of the flat. Electricity cables were coming out of the ceiling or the wall here and there. And even the living room was dark, although there were many windows. For some obscure reason the tenants had covered the windows with dark sheets so thick that no light would go through. The space on the walls had big shelves on which many empty bottles of alcohol were displayed like trophies. The place looked like a man cave. But then, I pushed one of the dark curtains covering one of the windows aside to see what was outside. There was a magnificent view on the Oslo fjord, with the sun falling in the sea and the clouds in the orange and blue sky.

I whispered "Aske, come and see."

No neighbors blocking the way, no noise from the road. We could even use the garden. I could hear the birds singing and the flowers blossoming. Aske smiled.

"We're taking it," I told the landlady.

"But I have other people who are interested," she answered.

"Yes, but we really want to live here and we can sign the contract right now. I have three months' deposit in my account which I can transfer anytime," I said convincingly.

So we had a deal. Being a French and a Dane helped a little I believe, as higher social classes in Norway seem to have a weakness for everything that is French: the language, the history, the arts, the champagne, the fashion, and the culture. And her four children had studied at a medical school in Copenhagen. I was no Coco Chanel and Aske was far from being a doctor, but that didn't seem to matter. I suddenly wondered whether we had had a chance of living there if we had been, let's say, refugees, or if we had Muslim names.

We left the flat and decided to explore the surroundings. Dagny, the landlady, said there was a forest called Nordmarka just a few minutes walk from the house. We started walking uphill and indeed, we found a forest. As we got deeper in the forest, the view was more and more dramatic. On our left we could see even more forest, with fewer and fewer houses, and on our right side a breathtaking view of the Oslo fjord. Aske was amazed that we were so high, he kept asking me how many meters over sea level we were.

"This must be a very high mountain in Norway," he told me. We were feeling so peaceful in this wonderful nature and continued walking. There were two lines in the snow from each side of the "road" we were walking on, and for fun I walked on them. Wondering what they were for. After a while, a person came down skiing and looked considerably annoyed. It took me three or four of those to understand I was walking on their skiing tracks. Oh well. The forest is for everyone isn't it?

The night started enveloping us. At first, we thought it was beautiful. Shades of pink and dark blue were adding to the moment's mystery and romanticism. We sat on a rock and hoped to see the Northern Lights. We were probably north enough for that, said Aske. We waited and did not see any lights at all. By now the sky was completely dark.

We had walked outside of the ski slopes for a while and had no idea where we were. We walked around for what seemed like an eternity, in pitch dark, only helped by the light on Aske's phone. We managed to get to the ski slope, which was illuminated by streetlights for skiers, but we were still completely lost.

We did not know whether we should go left or right and, of course, our phones did not get any signal. We walked and walked, and it was getting so cold. We had the wrong shoes for this. We were dressed to go visit a flat, not to survive in the wild in minus temperatures. I started getting angry at Aske and at myself. How could we be so reckless? I was already imagining that we would have to dig a hole in the snow to sleep until morning came. Which would be quite late the next day in my short experience of the Norwegian winter. Would we survive?

As I was imagining the headlines on the next day's papers, a man came down skiing. We waved at him and he saw how desperate we were.

"We are lost. How can we get back to the city?" we asked.

He skied next to us, using his headlamp, and took us there, it was really close. How embarrassing would those headlines have been "A Dane and a Frenchwoman found frozen to death one kilometer from the metro station." A great lesson was learned that day: know where you are going, and do not leave the house without proper clothing. Aske went back to Copenhagen the next day. He was also a bit shaken by this experience but seemed ready to move to Norway and live with me in Holmenkollen. It was just a basement flat, but we would only live there one or two years, and we could turn this into something nice.

A week later I met Dagny at the bank to sign the contract papers and transfer the money to a common account, which is what Norwegians use when someone needs to pay a deposit on a flat.

"One more thing," she said when we were about to part. "You must tell all the Norwegians you meet that you live in Jahn Teigen's home."

"Jan who?" I asked.

"Jahn Teigen. He is a famous Norwegian singer. He represented Norway in the famous Eurovision Song Contest 14 times! And he even got zero points at it. We bought this house from him twenty years ago. We kept everything as he left it, including your flat which used to be his rehearsing studio.

Tell the Norwegians you meet; it will impress them or make them laugh," she explained. Dagny lost her husband many years ago and was renting out this part of her house partly for the rent and partly to have some company in her huge house.

"Okay" I answered, trying to remember the singer's name.

Later I told every Norwegian I met that I lived in John Teagen's home, and no one was impressed. My new landlady has lost it, I thought, no one knows this man here. But then I got the pronunciation of the singer's name right, and indeed people's reactions were funny. Most people would start singing "*Mil eetttteeerr miiiiiil*" or "*Optimist*", two of his famous songs.

I owe many things to Jahn Teigen. The great and noisy parties I threw in his completely noise-insulated rehearsing studio. And the amazing view over the Oslo fjord, Nesodden peninsula, the islands of Hovedøya and Gressholmen, and the sailing boats on sunny days.

Other things were harder to get used to. The reaction of Norwegians when I told them I was renting instead of owning my apartment, and the kind of people who were living in my neighborhood.

After a while, I started calling my neighbors "the Orange People" because no matter the weather or the season, they were always tanned. The teenage girls from *Vestkant*, the richer part of Oslo, fascinated me. When I looked at them on the metro it felt like I was observing an endangered tribe in the forest: they had their own costumes which were so different from mine: big fluffy boots, tight sport leggings, very straight blond hair, a lot of makeup and a very strange orange skin. Many also had very expensive handbags although they were as young as 13 or 14 years old.

I learned by listening to their conversations that some Norwegians are so rich that they have yachts in Barbados. And they spend Christmas there, which probably explains the tan all year around.

The older people had a lot of dogs, but they rarely took those dogs out, as that was the role of the Filipino employees.

After some time, I noticed that the only foreigners living in Holmenkollen were 1) Filipinos taking the dogs out or taking care of other peoples' babies, 2) Polish workers or 3) partners of people living there, usually Spanish, Danish, or Cuban wives.

It seemed like they were used to having maids and gardeners and people doing their work for them.

Once I was carrying a bucket and a broom home from the shop as I had to buy supplies to clean my flat, and this lady with a big fur coat asked me, "Are you a cleaner?" She looked closer at me. "You don't look Polish, Serbian maybe? I'm really in need of a cleaner."

"No sorry, I am a lawyer. I also happen to be a very bad cleaner," I answered.

"Well, here is my card, let me know if one of your friends can help me out," she said.

Besides the uncomfortable questions, I must say I was transcended by the view every time I took the metro. The view over the fjord was just breathtaking and I never seemed to get tired of it, even though I could only see it from half of my flat, as the other half had no windows.

The other surprising thing was that, no matter who I talked to, they all seemed to be surprised that I was renting my home. It appeared that every single Norwegian I knew had bought their home. Even if it was a 35-square-meter one-room apartment, they seemed to find great happiness in owning it. People had all sorts of arguments to push me to buy a home in Norway and did not seem to listen to any of my arguments not to do so. That I was not sure how long I would live in Norway, that

I liked the freedom of being able to resign my lease contract in three months and that I did not have the responsibility of repairing things in my flat. The owner of the flat did. I also found it terrifying to take out a mortgage over 25 or 30 years. Norwegians certainly were not scared of taking loans. They were taking plenty of them.

Some of my colleagues were even going on websites to advise me on the banks with the best interest rates and looking at flats for me although I had no intention of buying one. All the homes looked exactly the same. White walls. Gray furniture. Wooden floors. Gray stones and candles in the bathroom, orchids in front of windows. Sometimes they were showing me different ads and I did not even notice. It was as if none of the flats (or the owners) had any character or personality. I just did not get it. Was plain and unoriginal the cool thing to be in Norway?

Sure, I was paying rent, but in France everyone pays rent until late in life. There was nothing wrong with that, I thought. It allows us to move more easily instead of committing, and we buy a house later in life – like my parents, who bought their first house when they were 35 years old, and it was not a brand-new house but an old rundown house they had to refurbish.

In Norway, things seemed different. Here, owning one's own home seemed to be a fundamental human right. One needs it as much as one needs to eat, breathe, and get enough snow to ski in the winter. I didn't quite understand why even 20-year-old kids were obsessed with "entering the real estate market."

It seemed to me like a very conservative dream for someone that young. Twenty is the age to travel the world, start a punk band, and rebel against society. I was obviously wrong, as this was not the case for 20-year-olds in Norway. It was more like what one aimed at having at 45 in France: a comfortable life in a new home one owns was expected by Norwegians (at least from Oslo) who had just stopped getting teenage acne.

In the meantime, I was very happy living on my hill, paying rent, looking at the view I would have never had the money to buy, and figuring out whether I liked Norway enough to stay here.

*Note to self:* to avoid annoying questions from Norwegians trying to convince me to buy a flat as if their family owned half of Oslo, always have a Finn ad on my phone to make sure to show pictures of a flat I'm going to visit this Sunday in what they call a *visning*.

# NORWEGIAN SKIING 101

Suddenly, the Winter Olympics took over our lives. I discovered that in Norway cross-country skiing, or *langrenn*, as they call it here, is not just a sport. This seemed to be part of the Norwegian national identity. I felt a change of mood in the air as soon as the skiing competitions started in February. These shy, humble, and discreet people became noisy, proud, and emotional about anything happening to their skiers. Or even to their skiers' skis. Or to the wax under their skiers' skis.

Any competition involving ice or snow, especially cross-country skiing and biathlon, made them become a little angry (when a Swede won), a little arrogant (when a Norwegian won), or a little depressed (when Norwegians didn't win three days in a row).

The first noticeable change was in the media. While normally covering regular news, Norwegian TV channels, radio programs, and newspaper articles suddenly started talking 80 percent about the Winter Olympics and 20 percent about all the other stuff happening in Norway and the world. Stuff like fires, wars, and floods. New debates came in the public arena which were surreal for anyone who isn't Norwegian. Should employees be authorized to watch the Games during working hours? Oslo's Mayor said that no, the 55,000 employees of the Oslo municipality would not be allowed to watch the games during working hours. Then a "leadership expert," whatever that means, was invited to say it's a bad idea to forbid watching the games. The best part is that all this was tagged under "labor conflict" by the newspapers. If a country comes to consider this as a labor conflict, it must mean all the other real conflicts have already been solved, which is impressive.

Second, I noticed the change in Norwegians around me. These skiing competitions revealed a new aspect of Norwegian culture: my colleagues who were usually very humble when talking about themselves, and were shy and calm in public, had suddenly no shame in bragging about how the Norwegian team was the best in the world.

"Yeah... in cross-country skiing. A sport you invented," I liked to remind them. They were surprised I had never heard of Petter Northug or never watched cross-country skiing on television as a child.

I was trying to update myself by reading the Norwegian newspapers which were available at work every day. I discovered jobs I did not suspect existed, but that have a huge responsibility in the collective happiness of Norwegian people. One of them is the *smøresjef*. I translated that to "butter boss" (*smør* = butter, and *sjef* = boss). I thought for a moment that the butter boss had the job to solve another butter crisis.

In 2011 there was a Norwegian Butter Crisis, with a shortage of butter at the crucial Christmas time where lots of butter is needed to bake the traditional cakes. People started selling it for ten times the regular price and smuggling it from Sweden. Maybe the butter boss they talked about in the news would make sure the supply matches the demand of butter is always ensured in Norway for Christmas. Why they would call the same man to help in a skiing competition was a mystery to me.

I was wrong: *smør* can mean many things in Norwegian. It can mean "butter" but also "wax." A *smøresjef* is a head wax technician, who makes sure the skis of the skiers are properly waxed. The waxing team and the butter boss were blamed for the Norwegian team losing. I don't fully understand what went wrong here, as there is apparently a team of 25 waxing experts who were in charge of this, with a budget of 25 million NOK in making sure the skis are waxed properly. How can one screw this up? I asked Torbjørn one day at lunch. How hard can it be to wax a few skis?

"Waxing is AN ART!" He answered, very annoyed. Okay, calm down.


But thinking about it, I give it to the Norwegians that the Winter Olympics are the only moment when they can forget about being humble and nice and be on top of the world for once. Good for them. We all need our 15 minutes of glory, even if it only happens for a few weeks in the winter. Everyone is allowed to be proud and arrogant and scream of joy for the success of the national sports team. Norway is a small nation and cannot produce as many high-level athletes as populated places like China or the US.

Norway is probably offering the best terrain in the world for all these cross-country skiing and biathlon competitions: Sweden is too flat. Let's not even talk about Denmark. Finland and Russia are busy trying to see who will die first in sauna competitions, and Canadians are too busy winning in ice-hockey. So the Norwegians have to win these competitions more than any other country, because it is their chance at being an international superpower. They just need to chill a bit, if you ask me, and remember that the definition of cross-country skiing is not "a game where Norwegians win every time."

Otherwise the other nations wouldn't bother participating. So yes, the Norwegians have to be prepared to lose at least sometimes.

*Note to self:* in Norway, it is socially forbidden to brag on an individual basis about one's own achievements. It is, however, acceptable to brag about the collective achievements of Norwegians.

Winning in sports, winning at Eurovision, winning at chess, being on the top of a UN chart on the human development index. However, it seems that foreigners are never allowed to brag. If they brag about their personal achievements, they are seen as not respecting the "don't think you are better than me" rule.

Remember it is highly encouraged for foreigners to learn how to ski because then you show interest in integrating into this culture. But, do not, under any circumstances, become better at skiing than Norwegians.

There was no risk of this happening in my case. I didn't intend to enter a competition — I just wanted to learn how to ski, because I had understood how important it was to the Norwegian culture. Ramu, the Indian engineer from my Norwegian course, and I enrolled for a beginner's class in skiing at the Oslo Sports Center.

He was from Pondicherry, a city formerly ruled by the French. He spoke some French and was a poet in his own native language, Tamil. We both enjoyed writing and playing with words. His family didn't consider poetry to be a good career path, so he became an engineer and worked for the Tata Group in Oslo.

He was as lost in translation as I was in Norway, and as eager as I was to learn more about this culture and integrate in this society.

First challenge: we had to get some skis and equipment. I bought a pack with skis, poles, shoes, and pants. It is crazy – those clothes cost almost as much or more than the skis themselves. As I had little time that week, I had to go to the shop on the Friday after work, the course being Saturday morning.

I got out of the sports shop with my skis, feeling very uncomfortable. I was in the middle of the city center trying to hold these skis without hitting someone in the head. I had planned to go to something called *fredagspils*, the "Friday beer," a social gathering with my colleagues.

What was I going to do with these skis? I would be too ashamed to take them to the bar, but then what else would I do with them? They were new, if I left them on the corner of a street to pick them up later, they would have surely disappeared.

I decided to get over my shame and take them to the bar. How strange and ridiculous I looked! Having a beer with my skis in a corner. For a French person this is the equivalent of going to a fancy party with your sweatpants on. You don't mix jogging and cocktail parties, so why mix skiing and beer drinking on a Friday with colleagues? It doesn't look professional.

To my great surprise, as I entered the bar called Justisen in the center of Oslo with my skis on my shoulder, trying to look as invisible as possible, people smiled at me. It was the first time so many strangers smiled at me. One man even talked to me! I could not believe it – he didn't even look drunk.

"Going skiing? How lucky you are!" he said, with a broad smile.

Another person hearing me speak English said, "Oh so wonderful, you will learn how to ski, good luck!"

64

These people were full of surprises. Next time I need smiles and human warmth in this country I will just put my skis on my shoulder and walk around bars, I thought. Maybe I could even make Norwegian friends like that. It seemed to be a great ice-breaker with locals.

I went home not too late after a few beers with my colleagues, asking them endless questions about Norwegian culture. The road was so long to understand Norwegians.

The next day we met up with Ramu at the metro station Majorstuen to go together to a place called Sognsvann. We met all the people in our beginners' course and the instructors, who looked like Norwegians from magazines. Tall, blond, and in skiing gear.

"Hi, I'm bored and he is odd," said one of them pointing at his colleague. The whole class exploded into laughter. This was a Norwegian joke, we thought.

"I am Bård and he is Odd. These are common Norwegian names," said Bård.

These names Norwegian people give their kids… it's as if they did not realize all these words have a different meaning internationally. Didn't any parents think their kids would meet foreigners or go abroad some day? He also had an assistant, with a much easier name to understand: Kaia. Bård introduced her as "one of those Norwegians who are born with skis on her feet, because she comes from Trøndelag." I didn't really get the link between the two, but there obviously was one.

To my great surprise, half of the class was Norwegian! Some of them weren't born on skis after all. Most of those who were there came from Southern Norway and Oslo. They had decided to stop pretending they weren't interested in cabin trips in the winter when their problem was they could not ski.

The difference between the Norwegians and the immigrants in the course was mainly the gear. Norwegians had expensive skis and were all in fancy clothes and sunglasses with "Swix" written on them. The immigrants like me were in old skiing pants their friends would lend them. Usually in flashy colors from the 1980s. But then again, what is the point in having all that great expensive gear if you cannot use it on a slope?

Bård checked the skis of all the participants to make sure we had sanded skis before we put the wax. He stopped at Ramu, who had apparently bought the wrong kind of skis. He had bought slalom skis.

"How was I supposed to know there were two types of skis?" he asked, slightly desperate. "I went into the shop and said I wanted to buy skis. This is what they gave me," he added. Luckily he hadn't used them, so he could bring them back and exchange them. But in the meantime, he had no skis. Luckily, Bård and Kaia had access to a room with a lot of old skis and found a pair to fit Ramu.

Once Bård made sure we all had the right skis, and that they were sanded, he went on to explain the different waxes and how to wax cross-country skis. He took out a red box which was the size of a toolbox and took out many little pots of different colors.

Red, blue, purple, silver, green. We all looked at the little pots and started taking one in our hands, to see what it looked and felt like inside. Then we quickly all chose one, probably feeling we would not have the color of our choice if we took too long to choose. I took the green one because I like green. The others chose the wax color matching their skis or pants. Some girls were fighting over the purple wax because they felt like it was better suited to their own skis, and there was only one purple wax in the box. Then the Kazakh guy started complaining because he felt there were only feminine colors, and he wanted a black wax. Ramu wanted a golden wax.

"Why is the choice of colors so restricted?" asked the Kazakh guy. "Why don't you prepare better when you go skiing?" he added.

I noticed Bård was irritated. I don't usually notice when Norwegians are annoyed, which means he was probably feeling even more annoyed inside, and just letting us see what he was unable to control.

"We do NOT choose the color of the wax which matches our skis. Waxing is not a fashion show," he said, snapping all the wax pots out of our hands. He put all the waxes back into the box.

"Everyone gets the same wax today" he announced, to our great disappointment. "The green one".

I smiled. My color won!

"Each wax is suited for different types of snow and temperature," said Bård.

"It is very important to have the right wax, or the right combination of wax. Otherwise the snow sticks to the skis, or they slide too much," added Odd. "Today we will all use this wax because it is cold and the snow is hard."

"How can there be different types of snow?" asked Ramu. "Isn't snow just snow?"

"There are many different types of snow density," answered Odd. It was like he was trying to teach quantum physics to a group of penguins. We weren't really his greatest crowd.

"Let's start skiing now," he said, starting to ski towards a flat surface behind the lake of Sognsvann.

Once there, he asked Kaia to show us the movements needed for cross-country skiing. Diagonal movements between legs and arms, while putting pressure on the feet to get speed. I was proud of myself because I could stand on the skis without falling. And also because some were worse than me. The guy from Kazakhstan could not keep his balance on his skis while just standing on a flat surface. Then when we started moving downhill, this girl from Australia got stuck in the middle of the slope. She had waxed her skis before coming, and the snow was sticking to her skis. Bård wanted to change the wax so that she could slide down, but she refused. She was so scared of going down the hill that she preferred not moving, being stuck.

To all the Norwegians saying cross-country skiing is just like walking... nonsense. I've walked all my life and never had problems with that. I have many problems skiing on the other hand: skiing fast, going downhill without falling. All of us fell, some of us hurt ourselves while skiing, by for example crashing into trees. Some hurt other people, like Ramu who almost beheaded a little girl when he clipped his skis off and swung them across his shoulder without looking. Her mother was very kind and just smiled, telling him to be careful.

I think the most depressing part of the course was to see small children as young as four ski like pros next to us while we were adults struggling to keep a normal speed without feeling exhausted. Skiing is very tiring if you don't have the right technique. At the end of the day, Bård said the rest was mostly about practice.

We went back to the city, and I felt like I was one step closer to integrating in Norwegian society. Sure I had been skiing only once, but it was a beginning, right? Kaia and I chatted on the metro on the way back to the centre. She showed me where Trøndelag was on the map, and her village next to a small town called Røros. She had just moved to Oslo and was very lively and friendly. She had lived in Brazil and spoke perfect Portuguese. She also worked in my field, NGOs. We hit it off, so we exchanged numbers so that we could maybe have a coffee.

When I got home, I was exhausted. I thought of Torbjørn, who comes back to work from his skiing weekends, having skied dozens of kilometers every day with a backpack. And I had been around a flat track 20 minutes from Oslo for two hours. Then down the same hill five times. And I felt like I ran half a marathon.

*Note to self:* as a foreigner, I will probably never reach the level in cross-country skiing of a five-year-old Norwegian child. Some Norwegians hate skiing, they just don't say it out loud. Others don't know how to ski, and they are even more discreet about it. Your outfit, with the right brands, is as important as your technique. To be like Norwegians, it is very important to count the distance one skied over the weekend in *mil* (the Scandinavian mile is 10 kilometers) and then brag about it at work on Monday. It is only after the sweat and pain of skiing over several dozens of *mil* that one can reward oneself with hot chocolate and a cinnamon bun locally called a *kanelbolle*.

# TROMSØ UNDER
# THE NORTHERN LIGHTS

Aske was busy with his exams and it was harder for him to come as often as he did initially. Now that our flat was sorted, all he needed before he moved to Norway was to finish his exams. I spent my lunches looking at my colleagues laughing at each other's jokes in Norwegian while I was trying to grasp what on Earth they were talking about. I understood bits and pieces of conversations but was mainly looking like an idiot by laughing at the wrong moment at something that was not a joke. I would also ask questions that had previously been answered, or just say something completely off topic. My social life was not very exciting. I had one friend, Ane, and I got some kind of social interaction through my Norwegian courses.

Sometimes I tried to invite my colleagues to drink a glass of wine or a coffee at my place but they all had busy lives and schedules. Many left the office early to take care of their families. It was dark and cold, and my skiing skills were obviously nothing I could occupy my weekends with. I was starting to get bored. Thankfully Kaia had called me back, and we met a few times for a cup of tea and cake. She made a point of always speaking Norwegian so that I would learn fast. My conversation skills were so poor, and I understood so little.

I was feeling a bit lonely but was not going to give up so fast. I wanted to travel and discover Norway, especially Northern Norway, the Northern Lights, whale watching, dog sledding, ice-fishing, reindeer-hunting, igloo-building, and bikini-skiing.

Ane's family was from Tromsø and she said her parents could host me for a weekend and drive me around if they had time off from work. So I booked the flights. Tromsø is roughly as far from Oslo as Oslo is from Paris. Around 2,000 kilometers. Norway is a long country, I realized.

When I went to the office the next day and told my colleagues I had decided to visit Northern Norway, they looked at me as if I was crazy.

"But it's cold up there. And dark. Why would you go there when you have time off? You come from the South of France. Go home to the sun!" said Åse, who originally came from Oslo.

"But it's so exotic, nobody in my entire family has ever been north of the Arctic circle," I replied, smiling. "I can go to France anytime, but this is a once-in-a-lifetime opportunity."

"So are you going to Trondheim?" asked Åse.

"Trondheim? Is that already Northern Norway? I am going to Tromsø," I asked.

"Tromsø! That's really north! Well, technically Trondheim isn't in Northern Norway but it is north enough. It's the furthest north I've been in Norway," she answered.

The others around the table nodded in approval.

"How many of you have actually been to Northern Norway?" I asked.

The only two who were eating lunch with us who had been there were Knut, our colleague who grew up in Kirkenes, and the guy from the administration department whose wife was from Bodø.

I was stunned. How can they not know their own country? They seemed to prefer going to a place called *Syden* instead of Northern Norway. From the pictures I found on the net, Northern Norway seemed much more attractive, with beautiful white sand beaches, Northern lights, whales, islands with high peaks and small red houses, while a Google search for *Syden* only showed me pictures of Norwegians holding beers on the beach.

The next Thursday, I did what some of my colleagues did and left the office early to take a three-day weekend. As I boarded the plane for Tromsø, I instantly felt the change in the atmosphere from what I had seen in Oslo. The voices, the noise. The laughs. Strangers sitting next to each other were actually having conversations. Making jokes, speaking loudly. I smiled. It reminded me of home.

Because let's face it, social interaction in Oslo is like a never-ending trip in an elevator. The only thing people are waiting for is to get out of the elevator and escape the terrifying idea of having to do small talk.

Northern Norwegians already seemed different. I had two ladies sitting next to me who were very happy to answer all my questions about the differences between people in Oslo and Northern Norwegians.

At first, they explained with simple words I could understand, but then after two beers they were using what seemed to be dialect words. At least none of these words were in my Norwegian books at my Norwegian class.

"The *Søringa* took all our wealth, our oil. Without us, they would be nothing. But they decide over us," said one of the women, who was named Toril.

I was taking notes. "Who are the *Søringa*?" I asked.

For any Northern Norwegian, Norway is divided in two, the border being the southern border of the Nordland county. Anyone coming from North of that border is a Northern Norwegian, and anyone coming from the south of that border is a *Søring*. *Søring* is not a very nice word, by the way. It turns out there is an actual region called Southern Norway (Sørlandet in Norwegian), located way south by the most southern coast of Norway, facing Denmark. But that is not the region Northern Norwegians refer to when talking about "Southern Norway" and *Søringa*. It seems the map of Norway is different depending on who you talk to, since my colleagues from Oslo believed Trondheim was already Northern Norway. This was getting awfully confusing. Norwegians, despite being a population of five million, seemed to think it's not worth learning the name of any city or town more than a few hundreds of kilometers from them. To add to this, I could feel resentment in Toril's voice regarding those southerners who had more power and more wealth. There seemed to be discrimination against those from up North.

"For the *Søring*, Northern Norway is a long coastal lane of land inhabited by people living in the dark who are exposed to too much moonshine. Can you imagine that when I went to Oslo in the 1960s I could not find a room to rent? The ads were saying 'Northern Norwegians are not welcome.'" she said. "*Jævla søringa.*" *Jævla* is a Norwegian swear word coming from "the Devil." This means something like "bloody southerners".

Ah! Exactly like when I was living in Denmark, I remembered, where most ads were stipulating "Room available for Danes only".

"I don't see any obvious discrimination against Northern Norwegians now in Oslo. When did this change?" I asked.

"When the Pakistanis came," she replied. "But it continues in a way until now. Did you know that Norway has never had a Prime Minister from Northern Norway? The only ministries we get are those relating to fisheries," she added.

This was very interesting. So there *was* trouble in paradise. The "Norwegian dream" sold to foreigners in the Norwegian course books was always about Norway being a heterogeneous society which all became richer thanks to the oil. Nobody ever told me there had been discrimination among Norwegians in the past, with some resentment still palpable among them nowadays. Marseille, where I come from, has this image among other French people and especially among Parisians, of being a rough city where everyone is violent, lazy, and uneducated compared to those from the capital city. So what this lady was saying was certainly something I could relate to.

We landed in Tromsø on a night where the sky had a very unique color. It was clear, and dark blue mixed with a shimmer of pink coming from the horizon. Ane's mother was waiting for me at the airport. Her name was Nina and she spoke with a very strong Northern Norwegian accent.

"*Katti kom du?*" she asked me.

"Excuse me? My name is Lorelou, not Katy," I answered.

"*Ka tid.* It means 'At what time did you come?' I know your name is not Katy," she said, smiling. "It's the way we say it in the North of Norway. By the way, although I have a strong dialect from here, I am actually from a small island in Finland called Åland. We speak Swedish there. I've been living here in Tromsø for over 30 years," Nina explained.

We chatted in a mix of Norwegian and English until we reached their home, which was behind a tall, white, pointy monument over a bridge. It happened to be a church, more precisely *Ishavskatedralen*, or Tromsø's Arctic Cathedral. Nina explained that this monument's architecture was inspired by an island called Håja, which she said she could drive me to the next day if I was interested. Of course I was interested, I just wanted to absorb whatever there was to learn about this new exotic place.

I realized after some time that every word that was supposed to have a H in the Norwegian Oslo people spoke became K in her dialect: "*Ka sa du?*" Instead of "*Hva sa du?*" (What did you say?) or "*Kofor fløta du til Norge?*" instead of "*Hvorfor flyttet du til Norge?*" (Why did you move to Norway?).

It had snowed a lot during the night, so Nina started shovelling snow. She gave me another shovel and it took us about two hours to clear the car out of snow, turn it on, and shovel the road for the car to get out. I think I sweat so much that I had done my physical exercise for the whole week with what seemed to be called "*måking.*"

***Note to self:*** remember that *en måke* is a seagull, and that has nothing to do with sweating in the snow.

When we eventually managed to have a clear way for the car to drive out, we put our bums on the seats which were pre-heated. I had never sat on a heated car seat in my entire life. What a luxury this car was!

We drove through the city of Tromsø which is an island. There are two bridges linking the island to the mainland on one side and to Kvaløya on the other side. She stopped close to the airport to show me a point on the horizon. "Look," she said "the sun has been coming up for a few weeks now. *Mørketida* is over."

We were just on the side of the road close to the airport, between a highway and some kind of lake or fjord, but the view was nonetheless breathtaking. The clear blue and pink sky reflected its light in the still water. The light was much sharper than I imagined.

"What is *mørketida?*" I asked.

"It's the word we use to call the period of the year where we don't have sunlight. It lasts for three months from November to January," she answered. I felt like Oslo was pretty dark already, how could it be here with basically zero sunlight for months? How can they survive this?

"But the rest of the time there are normal days?" I asked.

"No. It starts with one minute of daylight on the 21$^{st}$ of January, then *mørketida* is over. Then it comes back quite fast, we gain several minutes of daylight per day until the 21$^{st}$ of June when it reverses again to get less and less daylight," she said.

"Do you get depressed in the winter?" I asked.

"No, but we sleep more. And I need to do a lot of physical exercise. Otherwise, it's tough. We watch TV a lot as well. But then in the summer we have so much light, it's fantastic. Our mood changes. You should come back in the summer to see how it is!" she said. She wouldn't have to make that offer twice! I loved Northern Norway already.

We got back into the car and drove. We got out of Tromsø to an island called Kvaløya: the island of the whale. We drove inland for a while, on what seemed to be an old road, and then we suddenly saw the coast. We stopped at a place called Sommarøy (*øy* means island), where we sat on a beach. It was the purest landscape I'd seen in my life. The mountains far away were covered in snow, the light was pinkish and blue, and we could see an island that, indeed, looked very much like the cathedral behind Nina's house. Or more like the cathedral looked like the island.

"Haaøya!" she said, pointing at the island. We walked a bit, there was so much wind. Then we drove again, to a place called Brensholmen where her husband's brother lived. He had a very big wooden house with low ceilings and floors that didn't look very level. Most importantly, it was built above the level that the tide could reach. Nina's husband's mother was there when we visited; it was the house she grew up in.

"When I was a child, there was no road to come here. We had to go to Tromsø by boat," she said.

I looked outside. The sky was beautiful, and so was the low tide on the infinite horizon. But the wind, man the wind. Freezing one's bones, whatever one was wearing. I cannot imagine what a seven month winter feels like here, without a road to get out. What if the boat cannot come because of a storm, what would they eat? Sand and stormy clouds?

The old lady looked healthy enough. She survived the storms and the caloric restrictions she was probably subjected to.

"I live in Tromsø now and sold the house to my son. This big house is too much work for me alone," she said.

"I don't blame you!" I replied with a smile. I had trouble taking care of a forty square meter flat.

We ate pieces of flat, white, soft dough with what seemed to be butter and sugar and cinnamon inside. And coffee, of course. A Northern Norwegian house without five liters of coffee per person ready at any time is not a home. You need to be prepared in case someone drops by unexpectedly.

I would have loved to stay a little more and explore all the rooms. From the little I saw of the house (on my way to the toilets), all the rooms seemed to have lower ceilings than any modern house. I was sure three books could be written on what this house had seen over the generations of Northern Norwegians who had lived in it, the tides it had seen, the fishermen smelling like salt and sweat coming home.

Sadly, we had to leave. Nina had to go to the hospital for a few hours to work. She dropped me off in the city center of Tromsø, and I went to the information center to see which activity I could do that afternoon in this Arctic city. It was

2pm on a Saturday in February. And I was 344 km north of the Arctic circle and 644 km south of the North Cape. In other words, very far from home.

I had never been in a city with such slippery sidewalks in my life. The whole city was a giant ice-skating rink. How did people manage not to break their skulls every winter? It was a mystery. I was holding myself to everything I could see on the sidewalks: trees, metal ramps. My feet were sliding in every direction.

I could go on a trip to chase the Northern Lights, but for that I had to sit in a bus for six hours to the border with Finnmark and stay outside looking at the sky in the cold. I did not want to do that, so I booked a spot to go dog sledding on the Lyngen Alps. I managed to get to the meeting point without falling and waited there for the others. The other participants were mainly tourists. While on the minibus taking us from Tromsø to the location of the dog owners and where we would start the race, we all started chatting.

There was John, a tourist from England traveling to Tromsø to get some excitement and "meet people." People with long blond hair and a vagina, it seemed. But let's pass on that. There were also two old ladies from the Netherlands who were fascinated by the Northern lights and Norway in general. And a Chinese couple who spoke English like me when the dentist anesthetized half of my lower face: impossible to understand.

As we got to the location where our hosts, Anja and Gáppe, had their dogs, we were taken into a big room with dozens of warm suits in order not to freeze while riding. I'm so short I had trouble finding one my size, but it turned out fine in the end. We all went to meet the huskies and were shown how to steer the sleds. We patted the dogs a bit so that they could get to know our smell, and so that we could get used to them. I'm really not a dog person but these ones were really beautiful and friendly; they were living outside and running all the time.

We had to be in pairs: one had to stand behind the sled and steer, while the other would sit in front and enjoy the ride. Each sled had eight dogs. As the others were all in pairs, I had to be paired with John. We had to decide who would be steering first. That person was also the one braking, by putting all of one's weight on a metal bar on the bottom of the sled.

"I'm not sure I'm strong enough to brake," said John.

"If you can't, how could I?" I was half of his weight and strength. "But fine, I will steer first," I answered.

I took the lead. It was so exciting. At first the dogs were not running that fast, but after a while they were cutting through the snow like rockets. I looked away for some seconds: we were dog sledding on a white mountain under the dark blue Arctic sky. It was breathtaking. The frozen wind was whipping my face and I had to take control of the dogs and stop daydreaming. No northern lights in sight unfortunately. We continued like that for a while, and then it was time to swap. John took the lead. I was sitting on the seat between the steering person and the dogs, feeling like a queen being ported by guards.

Until the driver of the coach screamed. "No, this is too hard. Noo!" said John.

"What, John? What is too hard?" I asked.

As I was not getting any answer I looked back, the idiot had jumped off the sled and was in the snow. The dogs did not care; they were running, so happy not to have anyone stopping them.

I was on a free ride in the snow, without anyone to brake. I thought of taking control of the sled but from where I was sitting it was impossible to move back to where John had been standing. Or I could jump off, but the sled was going downhill very fast. So I started screaming, to alert Gáppe and Anja. Then the dogs in front of us stopped, but ours continued running, so we crashed into a hill of snow probably hiding a rock, and a piece of the sled broke. Anja checked it and it seemed it could hold for the rest of the trip despite the crash.

From then on, I took the lead of the sled and did not allow John to even look at the spot behind the brake. He was sitting under his reindeer fur looking very content.

We got back to Gáppe and Anja's place in one piece, and while the dogs were taken back to their homes and given food, we drank warm cocoa in the *lavvu*, the big tent that Gáppe and Anja had behind their house. We looked at the sky and talked about the four hours we had spent on the sleds, which felt like 30 minutes at most. The only thing that made us believe the time we had spent outside was the cold we felt on our bums, and on our cheeks.

We took the minibus back to Tromsø, and I took the bus to the other side of the bridge behind the Arctic Cathedral where Nina and her husband Svein lived. I was tired, cold, and hungry, and luckily Svein had baked something that smelled incredibly good. It was fish! Ane's brother, David, was there too with his girlfriend Ayta, who was a student at the University of Tromsø.

This fish was without any doubt one of the most tender fish I had eaten in my whole life. And I am from Marseille, a harbor known for its fish dishes like *bouillabaisse*. I have eaten a lot of fish in my life. There was something about this fish's meat which made it inimitable and so tasty.

"This fish is called *skrei*. It has traveled for 1000 kilometers from the Barents Sea to the Lofoten Islands. Some call it *torsk* but they are just ignorant. The regular cod does not travel that far, it just stays around here," said Svein while serving me wine. With that, there was a slice of what looked like fish eggs, and fish liver. It looked like a dream come true.

I told them how we grilled sardines in Marseille, thousands of them on the beach in what we call Sardinade. There were also potatoes, *kålrabi*, and carrots. And there were small glasses filled with golden liquid. Svein said "*Skål!*" and lifted his glass, so I assumed I had to do the same. I said "*Skål!*" and drank the golden liquid which I imagined being some kind of traditional Northern Norwegian drink people take with *skrei*, maybe a *skrei aquavit*? But to my great surprise, it was melted butter. As Svein saw my face when my throat had gulped the butter he exploded in laughter.

While the others were drinking *aquavit* (the real one this time) I made a chocolate cake from my grandmother's recipe. While the cake was in the oven, we cleaned the kitchen and sat by the fireplace with the television in the background. Nina was knitting a jumper for her daughter who had ordered a non-traditional pattern: brown skulls on a green mosaic instead of the quintessential red, white and blue woolen sweatshirt. I needed to find a man who has a mother or a grandmother who can knit those things for me, I thought. Svein was looking at the fire in silence while drinking wine, so I chatted with Ayta. She was Russian, from Siberia, and was studying at the University of Tromsø. She and David met at an ice-bathing club outside of Tromsø.

"Ice-bathing?" I asked, shocked.

"Yes, in Siberia we make a hole in the ice and jump in, but here we just walk in the water in the fjord. There is a little salt, so it does not completely freeze," she added.

The funny thing with Ayta is that she always felt warm in Tromsø. She came from the coldest inhabited place on Earth, Yakutsk in Siberia. In the winter, it was so cold smartphones would not work. It takes someone from Siberia to feel like Tromsø is semi-tropical, I thought.

I felt very close to these people I had just met, as if we had always known each other. They were so nice and friendly, and so funny – the dry humor that I liked. We ate the cake with a cup of dark coffee and went to bed.

I slept like a baby and woke up with great difficulty the next day as the sun did not rise. I decided to explore the city on my own, and left after a filling breakfast made of bread, salmon, eggs, and smoked mackerel. For some strange reason, I decided to walk over the bridge instead of taking the bus. Ah yes, the ticket was very expensive. The view was actually great, but it was freezing cold because of the wind. When I got to the other side, I walked to the city and explored Tromsø.

For a place with only 70 000 inhabitants, the city offers an impressive number of cafés, libraries, and movie theatres. Nina told me there was a famous film festival organized every year in mid-January: Tromsø International Film Festival. Such a shame I missed it by two weeks, I would have to come back next year.

I sat in a very – what do they say again in Norway – *koselig* café called *Verdensteatret* (The World's Theatre) and started writing postcards to my parents and my grandmother. "Hello from the North Pole!" It wasn't the North Pole, but close enough as far as anyone from Marseille is concerned.

While I was writing, David texted me and asked me whether I wanted to go out, it was Saturday evening. He told me he was meeting up with some friends in a student bar called Driv in the city center (as opposed to where? I wondered. The whole city was the center). There were mostly guys there, as Ayta was home studying.

The drunker they got, the more "dialect" they spoke and the less I understood. But at least they were friendly, offering the French girl some local Mack beer. I missed Aske. I was having so much fun and I wished he was there. Just when I was texting him, David's friend Mikkel spilled his beer over my phone and apologized with a great smile filled with black things on his teeth. Gum disease, maybe? I asked him what the little round box he kept on the table close to him was. The black thing from his mouth was coming from there. Oh, those were the licorice or chocolate boxes I saw people buy at the airport duty-free, I thought. I opened the top lid of the box and small wet black things were looking at me, smelling like dead rats. "This is not licorice, this is tobacco!" I realized. I sent an SMS to Ramu: "That thing you swallowed was not chocolate, it was tobacco. That is why it didn't taste good."

It turns out Norwegians' first mission whenever they go abroad, even if it is to Sweden, is to buy as much snus — tobacco to keep in one's mouth rather than to smoke — and as much alcohol and candy as is allowed by the Norwegian government's quota. Taxes on these products are high in Norway, so people love to shop for cheaper prices in foreign supermarkets or duty-free shops, even if that means missing their train home!

The evening was grand, and as I got more and more drunk, I also got hungry. Luckily, they were selling dried reindeer sticks at the bar which I chewed on all night. Not that I was having great conversations with everyone, but the atmosphere was great, and I felt involved although I spoke little Norwegian. David and his friends taught me a song, of which I did not understand the words but just repeated the sounds mechanically:

*Ka du sei, ka du mein*
*Har du pula mange rein*
*Var det en eller to*
*Var det han eller ho*


*What you say, what you mean*
*Have you f\*\*\* many reindeer*
*Was it one or two*
*Was it a male or a female*

I was so happy to speak Northern Norwegian that I repeated it all night to be sure to remember the lyrics. As the bar was closing, they decided to go to David's place. When we got there, they said they would teach me how to drink something called *karsk*. They had made dark coffee on the table, as well as coins and a bottle of unidentified alcoholic drink.

"The Norwegian way is to put a coin in a cup. Then pour coffee until you cannot see the coin. Pour moonshine until you can see the coin again," he said. As I was about to do that, he stopped my hand.

"But the Northern Norwegian way is to put a coin on the table. Pour coffee into the cup until you can't see the bottom of the cup, and then pour alcohol until the cup is full. Drink as many cups as you can, until you see as many coins on the table as the cups of alcohol you've had," he added. Everyone laughed.

"I remember once I drank *karsk* with some guys from Oslo. *Stakkars søringa* (poor Southerners). They did not even manage to get past the second drink," said Leif, David's friend from Karasjok. And they all laughed again.

We all fell asleep somewhere between the couches and the beds in the house. The word "hangover" took a whole new meaning the next morning. I felt like dying. "How do you guys get over a hangover in Northern Norway?" I asked.

"Northern Norwegians never have a hangover. It's called evolution," he answered.

"Oh, give me a break. Your liver might have seen more adventures than mine, but you look pretty tired too today," I answered.

Call it whatever you want, we spent the day sleeping, watching television, and sleeping more.

His parents put on the TV some supposedly "typical Norwegian" television shows. The first one was a fire burning show, live, where for several hours we watched the logs consume themselves in front of our eyes. I dozed off at some point but the great thing about slow television is that one quickly knows where the story is at. Not much suspense here, I was pretty sure none of the logs would survive a ten-hour fire.

At some point I opened my eyes because I felt a freezing breeze on my face. David had opened the door and was outside.

"Hey, not all of us were born to be sitting outside drinking coffee in -15 °C," I yelled for him to hear.

"Lorelou, come!" David yelled.

Covered in a woolen blanket, I walked into the snow. Above our heads a green dust of light was dancing in the immensity of the sky. The whole sky had become a huge movement of lights and dust which were green, purple and white. It lasted several minutes. It was one of the most beautiful things I had seen in my life: my first Northern Lights.

I felt so sad that I had to go back to boring Oslo. I wanted to stay – I still had to try out whale watching, visit the library, and eat at Tromsø's many wonderful restaurants. I hugged Nina one last time and gave her a little gift from home: lavender bags to put in her clothes so that it would smell like the flowers of my Provence. I boarded the plane to Oslo with a heavy heart. I fell in love with Northern Norway.

"Come back in the summer, when we have the midnight sun." Nina said as I was walking to the boarding area.

*Note to self:* Contrary to what my Norwegian teacher said in class, Noregian people are not that homogeneous. I only visited two areas in Norway, Oslo and Tromsø, and already found a wide variety of social codes, food cultures, dialects and even drinking games. I could not wait to travel more and discover all the variety the rest of Norway and its people had to offer.

# NE ME QUITTE PAS

When I returned from Tromsø I could not wait to tell Aske about my trip. I wanted to go back to Brennsholmen with him. We could rent bicycles and cycle to Senja in the summer. We could rent a boat and sail along the coast. We could take a road trip in Finnmark and follow reindeer in the *vidda*, or plateau. There was so much to discover in this country I initially thought had nothing much to offer. Aske had planned on bringing a few things from Copenhagen on every trip, and then moving for good to Oslo in the spring.

The night he arrived, I was waiting for him at the airport, expecting him to carry many heavy bags full of the belongings he needed to move here. He arrived with nothing, other than a four-kilo hand luggage.

"Weren't you supposed to start moving during this trip?" I asked.

"Yes, I was. But we need to talk," he answered.

In any relationship, one knows that the "we need to talk" is never very good. It means someone is pregnant, which I was pretty sure he wasn't. Or that your partner is leaving you for his yoga teacher, which is basically what he was doing.

When we got home, he pretended as if nothing needed to be said, and I had to get it out of him. Men are not so brave sometimes, especially when they have to face a woman who is potentially going to start crying. The whole thing boiled down to:

"I don't want to move here. All my friends are in Copenhagen. Oslo cannot become my home. It is too different from what I know. Too different from Norrebrø and too far from my friends."

I was speechless.

The next day he left with an early flight to Copenhagen. One-way. He called me a week later to tell me how relieved he was that he would not have to move to Norway. I realized this was real. I called my mother and explained. She seemed surprisingly happy for someone who is hearing the sad story of her daughter being left by the man she loved.

"Just come home. Drop the whole Scandinavia adventure. You can see this is not working out. There is a position at the post office down the street, I am sure you can still apply and get the job. We would be neighbors!" she said, enthusiastically.

I did not accept my mum's offer, but she had a point. What was I doing in Norway? It's not like Norway had ever been my top choice; it was a practical solution to maintain a relation-ship that did not exist anymore. I never dreamed of coming here, let alone live here on my own. Norwegians winters were so long. But I had signed a contract with my employer. I loved my job. This was going to be a lonely ride, I thought. I decided to give Norway a chance and leave if it became too tough. I gave myself one year.

# II

# SPRING

# SURVIVING WINTER

I remember, as a child, opening my bedroom window every morning before going to school to check the weather. There was always one day around the beginning of March when I noticed the sun was a bit brighter, the trees a bit greener. The Earth became warmer overnight. I smelled the air and closed my eyes: the first day of spring. Finally. The next Sunday, my dad would put Madonna or Maria Callas (he has a very eclectic music taste) very loud in the house, to wake all his four children. "Spring cleaning! Wake up!" he would yell, hitting on a pot with a wooden spoon, and opening our blinds. We would hate him for that – what kind of inhumane treatment is it to be woken up by Maria Callas at 10 am on a Sunday when one is 13 years old?

By the time we got up he had prepared some pancakes to lure us into cleaning with him and my mum, and then we would start. Everything had to be scrubbed and emptied and we would stash away our winter clothes, long sleeves and closed shoes, and take out our sandals and tank tops. When I say "winter clothes," this has nothing to do with what people wear in Norway. Not a single wool jumper was in our cupboards as it is never that cold in the winter in Marseille, down to five degrees, rarely zero degrees, but summers could be warm, up to 40 °C (104 °F).

The weather would be increasingly warm from that spring day, and summer was around the corner, with its promises of daily baths in the Mediterranean Sea until October.

It was already mid-March in Norway. I was opening my windows every morning with the hope of smelling that scent of spring I knew from Marseille, only to feel the chill of snow. Every other morning I was shoveling mountains of snow from the stairs in front of my flat to go to the office.

I did live close to the Olympic ski jump at Holmenkollen, where temperatures are two or three degrees colder than downtown. But still. Spring seemed to have forgotten us. I was looking outside and even when it was supposed to be daytime the sky seemed so dark. The hours of daylight were increasing every day, but still so little sunlight compared to what I was used to. I would leave for work in the morning in the dark and come home in the dark. No sign of Aske, who seemed to live a happy Danish life without me. My mother was calling; they were already eating in the garden and taking dips in the sea. Had I made the right choice in staying here alone?

I texted Ane to try to get out of my misery.

"Come to my place," she said. "I'll cheer you up."

She lived in an area of Oslo called Sagene. To get there, I walked up the Aker River which separates Oslo in two parts, the East and the West. I could not believe how beautiful Oslo was when I walked up that river, with its green areas and its waterfalls (!).

Her home was a perfect minimalistic Scandinavian home, just the opposite of mine. Where I would have painted a wall yellow or blue, her home was perfectly white with touches of gray. Even the orchid by the window was white, and the only touch of color was a dark blue Le Creuset pot on the stove in her kitchen. She served me one of those Norwegian coffees with lots of water in them, in a cup with a small angry girl painted on it. I recognized those cups from Nina's home in Tromsø and Kaia's home. They seemed to be a must-have for every Norwegian home. I later found out they were from the Moomin stories, written and illustrated by Tove Jansson, a Swedish-speaking Finn.

I told Ane about my longing for the spring, my break-up, and the darkness I had trouble carrying every day. I was so tired.

"I think you might have winter depression, but don't worry. It is curable," she said.

Ane was an always-positive kind of girl. She worked out an insane amount, had a killer body and was out every weekend to drink with friends if she was not traveling for work. She always had a new hot woman in her bed and did not seem to commit much in her love life. She just seemed to surf on life and always enjoy it.

"Do you take *Tran*?" she asked. I thought of it for a second. I had no idea what she was talking about. Was that some kind of sleeping pill that would make me hibernate until the first day of summer, so that I would not have to see these dark days anymore? She went to her fridge and took out a green bottle.

"Cod liver oil. You should take a spoon or two every day of every month ending in-*er* to avoid winter depression," she explained. Now it is March, you should have started in September." She took a spoon and gave me some to taste.

Oh gosh. Not recommended with a coffee taste in one's mouth. I remembered my grandmother telling me her parents forced her and her sisters to take cod liver oil as a child. This was disgusting.

"Yes, but it comes in lemon flavor too," she answered when seeing my distorted face after the terrible taste. Yuck! I could only imagine this fishy taste mixed with an artificial lemon taste, it sounded worse. "And capsules of course, for those who are *pyser*," she added laughing. I raised my eyebrows. "*Pyse* means wimp," she clarified.

I smiled and thought to myself that I will always be a wimp compared to Norwegians, no doubt about that. I gave up that fight on my first weekend here when I saw people skiing on a Saturday morning.

"There are many other ways to fight winter depression. You need to go out, be social, talk to friends, exercise. You can also do the Norwegian way of getting drunk every weekend, and having casual sex, especially now that you are single," she said with a wink. "Or you can go to *Syden* or get some sun in countries where it is warm during our winter. A cheaper option is to do UV light in a solarium here. Lighting candles is also important. To make things *koselig*."

I had heard it so often at the office and elsewhere in conversations. What did it mean?

*Note to self:* Norwegians do not cure winter depression with an ancient potion inherited from Norse Gods. Modern Norwegians use a combination of casual sex, artificial sun that can give you skin cancer, alcohol intoxication and charter trips to Mediterranean beaches. And fishy-tasting oil to take with your morning coffee.

Man, what a deal I made trading my mild winter in Provence for this.

# MAKE EVERYTHING *KOSELIG*

I sensed right after my arrival that *koselig* was something very important to Norwegians. They said it all day long and in different variations: *"kos deg!" "Det var så koselig," "kosemat,"* Så *koselig!"*

What did it all mean and why was it so important for them to make things *koselig*? As the weather got colder and the nights got longer, the quest for *koselig* reached a new level.

At first I really didn't get it. So I asked Ane:

"What is *koselig?*"

"This is *koselig!*" she answered, showing me a lit candle on the kitchen table.

"Being *koselig* is about candles?" I asked.

Of course not. It was much more complicated. And it became even more important to make things *koselig* during the winter, when the sunlight and warmth of the summer were gone. It seemed like making things *koselig* was a defense mechanism Norwegians had created to prepare for and survive the winter.

Being *koselig* is an important concept one needs to understand and embrace when living in Norway all year around. Most English speakers translate it as "cozy", but that term doesn't even begin to cover everything that *koselig* can express.

Anything in Norway can (and should) be *koselig*: a house, a conversation, a dinner, a person. It describes something/an atmosphere/a moment that makes you feel a sense of warmth very deep inside in a way that all things should be: simple and comforting.

I asked many different Norwegians for their definition of *koselig* and I realized it is not only hard for us to translate, it's also hard for them to explain.

"So *koselig* is the same as *hyggelig*?" I asked at lunch time.

That question lit endless discussions. To add to my confusion, Danes only have one word (*hyggelig*, which seems to be the equivalent of *koselig*) whereas Norwegians have two words: *koselig* and *hyggelig*. *Hyggelig* is apparently less intimate than *koselig*. One can, for example, say, "*Det var hyggelig å treffe deg*" (It was nice to meet you) at work. But saying "*Det var koselig å treffe deg*" has a whole new intimate meaning and is inappropriate in a strictly professional setting.

After a while I figured out some patterns of *koselig*. If a person left my house saying "*det var kjempekoselig*," and gave me a *klem*, a Norwegian hug, then I knew I was probably on my way to making a new friend.

A Norwegian hug, if you wonder how that differs from a regular hug given anywhere else in the world, is a hug where the person has a grip on one of your arms and presses their cheek on yours. Very strange at first, but a sign of high intimacy, or friendship amongst Norwegians. Making friends is however a complex process, which involves being invited to the family *hytte*, getting drunk together and much more.

So how to make things *koselig*? According to my experience in Norway, a *koselig* evening involves candles, good music and as few awkward silences as possible. No topics that will offend people. No heated discussions like we would have in France at any given occasion. Warm colors around you, a fire in the chimney, good food on the table, wine, and people you like and feel comfortable with. Chatting away the evening and the night with a little drunkenness and inner warmth.

Said like that, it sounds very easy to figure out what makes a *koselig* evening, especially in wintertime. But then it gets tricky because in Norway virtually everything needs to be *koselig*. And there is no manual for us to know how to be and make things *koselig* in all circumstances. So for example what is a *koselig* decoration in a house? What does a *koselig* kitchen look like? A *koselig* cup? What is a *koselig* thing to do on a weekend?

And to make it even harder, I realized that one needs to be *koselig* also in the summer. I thought it was all about finding comfort and warmth when there isn't any sun outside during the long and dark Scandinavian winters, but then if everything also needs to be *koselig* when it is light outside and summery…

What is a *koselig* day at the beach when there is no fireplace, no candles, and no woolen socks? I gave up.

Norwegians do it very naturally, and it is very obvious to them what is koselig and what isn't. Who is and who isn't. But for us foreigners, it's a different story. Could it mean, maybe, that doing things in a *koselig* way is cultural and not (at all) universal?

To be honest, before living here I had never felt the need to do *koselig* things. In any Southern European country like Spain, Italy, or France, we don't feel the urge to have nice things inside our houses because the whole point of social life is to be outside: at the beach, in a garden, in the street, on the terrace of a café. There are very few months where it's too cold to be outside, and therefore we wouldn't think to put a lot of money into refurbishing our interior every second year, or to put extra effort into making it look more welcoming and warmer. It is already warm outside, the windows are wide open, and we are eating fresh tomatoes and mozzarella salad with basil from the garden. No need to make a concept of coziness out of that; it's just called living.

But in Norway, it is completely different. The winters can be long, the nights too (especially in Northern Norway) and then one never knows what spring and summer will be like. In summer in Marseille, we knew for sure that tomorrow will be just as sunny and warm as it was today.

I could wake up and hop in my bathing suit without looking out the window or checking the weather forecast. The winter clothes would be buried deep in my closet and would not come out until next November.

But in Norway one can never be sure, even in mid-July or August, that it will be equally warm and sunny every day. So Norwegians have learned to seize the moment. The moment, in the summer, when the sun is warm enough to go lie in a park or on an island and bathe, or the moment one can wear a light dress or shorts. The moment, in the winter, where there is enough snow to go skiing with one's friends or kids or dog and enjoy some waffles in a cabin on the way.

One has to seize it because tomorrow it might be rainy and gray, and we might have to get our autumn jacket out of the cupboard and say goodbye to the summer for this year (and it's July!). For all these uncertain times Norwegians need other forms of warmth to hold on to: tequila (or gin and tonic, or *aquavit*) and *koselig*. It is an inner summer that Norwegians create for themselves to feel like it is warm all year long no matter the circumstances.

Another option is to think that Norwegians, not being culturally raised to express their feelings too much, made up a single word to express all at once love, friendship, comfort, trust, and most of all happiness. So practical!

*Note to self:* I can imagine an exercise to see if immigrants have managed to integrate in Norway with a *koselig* scale; in order to assess your ability to make life *koselig*.

You invite people over for dinner and you don't light candles? You definitely lost at least two points on the *koselig* scale. But then the next Sunday you make waffles (not from a box please, you made the batter yourself), that you serve with a homemade jam with berries that you picked yourself in the forest next to your cabin? Congratulations, you've just won three points on the *koselig* scale. You came back from a day of skiing and sweating in Nordmarka with your partner and offered him or her an iced tea and a doughnut? Minus three points on the koselig scale. Then turned on the heater and left the fireplace empty because it's much easier to just switch a button on than to actually light a fire? Minus three again points on the koselig scale. You were supposed to offer them warm chocolate with *pepperkaker*, Norwegian gingerbread, which was left over from your Christmas baking session, put wood in the fireplace, and crash on the sofa with them while watching the fire light up in silence, still wearing your sweaty woolen underwear.

Nobody said it was easy to be *koselig*.

# TACO FRIDAY

What Ane told me about having a social life to combat my winter depression and survive my first Norwegian winter hit home. I rang Kaia, since she was the closest I had to a friend in Oslo besides Ane.

"Come over to my place for dinner on Friday, 5pm. I will ask Pål to cook his specialty, a killer traditional Norwegian meal."

That sounded amazing. Pål was the guy she had been seeing a lot lately, without them being officially boyfriend and girl-friend, an in-between status I had issues understanding.

Meeting people around a warm traditional Norwegian meal was exactly what I needed right now. Kaia lived in a *kollektiv* or shared apartment in an area called Gamlebyen, the Old Town. I got there at 5pm sharp, as I had learned never to be late when invited by Norwegians.

Being invited for dinner in a Norwegian home happened to me once before. Ane's family in Tromsø, because I was staying

99

at their place. At Kaia's place I was hoping to taste original homemade traditional Norwegian food. Maybe Pål came from an area I had not visited yet? Maybe he would cook those sheep heads I had heard of, *smalahove*, from the Voss area? Maybe they had hunted the game meat themselves or fished the fish by their family cabin? Maybe the berries they would serve me would come from the forest nearby? I just couldn't wait.

When I got there Kaia opened the door and gave me *a klem*, and a tall broad man from Harstad called Pål shook my hand. I hung my coat and smelled the air to try to guess what they were cooking. There was only the scent of vanilla from the candles lit all over the living room.

I looked in the kitchen, nothing was out or in the oven. Apparently, they had not started cooking. What kind of traditional dish takes ten minutes to cook, I wondered? I sat on the sofa and started chatting with those already sitting there while politely eating the potato chips available on the low sofa table.

Three of them were nursing school students who lived in the flat with Kaia, renting a room and sharing the common spaces. Ante was Pål's friend and worked as a washing machine salesman at the big electronic shop Elkjøp.

He was very friendly and had a lot to talk about since he came from Northern Norway, which I had just visited. He came from a place called Kautokeino in Finnmark in the North and told me about a festival that involved reindeer that took place every Easter in his hometown. The World Championship in reindeer racing. How exciting! I thought. I wanted to invite myself, but of course that would be rude since I barely knew the guy. He was more outspoken than most Norwegians I met, and he laughed a lot. He actually seemed comfortable in social settings without having to make any effort. How refreshing!

After a while, Pål diced two tomatoes, lettuce, and a

cucumber, poured some corn out of a can, and grated a cheese called Norvegia. It is this Norwegian cheese that comes in a big hard block, looking like light yellow hard plastic (and tastes that way, too). My heart sank when he opened a bag of powder called Toro. He poured the powder into raw minced meat and put it in the microwave.

"This is where the magic happens," said Pål excitedly.

By then, I was hyperventilating.

Then he opened a jar of red sauce and put it in another bowl. Got a box of cream out of the fridge. And that was it. The table was filled with small bowls with one ingredient in each: corn, minced meat, cucumbers etc.

"Tada!" said Pål proudly. "Here is our famous Norwegian meal! *Taco Fredag!*"

Wait, did the man just say "Taco Friday" and Norwegian in the same sentence? He served it all in ready-made tacos, freshly out of a plastic bag.

While all the different ingredients were lying cold on the table, everyone happily composed their own taco. As I was eating my first ever taco, I wondered when on Earth this meal became part of Norwegian food culture. In my culture, cooking, especially for guests, involves time, good produce and especially love. Despite all of Toro's efforts, that taco sauce in a bag didn't taste like love at all.

"Why is this typical Norwegian food?" I asked.

"This is a tradition in Norway. *Taco Fredag!*" said Pål.

"A tradition? When did it start?" I asked, wondering after how many years of practice something can be called a tradition. I was pretty sure the word "tacos" was not inherited from old Norse.

Someone else at the table did not seem too impressed: Ante. He was politely chewing on his food and laughed a little when I asked all those unsettling questions.

"Since the 1990s, maybe," said Pål. Right... Tradition...

When one first gets to hear about traditional Norwegian cuisine, one hears about cabbage and sheep and pepper cooking for hours (*fårikål*), fish being rotten in the ground for months (*rakfisk*), and the head of a sheep served to you on a plate (*smalahove*), or some very old cheese that would make any French cheese smell like fresh rose (*gamalost*).

Quickly enough, I understood that lamb ribs (*pinekjøtt*) and pork belly (*ribbe*) are eaten once or twice a year, and not during the same meal; and that Norvegia is what people want in their *matpakke*, not *gamalost*. *Matpakke,* or "packed food" as literally translated, is the lunch Norwegians pack every day for school and work as there are few cafeterias.

I tried to compose two tacos and put the right amount of cream and meat and whatever was on the table. At the end of the meal, everyone took out their beers and we started drinking. Kaia put some candy out on the table, and we chatted the night away.

What a strange traditional Norwegian dinner I had, I thought on the way home in the snowy night.

On the metro, I called Ramu. He was from Tamil Nadu, which has a very rich food culture. I had to share this story with someone who would understand my despair.

"Guess where he put the powder? On the raw meat in the microwave!"

I told him everything. He could not believe it.

*Note to self:* Norwegians seem to have a very broad and short-term definition of "tradition". They do not mind inviting you for dinner to serve you food from several bags and heating them in a microwave. When their country has so much wonderful food to offer. Norwegian food culture is a mystery to me.

# *SKÅL* TO FRIENDSHIP

My closest colleagues, Ylva and Torbjørn, were always busy with their own lives and friends. Torbjørn left around 3:30pm almost every day to pick up his daughters at the kindergarten. Ylva always had a spinning class to attend, a friend to meet for coffee, or a choir rehearsal. My other colleagues, like Åse, were older and took the same train home every day.

There was not a minute to waste in their workday or later for side activities with a foreigner who had no activities. I was meeting Kaia quite often, but she was also making a life of her own with Pål and was practically living at his place now.

I was in full winter mode, sleeping a lot and leaving the house just to go to work. Finally, I saw a light at the end of the tunnel when I received an invitation to the party Ane had been talking about since I moved to Norway. As the party got closer, I was getting so happy. I had been waiting for a Norwegian to invite me to a party for a long time, but it never happened. I might not have been born on skis, but I knew how to mingle.

That Saturday, despite the cold, I tried to keep my motivation high in order to be awake to go to that party. I easily found my way back to Ane's flat. I rang the intercom, and someone buzzed me in without even asking my name. The noise of the music and chatter guided me through the stairs.

When I got to the flat, the door was slightly open and dozens of shoes and jackets were piled up in the hallway. After taking all my winter gear off I literally had to climb my way to the rest of the flat. It almost seemed like a different place from where I had coffee a few weeks back. There were people standing everywhere, with a glass in their hand and a smile on their face.

I had not anticipated that I would have to take off my shoes, and my stockings had holes in them at one of my toes.

I looked around. The guys all had messy moustaches and checkered Canadian timber shirts, and the girls had knitted woolen jumpers with Scandinavian patterns and tights. This was obviously not a Parisian fashion show, my naked toe would fit in.

The first person whose speech I clearly heard among the mumble of chatter was a Norwegian guy.

"Oh no, I don't know anyone at this party. I have to get drunk really fast" he said out loud.

Why would anyone think like that, I wondered? I found it exciting not to know anyone. What is the point of a party with only people one knows from before?

I had brought a bottle of wine that I left on the table to share with everyone else. I then started pouring myself drinks from other bottles. Until someone looked at me as if I had murdered their friend.

"This is my bottle," said the guy.

"Okay, is it a good one?" I answered, with a smile. In France, everyone brings a bottle of some alcohol, or a bag of chips, or a homemade baked cake. We all put everything on the table and we share. From the moment we get to a party and put whatever we brought on the table, the private property over that bottle of wine does not exist anymore. It is a collective good, like in communism. I was not getting a communist vibe from this party though. I realized after a while that everyone was staying close to the one bottle they had brought. Where is the fun? Then one has to drink the exact same thing all evening, and no one shares with others.

To excuse my foreign behavior, I offered the guy a glass of my wine. He then explained:

"Alcohol is so expensive in Norway that it's easier to bring what you will drink to parties. Nobody can afford to have drinks for everyone, and then people want to make sure they will have enough for their money," he said, smiling.

That evening I even saw people take the beers they had not drunk back home after the party. That is among the rudest things one can do in France: you have to leave those things for the host.

The guy smiled after his little explanation, said he was getting potato chips in the kitchen and never came back. Then I talked to this girl, and then a few more people.

I realized that everyone asked exactly the same questions in what seemed to be the same order.

First questions: "Who do you know here?"

Second question: "What do you do?"

Third question: "Where do you come from?"

Then they would add something like "*Ååhhh så spennende,*" (so exciting!) when I said I am from France. They asked where from and evaluated the distance to the place they'd been to (usually Nice or Paris).

When they ran out of topics, they'd go get a drink and

never come back. Or go to the toilet and then sit somewhere else to talk to a more interesting person. I had traveled the world, spoke three languages, and had many friends outside of Norway. I had always seen myself as someone with conversation and wit. How was I so boring to these people?

I was looking for Ane, but as it was her party, she was always busy fixing some drinks or talking to all these people who were never hiding from her.

There seemed to be codes to these conversations I was not understanding, and my answers to their questions were probably the wrong ones. Maybe it was because after a few words in Norwegian I asked them to switch to English? Maybe they could smell the winter depression on me? Maybe Norwegians had such an interesting life that mine was dull in comparison.

At some point I even saw a cute guy looking at me across the room and thought maybe someone would take me out of my social misery and flirt with me, but he just looked and never came over to talk to me. Obviously not interested. After a few hours of polite beer drinking and saying "*så spennende*" every five minutes, people started getting much more drunk and more… liberated. Speaking louder, dancing. They all decided around 11:45pm that it was time to go downtown. Why so late? I wondered.

We went to a bar/nightclub called Jæger, which apparently means "Hunter." I only remember there were many tall and drunk men and I got scared they would forget I existed and hit their elbows against my head. I'm too short for parties in this country, I thought. But they were becoming so social this felt more like a party in France or Spain. Around 2am, I was talking to some of the people from the party at Ane's place.

A girl called Berit told me she is a singer. She invited me to her concert in a museum the next Friday. My God, I was entering a group of friends! I was invited to a concert by the lead singer! How exciting this Norwegian life would be.

I could see the cute guy carefully moving in my direction, looking at me and then looking away. What was going on here? He was maybe interested after all. Ane was getting drinks for me at the bar, obviously trying to cheer me up and get me out of my winter depression.

I had trouble keeping up with her, she was getting them in pairs: a glass of beer and a shot of something dark, either Jägermaister or something called Fisk. Fisk is a bottle of alcohol with a fisherman drawn on it. It's black and has the taste of licorice. I was getting more and more tipsy, and I could see people getting more and more friendly, laughing out loud in a much more natural way.

The guy who was so offended I drank from his bottle of wine earlier was suddenly much less shy to share his glass of alcohol with complete strangers. The cute guy was now a meter's distance from me.

Suddenly around 2am or 3am, a bell rang in the bar.

"What is happening?" I asked Ane.

"The last drink," she screamed at the top of her lungs.

"What? Are they closing after this?" I asked, astonished. Wasn't it a bit early to close a bar on a Saturday evening in an European capital city?

It feels like the second that bell stopped ringing, the cute guy's thigh was touching mine.

"*Hei, du.*" he said with a broad smile.

"*Hei!*" I smiled back. His name was Nils. He was very funny and interested in the fact that I was French. He asked a lot of questions about my life in Norway, something not many had been interested in until now. When everyone had their last drinks on the table, our little group cheered the last "*Skååååålll*" and drank all we had.

"*Skål*" means "cheers" but it also means "skull" in Norwegian. I had heard stories saying that it came from the skulls the Vikings used to drink alcohol from in the olden days in Scandinavia. Others say it is because *skål* also means "a bowl," from which alcohol can also be drunk.

At some point, not sure how long after we had started talking, the lights were switched on in the bar. I looked around. My eyes had to get used to the bright light again. It felt like we were all night creatures who would burn if exposed to bright light for too long, and the bar emptied itself at the speed of light.

Everyone was suddenly in the street. People were chatting and smoking, by what seemed to me like very cold temperatures to be standing outside in a T-shirt.

Some people eventually took a cab, others walked away alone or with others to some exciting party. My vision was a bit blurry, and I could barely walk straight. I was not used to drinking so much in one evening.

While I was checking my phone to find the time of the next night bus home, Ane grabbed my arm. She was laughing and dancing in the street, obviously drunk.

"Come with us, Lorelouloulou," she said laughing.

She was with a group of several people including Nils, who smiled and waved at me. Berit the singer was also there.

"What's the plan?!" I asked Ane.

"*Nattspiiiil!*" screamed Ane. Was that a place in Oslo? I wondered. It sounded like a bar called "Night game" (*Natt* means night, *spill* means game).

"Cool. I've never been to Nattspill. Is that another bar that stays open after 3am?"

The five people in the group exploded in laughter,

"Yes, just come and see the bar. *Nachspiel* is a special bar," said Berit, correcting my pronunciation.

It was supposed to be a 30-minute walk to the area of Oslo

called Birkelunden, according to my GPS. That was probably the time it took on a normal day, but everything took much longer. There was always someone stopping to yell at another person, or laugh, or ask for a cigarette from another person in the street.

Nils was walking close to me.

"So you've never been to a *nachspiel*? Norwegian parties start with a *vorspiel*, a pre-party, in somebody's home, like we had at Ane's place earlier. Then we move to a party in a bar, like in Jæger, and then Norwegians move on to a *nachspiel*, an after-party," he explained.

"Okay, but why do people bother to have three parties in one night? Why don't they just start in the bar and stay there?" I asked.

"Because alcohol is expensive. So it's cheaper to drink at home with alcohol we bought duty-free in airports, or in Sweden. Then we try to spend the least possible in bars, and then we drink again at home," he added.

Why did they need to drink that much? I wondered. Was everything social in Norway around alcohol, rather than around food like it is in French culture? As I was about to ask him, I was interrupted by Ane who yelled, "Keebbbaaabbbbb."

"And there is no *nachspiel* without kebab," said Nils.

A surprising number of people were in the queue to buy kebab in the middle of the night. In addition to the queue, there were many Norwegians eating their newly bought kebab as if they had not eaten in 3 days.

What a horrifying picture it was seeing them throw themselves on these kebabs. Brown mayonnaise dripped down their chins and coats while they tried to have conversations with each other. After what seemed like an eternity, everyone was holding a kebab and we carried on walking to Birkelunden. The walk there made the effect of alcohol disappear for me, as it was a cold night and wet snow started falling.

I was getting further and further away from my home, and suddenly wondered how I would get home eventually, with no public transportation between the last night bus, around 4am, and the first metro around 6am.

We continued our walk to Birkelunden and when we got to the heavy front door of the building where we would have a *nachspiel*, to my great surprise Nils took a key out and opened the door. It was his place! I turned around and found that we had lost Berit and another guy, who had left without saying goodbye. There were still five of us, with Ane, a blond girl who looked like she was sleeping while standing, and a tall guy with black tobacco that ran down his gums while he spoke.

The flat was tiny. We all sat on the kitchen floor listening to music and drinking some beer Nils had in his fridge. He also got out a bottle of aquavit and served small glasses of it to everyone. Nils and I continued talking, and as we were moving closer, I could see his cute freckles. I had always dreamed of being a redhead, and here he was with his green eyes and his eyelashes the color of the sun.

I was pretty sure he liked me by now. I thought I would need some courage to lean in and kiss him, or let him get closer to me, so I went to the bathroom to put fresh water on my face. I was wondering where this would take me. Maybe we would kiss, maybe he would be my first Norwegian boyfriend.

When I came back, the tall, bearded man was sleeping on the kitchen floor. Nils and the other girl were kissing like teenagers on fire. I must have been in the bathroom for maybe five or 10 minutes? I was standing there so confused. Wasn't this man flirting with me 15 minutes ago? What happened? I took my coat and left. Outside, in the cold weather, looking at the night and hoping not every *nachspiel* is as lousy as this one. Well, this night was not a total disaster, I thought on my way home. I had to catch a taxi which cost me a week of groceries. I obviously had no idea how to seduce a Norwegian man, but at least I had made new friends. That was not too bad for a first party in the city.

I called Kaia and when we met again, it clicked as if we had been friends forever. I told her all about Nils and the others. I could not wait to introduce her to my new group.

I asked Kaia what she thought about what had happened with Nils. It was not that I was heartbroken, as I barely knew him, but I must admit my ego was a bit hurt and I was extremely confused. I was so sure we were flirting. I didn't understand how he ended up with another girl in such a short amount of time. Did I misread the signs?

"He probably did like you, and you probably read the signs right, he was probably flirting with you," said Kaia. "But how did you show him that you were interested?" she asked.

"The usual. I laughed at his jokes and batted my eyelashes," I answered.

"Okay, well, that's not enough. In Norway, women are fierce. They don't wait for a guy to flirt heavily with them. They go and get the one they like. And men don't waste time with women who aren't that interested. They are too afraid of being seen as potential rapists. They want to see consent very, very clearly. And interest. Norwegian men are a bit lazy in that sense. They have a choice – there are many women interested in them, so they don't have to do as much work as, let's say, in Brazil, to seduce a girl. You know just how you want to be swept off your feet? Men want that too," she said.

I was more and more surprised. It made me feel like I was not that special.

"But why did he not wait for me for the five minutes I was in the bathroom, then? Is that so much to ask from a man?" I asked her, feeling hurt as I recalled the events.

"Well, think about it. When you disappeared, he had a choice between someone as drunk as he was, showing clear interest, and an exotic yet complicated French woman. The choice was easy. Also remember that many, both men and women in Norway, will prefer the drunk one as there is a social rule among us that if we were drunk. We can pretend it never happened. It just makes things easier for everyone."

Great. I looked into my future and saw a long, lonely life in Norway. I had to unlearn years of being taught women had to hold back, smile subtly and not show too much interest.

The next Friday was the concert Berit invited me to. I decided to go and invited Kaia to keep me company. Maybe I was lousy at making a Norwegian boyfriend, but I was sure I had made friends that night. We got to the concert which took place on a small stage in a museum café. Most of those who were at the party were sitting there while Berit was singing. I came their way, with a broad smile.

"*Hei!*" I said. Ane was abroad, but I recognized most of her friends from that night. "A fun *nachspiel* that was, right?" I said to the guy who had told me about his love life during the party. I was about to continue this conversation – or rather monologue – when he left for the bar, rudely avoiding me. Unless he had not recognized me.

At last, Berit finished singing. I clapped enthusiastically and went to see her.

"Great show! Thanks for inviting me!" I said cheerfully.

She looked at me as if I had come from out of space. Her eyes said "Who are you and what the hell are you doing here?"

Oh no, did I misread something again? Aren't these all the same people who were so friendly just a week ago, and invited me here? It's not like I saw light from the outside and broke into this (by the way, public) place. She smiled faintly and said

"Yes, *skål*," and left me without another word. As I was

about to lose faith, I saw Nils. He looked at me briefly with no expression on his face and walked past me as if I was transparent. Okay, people from the north, I get it, I'm out of here.

Kaia and I finished our beers in the blink of an eye and left the place without a goodbye from my "friends." I kept silent as we walked down the street to the metro station.

Eventually she said,

"It's not easy to make friends in Oslo."

That is a freaking understatement. Like my mum says, with friends like those, one does not need enemies.

"It is not like that in Trøndelag, you know. It's also hard for me to make friends here, and I am Norwegian. City people are different," Kaia added.

Maybe Kaia was right, or maybe I was just not interesting enough for Norwegians, I thought.

*Note to self:* do not, under any circumstances, believe that you have made Norwegian friends unless they talk to you when sober about very intimate details of their lives. If they invite you to anything when drunk, do not take it seriously. Say, "Yes, that would be great," and do not show up.

At my next Norwegian course, I asked our teacher a question about friendship.

"Do you think foreigners can make friends with Norwegians?" I asked.

"See I told you!" said Mario. "It is impossible. They don't need us here in their lives."

The teacher did not seem too interested in answering these questions, as it was not in her textbook. But seeing the motivation of all the students in speaking Norwegian on this topic, she gave up and opened a discussion. All of us could say whether we believed it was easy or not to make Norwegian friends. I noticed that Ramu was not in class.

"What I have heard the most from Norwegians is 'You are nice, but I have enough friends'," said Gerda. "Does that mean they don't like me? Is that their polite way of saying it?" she asked the teacher.

The teacher explained: "No, it is because Norwegians often feel like they are in something called *tidsklemma*, the "time squeeze". They have a lot of activities after and sometimes before work. So it might be that they do not even manage to see their own friends, so they don't know how to squeeze you into their schedule," she added.

What a strange way of seeing friendship, I thought. In France one meets new friends all the time, some stay friends for life, some just temporarily because people change. Maybe every Norwegian had set a quota of friends for themselves, just like the government set an alcohol quota for those entering the country?

"Have you made new friends in recent years?" I asked our teacher.

She thought about it for a while. "No, I haven't since university," she admitted. Exactly what I suspected.

Norwegians seemed to make friends in kindergarten, primary school and later in high school. Those would then be their friends for life and then make friends in different predefined circles: chess club, mountain climbing, university. They had parties or dinners with the same friends without accepting anyone new in the circle. I was 26; if I wanted to make a best friend in this country, I was basically ten years late.

I tried to stay positive in this sea of negativity.

"Maybe we need to make a real effort to get them to include us in their busy lives?" I said.

"Maybe we need to be extra nice so that they make space for us? I have two Norwegian friends."

The other students were amazed. Two friends! I didn't mention that neither of them was from Oslo. My few days in Northern Norway made an impression on me that it would have been much easier to make friends up there if I had moved to Northern Norway instead of Oslo.

I was noticing something else. It seemed that Norwegians around me needed to be sure I would be around, so I was worth "investing time in," which was not the case if I was there for one year. Like with flats, it seemed like Norwegians only wanted to make good investments in people. I met people who had friends from kindergarten they did not like that much anymore, but for the sake of history and group cohesion, they would never say anything and continue meeting them. They would rather have old "safe" friends they had almost nothing in common with rather than new exciting friends. All this was not very comforting for me.

*Note to self:* considering how hard it is to make Norwegians friends, be nice and funny, don't complain, learn the language, learn how to bake cakes or pizzas Norwegians like in order for them to invite me over and like me. Never say no to an invitation to a Norwegian home, as it is so rare and might not come around anytime soon.

I realized Ramu was not late, he was absent. When I got out of class I called him.

"Why didn't you come? You missed a very interesting discussion on friendship in Norway!" I told him joyfully.

"Oh Lorelou, that sounds great. But here it's not going so well. I am at the hospital."

"What happened? Are you okay?" I asked.

"Yes, I'm kind of fine. My friend is not so fine though," he said.

"Do you want me to come to the hospital?" I asked.

"Yes, I can text you the address. But I must warn you, we are way outside of Oslo. You need to take a train."

It took me an hour and a half to get there, to a town called Hamar. He gave me the address of a hospital called Innlandet Hospital.

I met Ramu in a shared room. He was sitting on a chair with stitches on his face, and his friend was lying on the bed next to him. They both looked as if they had just seen death.

"What on Earth happened? Did you have an accident?" I asked.

"Well, do you remember Kevin?" asked Ramu.

I looked at the tumefied face of his friend. Even if I had met him, his face was so distorted by the bruises, the stitches and the blood it would have been hard to remember.

"We met at the improv and poetry class. I told you I had enrolled in those, right?" said Ramu.

He continued without waiting for my answer.

"We went to this place called Elverum, about half an hour from here. Kevin was invited by the Innlandet Theatre. We went to this masterclass on acting. Anyway, we went to have a beer after the masterclass, and we got cornered by five guys in a dark street. They attacked Kevin and kicked him to the ground. I tried to defend him but when I saw they were outnumbering us I ran out to get some help. By the time I came back he was on the floor, bleeding. He did not want to go to the hospital there, so we drove to Hamar real fast and they agreed to check on us here," said Ramu.

I looked at his friend. Kevin seemed to carry the sadness of the world on his shoulders.

"What did they do to you? Did you go to the police? You need to complain formally. Can you identify your attackers?" I asked him.

He looked at the wall behind me.

"They kicked me and kicked me. I tried to protect my head. They kept on yelling '*jævla neger*' and 'we don't want people like you here.' Then I tried to pretend I was dead so that they would stop. It worked. Then they spat on me and they left me on the floor. Ramu found me there and helped me to get up," said Kevin. He burst into tears.

Jesus. Are we living in the same country? It did not seem like it. I suddenly saw my whole journey run before my eyes. How welcoming would Norwegians have been if I was Black or had a Muslim name? Every time I met someone they said,

"Oooohh, you come from France! I love France! Why are you here in Norway when your country is so beautiful?"

I would bet Kevin didn't get that very often. I took his hand.

"Listen, you need to file a complaint. The police will help you," I repeated.

"The school helped me report it. They even went out to the local press. But the police do not seem to want to do anything. This is a small place; everyone knows each other, and they don't want trouble. Especially not for someone like me, who's just passing by," he said. "But who knows, NRK called me so it might be on national news."

"Are you from Northern Norway?" I asked. I could recognize his dialect from my travels up North.

"Yes, my parents are from Kenya, but I was born and raised in Tromsø. People are always surprised when they hear a Black man speaking with such a thick Northern Norwegian dialect." He laughed.

"They speak very slowly because they think I cannot speak Norwegian and then their mouths hang open when I start speaking," he said in another laughter. He held his torso as they had cracked two of his ribs and it hurt to laugh.

"These things should not happen. Not in Norway nor any-where else. If I can do anything to help you, please let me know,"

I said, feeling completely useless. "Have you experienced much racism in your life?" I asked him.

"Well, I am only 25." he said. "But yeah, some. I mean my neighbors in Holmen never say hi to me. Then again, *Vestkant* is not exactly a paradise for Black people," he said. *Vestkant* is the West part of Oslo, the richest of the city. "Once my pass for the front door did not work and the neighbor acted like she had never seen me before and refused to let me in. Small things. It's hard sometimes, it's like they pretend we don't exist," he said.

*Note to self:* everything is not sunshine and flowers in Norway. Like everywhere else, there is racism and individualism. Despite claiming equality is an important value in Norway, underlying racism is visible. Words which seemed from another era, the colonial era, seemed to be used by Norwegians as if it was okay.

This country was after all much more complex than what they told us in Norwegian textbooks.

Will I ever manage to fit in? My year is not over, the one I gave myself to decide whether I would live here. Maybe I would also have good surprises along the way?

# WORK-LIFE BALANCE

Work life in Norway was definitely different from what I was used to. One main difference was that people seemed to be at work like on a mission. My colleagues went through a day at work with a very specific schedule.

They arrived in the morning, sometimes as early as 7am, and raised their eyes from their computers only to get more coffee. At the coffee machine, they would not stay 15 or 30 minutes like in many French offices. They would go back to work and move again from their desks around 11am to have lunch. Lunch would last 30 minutes maximum, during which they would have time to eat their *matpakke*, with pieces of bread and various *pålegg* on them, and chat with colleagues.

Lunch break was the best time of my day for me. Not because of the food, but for the company. It was the moment when my colleagues socialized and read the daily quiz in the newspaper

*Aftenposten* - to which I hardly knew any answers, especially since I didn't even understand all the questions. People would chat very freely about their families and hobbies. I would learn so much about how Norwegian people live. These insights were important to me since I did not have a very Norwegian life and did not live with any Norwegian people. These lunches were a great occasion for me to practice my Norwegian and have casual conversations with my colleagues.

After this 30-minute break they would take another cup of coffee on their way back to their desk and hardly stop working until it was time to go home. There was also the occasional meeting, which made them leave their desk, but that was it.

Sometimes as I came in the morning I would say "hi" to every colleague and some would not answer. I thought they were so rude at first, but realized they were just absorbed by their work and did not feel like greeting every single person who came in after them every morning. Fair enough.

Once the hours were done, their work advanced as planned, and the meetings finalized, they would go home to their family. Kindergartens and schools seem to close very early compared to France. For example, colleagues with small children under the age of six had to leave around 3pm to fetch their kids at kindergarten.

"If I am late, even by 5 minutes, I need to pay a fine," explained Torbjørn once.

Primary school finished around 2pm, so kids would either go home and stay there alone or would attend after-school activities. Very different from what I was used to as a French child, being at school from 8am to 5:30pm Mondays, Tuesdays, Thursdays and Fridays, with half days at school on Wednesdays and Saturdays from 8am to 12am.

Even babies could be picked up around 6pm by their parents, because French parents have longer days at work. All these differences in logistics and schedules meant my colleagues with kids under the age of 12 often left work early, and sent emails in the evening, when they worked to catch up on work from the day.

I noticed many other differences. During meetings, everyone was asked for their opinion about a matter. Bosses were managers more than leaders, and definitely not authoritarian.

Trust in management seemed to be a very important value. A manager being too bossy, or deciding without consulting or involving their staff, would lose the team's trust. That would mean losing their own management's trust. That meant being a bad manager.

For an employee, it seemed okay to disagree with one's boss. As long as the tone was friendly almost everything could be said. For me, a woman who grew up in a more hierarchical and patriarchal work system where bosses could be bossy if not moody, this was a breath of fresh air.

At my workplace, young women got promotions and reached leadership positions. They were trained to be good leaders, and male leaders would go on paternity leave for months. My own boss left for seven months of paternity leave. He was replaced during that time by another one of my male colleagues who happened to work for only 80 percent of the time. His child was often sick, and he and his partner had been advised to put him in kindergarten only part-time.

The fact that someone not working full-time got this job was surprising in itself, but the fact that his partner was not the one who would be working reduced hours when he just got a promotion was even more surprising. The last surprise was, of course, that my boss didn't answer a single email during his seven-month paternity leave. The day he came back to work he picked up where our colleague had left things, and everything came back into place. I was used to male-oriented workplaces and societies, where women were "naturally" expected to step down for the needs of their family. I was suddenly seeing a possible career and work life that I never imagined possible.

In Norway, we are expected to work, and put our heart and time into it. However there are things more important than work: life, family, our sanity. People leave work to go skiing, and bosses encourage their staff to take "real" holidays, not checking their work emails. Work is not a sacrifice; it is just part of life.

In France, there are protest marches and strikes every time a government wants to push the retirement age to anything later than 60 years old. In Norway the retirement age is 67, and I believe it will be even later by the time I retire. If I have a work-life balance the Norwegian way, working until 70 is not a big deal.

There is more to say about the differences between work life in Norway and in other countries I worked in such as France, Canada or Indonesia.

I think the last element I will mention about Norwegian working culture is the importance of transparency and trust. Trust is key. The trust colleagues have in each other. The trust employees have in their leadership. The trust regular citizens have towards their government, tax authorities and all public institutions. The trust managers have in their employees.

It is expected for example that all employees say the truth. Norwegians trust people to admit they've made a mistake. It is socially acceptable for people to make mistakes in Norway. Even people in power can make mistakes. The unacceptable thing for Norwegians is to lie about it and cover it up.

This means making a mistake at work is acceptable. The Norwegian thing to do is then to contact your manager and explain your mistake. Apologize. And explain you will do everything in your power to fix it. Covering it up will make your mistake unforgivable. Because honesty and transparency are key for the Norwegian society to function.

Arrogance is to be entirely banned. As I like to remind those who have issues understanding this element: when is the last time you thought someone was smart? Was it because the person told you "I am smart" or because you found out on your own?

The CEO of a Norwegian company needs to be as humble as the person cleaning the floors. Both have a job to do. Both are important to the company. Their salaries are not even that different, not as much as in French or American companies at least. According to the Norwegian system, a living and decent wage is something everyone should have. Respect for their work is too. Even the King cannot afford to be arrogant.

After these months working in Norway, I have to admit some things still annoyed me: the never-ending meetings and the compromises that took forever to reach. The worst are those who don't say what they think directly not to offend anyone, but then talk about it for months.

The codes were still so hard to learn, and the messages between the lines so hard to read. Besides those small things, working in Norway felt like utopia. When my boss asked me

"So, Lorelou, what do you think of the organization's new strategy?" it felt amazing.

The best part was being seen and respected for my work, without anybody patronizing me because I was young and female. Although finding a man in this country seemed like mission impossible, maybe a fulfilling job would be enough?

Around the beginning of April, my colleagues seemed excited. They were laughing and chatting loudly at lunch breaks and had livelier discussions than usual. The word "*posque*" was being repeated often around me every day. "*Posque*" was a word they combined with "*hutta*" at lunch time, or "*chi*." I had no idea what was cooking.

I was working on a file where I needed Torbjørn and Ylva's input. All decisions need to be made by consensus in Norway, and this was no exception. I sent them a meeting invitation for Thursday that week at 2pm and both rejected it, despite having nothing else planned in their calendars. Torbjørn suggested another date for that meeting: two weeks later. Ylva was more "flexible" and suggested a date 12 days later. Wait, what?

I found Ylva by the coffee machine, pouring herself what seemed to be a weekly dose even for a coffee-drinking Norwegian like her.

"Everything okay?" I asked her politely. "Can't we try to fit in that meeting before the end of the week? I need to finish the report," I said.

"But I'm leaving tomorrow," she answered. "Back in two weeks. And I'll be offline, so no meetings will be possible for me. I'll be enjoying the last snow of the season with hopefully looottss of sun," she said, looking into the distance.

It seemed she was there already in her mind.

"No time to waste! I have lots of stuff to finish before tomorrow," she said while running away from the kitchen.

"Wait. Are you off on holidays from tonight already? But it is 11 days off??" I said.

"Yes! We don't even use our holidays, just *avspasering*!" she answered.

"What? *Avs*-what? And two weeks? When did we get two weeks off?" I asked.

"*Avs-pa-se-ring*. It means all the hours you worked extra, can now be used to take time off," she said. "If you count the bank holidays and strategically use your *avspasering*, you get around 11 days off. Isn't Easter great for that?" she said, running to her desk.

If only someone had told me about this "free" holiday as well as this *avspass* thing. I checked the calendar, and indeed there would be a few bank holidays for Easter. I counted six of them: Palm Sunday, Maundy Thursday, Good Friday, Easter Eve, Easter Sunday and Easter Monday.

With the weekends and a few days off, indeed it was 11 days off. I found out that the Norwegian way of calculating time off is quite a strategy in itself. When working in Norway, one gets an automatic five weeks of paid holidays per year (after one year of work though), and one gets all the bank holidays.

Then Norwegians look at the worked days between the bank holidays for something they call "*inneklemte dager*" or "the days squeezed in between", i.e. squeezed in between bank holidays. They calculate how many hours of *avspasering* or holiday days they will need at the minimum to get the maximum time off. Articles are written about this every year in January to let you know how many "*inneklemte*" days there will be that year.

Needless to say, my strategic thinking on "days squeezed in between" and best utilization of *avspasering* was nonexistent. I discovered all of this the day the office was emptying itself. That Friday, I decided to come to the office anyway. Not like I had anything better to do.

I found myself turning the lights on and starting the coffee machine. I was finding this quite refreshing and was able to get a lot done since I did not have any meetings to attend for once. Around 2pm my CEO Bjørn passed by the office to pick something up before going to his cabin to ski. He came to my desk and asked,

"Lorelou, what on Earth are you doing here?"

"I am working. It is only 2pm. Still working hours, right?" I answered.

"But it is *Påske*! Go out, meet friends, this is a national holiday in Norway. Get a life," he laughed.

Yes, but Easter break is *next week*, I felt like saying. Next Thursday actually, in almost one week. You guys don't seem to look at the calendar the way I do, I thought.

Still, a CEO telling his/her employees to stop working and get a life is something I never thought I'd personally witness in my worklife. I looked at my empty office, which was usually buzzing with over 50 employees. I recalled that not so long ago there were other holidays, the so-called winter holidays during which all my colleagues who have kids were absent from the office. Why do Norwegians work so little?

I know many have this preconception that the French don't work much. We are supposedly on strike half the time and spend two hours every day on lunch break eating frog legs and snails at the restaurant. The truth is I have never seen people work as few hours as Scandinavians. My friends working in Paris would only dream of leaving their office before 6pm. I remember a French colleague in one of the few Parisian offices I worked in telling me,

"Well, have a great free afternoon" in a passive-aggressive way because I had to leave the office at 4.30pm.

French parents get nannies as soon as their kids turn two months old because that is all mothers get as maternity leave. When the kids are older, they get babysitters who fetch them from school at 4:30pm. The babysitters bathe the kids, feed them, and get them into pajamas for when the parents come home from work. They barely get time for a kiss good night before the kids need to sleep.

Already when living and working in Denmark, I noticed a huge difference between the work culture in Paris and in Copenhagen. When I talked about it with Aske, he told me, "Here in Scandinavia we work to live, we don't live to work."

Are Norwegians lazy, or was I just jealous that they all had exciting private and family lives outside of work? I noticed much shorter lunch breaks and way less breaks during the day to chat in front of the coffee machine here than in France.

*Note to self:* some may say Norwegians are lazy. They take time off as soon as they can, leave the office early and calculate their long weekends one year in advance.

When thinking about it, if it is 2pm and you know you have two hours left of your workday to be done with everything, the need to be efficient is much higher than when it is 2pm and you know you have five or six hours left.

In French offices, one is often expected to stay until the boss leaves. In Norway it is quite the opposite. A Norwegian boss would rather have you enjoying your afternoon if you believe you don't have much work to do. And then when the busy time of the year comes, you'll be expected to put in the extra effort.

Is it so hard to be honest about one's mistakes and not be arrogant at work? Maybe for some. For me it is the most relaxing work life I could dream of.

After two days in Oslo, my colleagues weren't the only ones who had taken off. The whole city was empty.

Easter was a religious holiday. Were some of them in church thinking of Jesus and his resurrection? I doubted that because what they were packing in their cars before leaving the city were not Bibles but skis and wine in boxes.

# THE CABIN TRIP FROM HELL

I started chatting online with Ramu and found out the people I had been skiing with were organizing "a typical Norwegian Easter cabin trip." The catch was that this typical Norwegian trip would be without any Norwegians. Not that they weren't invited, they were just unavailable, on real typical Norwegian Easter *hyttetur*. The Australian girl who was stuck on the hill with the wrong wax under her skis was organizing the trip to a cabin north of Oslo that is only accessible by train and then walking some kilometers.

We did not need Norwegians to invite us to their cabin or to spend a typical Norwegian Easter. All of it was very simple. We just had to become members of DNT, the national trekking association, and plan a trip to the wild. We needed a map in order not to get lost. A backpack each. Some food. Warm clothes. How hard could it be, really?

I was happy to go out with foreigners, because when going

on short trips with Norwegians I noticed they forced everyone to follow a lot of their rules. Waffles could only be eaten with jam and cream or *brunost*, this brown cheese with the taste of burnt milk. Nothing else was ever an option. Whipped cream and melted chocolate? No. Mango chutney? No. One had to walk for a long time without any option to stop and check out the scenery before reaching the top. And of course, the annoying five-year-old skiing very fast and the 70-year-old grandparents hiking faster than us 25-year-olds. A trip among fellow foreigners would be less stressful.

The meeting point was outside of the city, close to a train station in the woods. We would hike three hours to reach the *hytte* or cabin. Ramu, the Australian girl, and the Kazakh guy from the skiing course were there. There was also a family from Great Britain whom we had never met before.

First of all, we were obviously badly trained for such a hike, compared to Norwegians who climb mountains before breakfast since childhood. Norwegians are used to walking steadily without stopping or complaining and covering dozens of kilometers per day.

After less than 15 minutes the complaints started.

"Are we theeeeere yet? Is that the cabin?"

(It couldn't be, we started walking 10 minutes ago and we are covering 11 km).

"I am tiiiired, why is this mountain so steep?

(Because it's a mountain).

Others were not necessarily tired but wanted to enjoy the scenery. So it took us much longer than two hours to get there, because we stopped often to check the view. And eat chocolate. And take peeing breaks. Why do Norwegians have to rush it all the time? Even in nature, they seem to be going somewhere and have a schedule for it. That was the case of all of those we met on the way to the cabin, at least.

Secondly, the foreigners on this trip did not know what they were getting into. I had not checked the weather forecast, and I was not the only one apparently. At least I brought woolen clothes, as Kaia made me buy something called woolen underwear or *ullundertøy* so that I wouldn't get cold. She taught me how to layer clothes to keep warm without sweating.

It involves having a thin layer of wool directly on your skin for your whole body, i.e. woolen socks, some kind of leggings, T-shirt and woolen hat. They even have something called a *buff* to have under your scarf. Yes, also in wool. It is important here not to have synthetic or cotton fabrics on your skin as it is not breathable and makes you feel cold when the fabric gets wet. The second layer could also be wool, for example a sweatshirt, or some fleece or a light down jacket. Then a shell in some kind of waterproof fabric. This was spring gear, ready for both warmer and colder temperatures.

Not everyone on this trip got that kind of training, as Ramu had three layers of cotton T-shirts, a jumper, and a thick down jacket. He also had thin cotton socks and running shoes. After one hour he was sweating on his upper body inside his down jacket and his feet were freezing. He started shivering and we weren't even close to the cabin. Many of us brought heavy, unnecessary things such as glass bottles and bananas that got mushy after an hour of hiking but forgot the essentials like a good knife and a head lamp.

When we eventually got to the cabin after several hours of hiking, the guy from Kazakhstan wanted to go to the toilet. We heard a scream from the little outhouse. He came back petrified at the idea of peeing and pooping on top of others' own offerings to nature.

"I thought Norway was a developed country," he said.

The British couple were not aware there would not be running water in the *hytte*.

Thirdly, and this was the most worrying part, we were carefree and did not realize the dangers of being out there. The cold, the night and the fire. When we settled down in the *hytte*, we made a little fire. The British lady thought making it bigger would make the cabin warmer. By grabbing any branch she could find outside, she did make the fire bigger, but it suddenly started giving off thick smoke. The fire was uncontrollable, and, for the first time, I got scared. I imagined all of us outside, in the snow and cold temperatures with children, looking at a burning cabin, and later explaining to the fire department that we made a great fire with wet wood, which the woman took from under the snow. She wanted to pour water over the fire to put it out, but we managed to stop her from doing it just in time.

We spent a few hours with the windows fully opened, pieces of cloth over our mouths, trying to get the smoke out while the fire alarms were screaming. We had trouble breathing and seeing, but we managed to get the situation under control, and eventually we all got back inside the cabin. The cabin had a thick smell of smoke, and the temperature inside was now close to zero degrees. I was sure this was not the way Norwegians spent their Easter vacations. I later learned that whole books had been written by Norwegians about how to make a fire.

*Note to self:* next time I go on a cabin trip with foreigners, send them a PDF document with all the rules relating to fire-making, including not using wet wood, and opening for aeration for the smoke to be evacuated elsewhere than inside the house. Another document could be about how to behave in a cabin, with a potential two-day training teaching you how to pee in the woods, how to identify edible berries if you get lost, and how to layer clothes in order not to get too hot or too cold. This information is all part of the package Norwegians are born with.

The next day, as we were leaving, we all wrote our names on the book so that DNT would send us the bill for the night we had spent there. The British lady refused to write her name. She and her family were supposed to camp, but they had found it much nicer to sleep in real beds than outside in a tent.

"Nobody will know we came here," she said.

I started getting annoyed.

"Look, this is not how it works here. The whole system is based on trust. If we all start not writing down our names, DNT will have to put a person in each cabin to check us in, and everything will get more expensive. Isn't it nice that we can have access to all these cabins just by being members of this association? This network is genius!" I told her.

"But you won't tell them. It's only a few hundred kroners. Nobody will even notice," she answered.

Ramu was on my side.

"These people really trust you to do as they do. Do we want, as foreigners, to break that great cycle of trust? No. You have to do the same thing. Write your name and pay the bill," he told her.

She was still not convinced but we forced her. She wrote down hers and her family members' names. Un-freakin-believable. Not only did she almost set the place on fire, now she did not even want to pay for the night.

After this unfortunate experience, I realized that it is not the Norwegians who are annoying, it was the rules (don't enter the cabin with your shoes on, don't leave candles burning during the night, and so on). I understood that these rules were there for a reason: that's because they will save your life. Fire is not a fantasy-fear; it is real. While I was fighting against the smoke and hoping the cabin wouldn't burn down, I was thinking to myself that this would have never happened if we had brought a Norwegian with us.

*Note to self:* one of the greatest things about Norwegian culture is that people trust each other. Like giving you the key to a cabin in the woods and expecting you to hand it in as clean as you would have your own home, expecting you not to burn it to the ground, and expecting you to write down your name so that they can send you the bill. Most importantly, you are trusted to tell the truth.

# A PERFECT NORWEGIAN EASTER

When I returned to the office after the long break, I used the opportunity to ask my colleague Åse about these long Easter holiday activities.

"Usually we go to our cabin, ski, and eat lots of eggs," she answered.

"Eggs? You mean chocolate eggs?" I asked. Ahh, that was where they were: chocolate egg hunting.

"No, regular eggs," she said.

"Like real eggs? Do you also eat real rabbits instead of the chocolate ones?" I asked.

These people take the whole Easter thing way too seriously, I thought. I did some research. NRK reported that in 2011, Norwegians ate 35 million eggs just over the Easter Holiday.

What I understood is that as soon as Christmas is over, Norwegians are only waiting for one thing: Easter holiday. The wait is long: three to four months until *Påske*, depending on whether it is early or not that year. All these bank holidays give everyone the possibility to enjoy a full week (and a bit more sometimes) of pure holiday.

It is very important that there is snow at that moment, as this is considered as the last skiing holiday of the year. At least for those living in big cities. It turns out most people couldn't care less for the religious reasons for Easter. All they want is a break. Before the real break: summer holidays.

How does one prepare for a perfect Norwegian Easter holiday? Like many things in Norway, it's not just about what one eats or does, it's about the whole atmosphere. It needs to be *koselig* of course, which means it will involve family meals, evenings by the fireplace, hikes, skiing trips in the woods, and lots of sun. At the Norwegian course, Ramu and I even learned that there are a whole lot of words associated with Easter in Norwegian.

*Påskekrim* were the crime novels Norwegians brought with them on *påskeferie* (the Easter holidays). There was the *påskeøl* (Easter beer) they bought for that holiday specifically, not to be mistaken with *sommerøl* (summer beer). Do not ask me the difference between all of these, I have no idea. The foods to look forward to during Easter are the *påskesjokolade* (Easter chocolate), *påskeegg* of course (Easter eggs) and the traditional *påskelam* they served (Easter lamb). Their favorite Easter fruit are oranges, because according to Åse, "oranges are the sun of Easter," whatever that means. It makes sense that the favorite Easter soda is Solo, the Norwegian version of Fanta, which also tastes like oranges.

It is crucial to drive to Sweden to get all these necessities, as Norwegians believe everything is always cheaper there. By the time a Norwegian Easter ends, one needs to be *påskebrun*, a tan one gets from skiing in the sun.

*Note to self:* everything I discovered about a typical Norwegian Easter had nothing to do with what I had been doing with my foreign friends, no matter what the organizer said.

Norwegians have a very clear idea of a typical Norwegian Easter, as if they were all doing the exact same thing. If it is the case, they really like conformity much more than the French or other people I've met elsewhere.

Coming back from their Easter holidays, they compared how many kilometers they skied, how much sun they had here and at their own cabin. They were all eating eggs, oranges, as well as the same chocolate bars (Kvikklunsj, a Norwegian version of the KitKat, although they pretend it's different) and reading the same books also at the same moment.

After my colleagues were done talking about their great Easter memories of the year, they started talking about the next big thing happening in a Norwegian year: the 17th of May (Constitution Day).

The many milestones in a Norwegian year gave way to many topics of conversation, alongside how much their house price increased and whether their kid got a spot in the local kindergarten. After Easter they were longing for the 17th of May, then longing for the summer holidays, then for so-called fall holidays, then for Christmas holidays, then for Winter holidays, then for Easter again, and so on. I call it the Norwegian circle of life.

I found this obsession with tradition fascinating.

Sometime between Easter and Constitution Day, around the beginning of May, spring finally came along. It was not stable sunny weather like in my hometown Marseille. Once spring was there, we were sure it would only get warmer.

Weather all year long is unpredictable in Norway, but spring in Norway is under the influence of Freyr, the Norse god of sacral kingship, prosperity, virility, and mostly sunshine and fair weather.

During the spring Freyr changes moods very often, submitting the weather to radical changes: from hail to rain, and then beautiful sunshine on the same day.

Spring in Norway is like living with a manic-depressive man who has an influence on the mood of the whole country. One would think Norwegians are aware of this, since they were born and raised here, but they don't seem to be. They were going around in summer clothes and catching pneumonia. At some point in April, the weather warmed up for one day (read: it gets above 0 degrees Celsius), Norwegians literally started stripping, getting out their tank tops and sandals. Hey guys, it's not warm, it's just a tiny bit warmer today. For two hours. Three days later, half the people had caught a cold. We really wonder why.

It turned out I was hardly noticing that spring had started because just like Norwegians show their feelings with subtle signs, so does the Norwegian spring. To know that spring is coming, one can also watch out for Norwegians' change of attitude in everyday life. And change of vocabulary. For example, instead of staying at home making things *koselig* and walking fast from one point to another with a clear destination, I saw people standing in the street, or sitting on a bench with their eyes closed and sometimes a smile on their face, directing their face into a ray of sun. At first, I wondered how these could be the same people who look at small candles in the comfort of their home all winter. I was told this is called *solveggen*, another untranslatable Norwegian word. Say "wall of sun" in English to any foreigner and they won't know what the heck you are talking about.

Another thing that seemed to announce the spring were the billboards bars put outside on the street: "Come and enjoy this year's *utepils*." I did not get it at first. As "*ute*" means "outside" and "*pils*" means beer, in other words, an "outside beer." Following this simple translation, a beer one drinks outside by -10 °C in January because one wants to smoke (and therefore has to leave the bar and go outside) is an *utepils*, right? No no no. An *utepils* involves something else: sun. Spring, the promise of a warm summer and of many future *utepils*. It is the word to describe the beer one drinks outside when the weather is "warm enough" to drink it on a terrace with sunglasses on one's nose.

Another new word I learned when the spring came was *våryr*. I saw it written on a shop's window: "*Våryr?*" I had asked Torbjørn for the meaning of this word, which led to more laughs. "Why are you asking, Lorelou? Are you *våryr?*" I understood what it meant, eventually, when Ramu came back from a club one Saturday night and told me: "Lorelou, this is insane. You have to come to town and see what is happening in these bars. I've been here for a year and I have never seen Norwegians this wild. They were kissing all over the place, then there were lap dances. I think someone lost their panties. Everyone was looking at each other and going home together, more and much faster than on usual nights earlier this winter," he said.

"Ah. I guess that is what they call being *våryr* or *vårkåt* in Norwegian," I answered. Norwegians seemed to be extremely affected by the weather. People were "spring horny" (*vår* = spring and *yr* or *kåt* = horny) because it's light outside. Yes, surprisingly, enough *yr* means both "fine annoying rain" and "horny" in Norwegian.

Can one justify being *vårkåt* in a tropical country? In Mexico, Thailand, or Ivory Coast there is no such thing as spring. Let alone horny spring mood. Nope. It is here, because we are so happy the sun is back. The promise of a warm summer. Of beaches and bikinis. Of Norwegian tans. Dream on. I'm not really sure when the spring ends and when the summer officially starts in Norway. Some say it depends on the actual weather.

Around the beginning of May, my Holmenkollen neighborhood started being invaded by teenagers in red, blue, and black pants. This was extremely surprising, as the usual crowd was mostly old women with real fur and fake noses. I saw a few, and forgot about it, but then I saw more and more.

Every time one appeared, hordes of screaming children were running towards them. The third strange element in this equation were the buses. Huge graffiti tagged buses started driving around Holmenkollen, all with different drawings on them, and different names. Some had psychedelic colors, like those drawn in the 1970s on LSD.

Others had very good reproductions of famous dead singers like Elvis Presley, or very large-breasted cartoon women. Others had a statement: Magic Drunkdom, Billig MILF-shakes, The Hangover, Sluts with Nutts, Big Titts of Fire, and so on. Most were connected either to sex, to alcohol, or to both at the same time. These buses were extremely noisy, as if there were nightclubs in them (believe it or not, there were).

How could these kids drive these huge buses? They all looked like they were 16, therefore not old enough to have their driver's license, let alone have a license to drive a bus. And they seemed to be continuously drunk. Drunk driving in Norway leads to a heavy fine calculated on your salary: the fine is one and a half months of salary if you have more than 0,2 grams of alcohol. If you have anything more than 0,5 grams you will pay the fine and have your driver's license confiscated for one to five years. Even go to prison.

In any case, knowing Norway's strict rules, there was no way these kids were driving. It turned out the buses are driven by paid drivers. The kids in red and blue pants are all what Norwegians call "*Russ*": teenagers who are about to graduate from high school (around 18 or 19 years of age) and are therefore celebrating.

The worrying part here was that they got insanely drunk. Like close-to-a-coma kind of drunk, and that this happened just before exams, not after.

Anyway, this lasted a long time. The "*russetid*" as they call it, or "*Russ* time". Party buses filled with these kids wearing pants they did not seem to clean very often, giving away their personalized cards to children who could not wait to be *Russ* themselves. Sometimes because of bets and to get knots on their hats, they had to do stuff like take off their clothes and start racing in their underwear and show their asses to cars on a roundabout. In any case it seemed like they never slept, as they were having big parties just above where I lived, with the echo of their beats being heard in the whole valley.

I saw this lack of knowledge of mine as an opportunity to engage in a conversation with my neighbor Dagny.

"When will these kids go away so that we can sleep again?" I asked her when I saw her open her blinds one morning.

She answered that the 17th of May would take us out of our misery.

"May this day come soon." I prayed.

*Note to self:* I don't understand how a society which does not socially allow parents to have alcohol in the presence of children have no problem with teenagers poisoning themselves with this amount of alcohol.

I know the *Russ* are adults, and of legal age, but obviously something is not working in keeping youth away from alcohol. Maybe Norwegians parents need to try another strategy?

# THE HAPPIEST DAY OF THE YEAR

Everyone had been waiting for this day since Easter. Norwegian flags appeared everywhere, shops started selling just about anything with the red, blue and white colors of the Norwegian flag: candles, napkins, flowers, banners.

The shopping center Glasmagasinet had been showcasing the new *bunad* trends and black shoes with silver stuff on them for weeks. *Bunads* are traditional Norwegian dresses which Norwegians wear depending on where they came from in the country. They have different colors and patterns, with lots of silver accessories and embroidery.

I read a lot of things in foreign newspapers about Norway's national day – known as Constitution Day - and could not put my finger on what was happening that day, and why Norwegians were so ecstatic about it.

In France, the National day is on the 14th of July, the day we remember when rioters took La Bastille, in 1789. We watch military parades on television and go see fireworks in the evening. There are few flags except for public buildings. And that's it. We don't plan our holidays according to this day. It's just another summer day with bad programming on television.

Not only are Norwegians very keen on celebrating this day wherever they are in the world (go check a Norwegian Embassy on the 17th of May and you'll see what I am talking about) but it also raises many heated debates. Every year at least one Scandinavian paper raises the debate of the use of the Norwegian flag during the Norwegian national day.

Because here it is not just a few flags which are waved, there are literally tens of thousands of them being waved, pinned, drawn on cakes, and on faces. For foreigners like me, this exaggerated use of flags was very strange at first, if not shocking.

In most European countries, there aren't many groups who use their national flag. There are the football fans who wave it to support their national team on stadiums, and there are the far-right parties who wave it in the streets to demonstrate their nationalistic views, sometimes linked to ethnic purity and xenophobia.

The challenge with Norway's national day is that when one sees tall blond people with blue eyes dressed in traditional robes, waving their flags frenetically, and making their children march in the street in front of the King and Queen, it is easy to conclude that this is the reflection of strong nationalism and a reminiscence of national socialism-inspired propaganda.

It is quite different in reality, because Norway has a specific history and culture that one needs to keep in mind when looking at them waving their flags on and making their children march on their national day.

Firstly, while other European nations like France and Great Britain were getting rich from colonialism, Norway's fate was negotiated between the Danes and the Swedes. "Whose turn is it to occupy Norway?" they seemed to ask themselves.

Norway had a combination of elements which did not help: rough weather with a long freezing winter, unpredictable sun exposure, and very little land suited for agriculture, therefore giving little food security to its people.

A population spread over a vast country with a difficult topography to cross and, again, difficult weather making many transport channels problematic in the winter. Despite all those difficult factors, Norway was doing okay until the 14th century, thanks to dynamic trade. In 1349, the Black Plague entered the country through Bergen and two-thirds of the Norwegian population died in less than two years. Those who survived were those who lived so far from communication with merchants and the coast that they were not infected. Guess how Norway did after that?

Sure, there were many empty farms that the survivors could settle down in. But all in all, it weakened the nation on an economic, social, demographic, and political level. After that, the Swedes and the Danes decided the fate of Norway by taking turns at occupying it for several centuries. Norway wrote its Constitution on May 17, 1814 (which is what they celebrate on the 17th of May) but their true independence was not until 1905, two years after Panama became independent.

Between 1825 and 1925 approximately one million Norwegians emigrated to North America; roughly half of the country's population at that time. In other words, in its recent history, Norwegians have been a poor and colonized people. And they made it. They became free from Denmark, and then Sweden. They were occupied again during World War II, bombed by the Germans and became free again. But still poor. Then they found oil.

Secondly, despite the fact that nowadays Norway is one of the richest, if not the richest country in the world, Norwegians kept some features and language from this history of poverty and of being vassals, not masters.

The expression "*svin på skogen*," for example, means that there is something hidden (literally pigs in the forest). It refers to the time when Danish officials came to collect the tax which was calculated on the farmers' wealth and assets. The farmers would send some of their animals into the forest to avoid paying tax on their total livestock.

Another expression is "*å ha lua i hånden*" (to hold your hat in your hand) which is a typical Norwegian attitude according to many people I've spoken to who are over 50 years old and grew up in the countryside or in the North of Norway. They felt maybe some kind of inferiority complex. I'm sure that the younger generation born in the 1980s and later, who lived a different life influenced by a much richer society due to oil income, would not find this as typical Norwegian anymore.

Some might say many of the "oil kids" have a superiority complex that is in total contradiction with how their parents and grandparents saw themselves in the world. All that to say that Norway being an independent, proud, free, and wealthy country is recent.

I personally love this day because the joy that one feels in the streets of Norway is so intense that it feels like pure collective freedom. I would advise any foreigners living here to stay in Norway for that day or even invite people over. It is not a military parade; it is a people's celebration. Don't take a get-away weekend to your home country on that day, because it is not just another day in Norway, and it is definitely worth it!

When do you get to see the Queen and King waving at you from the palace balcony if not on the 17th of May? The only challenge with this day is that if your family is visiting you they will probably think that this country is inhabited by euphoric people who love dressing like it's the 18th century. If they came back mid-January the same year, they might be in for a shock.

What I did not expect was the 17th of May to involve so

many preparations. For my first 17th of May, I was invited to Kaia's place, and she asked me to come the day before. We first went shopping and she bought an impressive amount of butter, sugar, berries of all colors, eggs, all kinds of ham, Norwegian flags of all sizes, cheese, flour, and smoked salmon.

We got out of the regular supermarket and went to *Vinmonopolet*, the alcohol monopoly shop managed by the Norwegian state. I heard of that shop before but had never been inside, as it was difficult for me to buy a bottle of wine for 150 Norwegian kroners when I could buy the same for 3 Euros in France.

Kaia literally stocked the trolley with many bottles of Cava and other bubbly alcohol. Cava is like champagne but cheaper. We went home and started baking the cakes and homemade bread. She seemed very well organized, so I followed her lead.

"How many cakes are we making?" I asked.

The unbelievable amount of strawberry and blueberry baskets we bought seemed to be enough to bake one cake per person.

"Don't worry," she said. "Berries will also be needed for the champagne."

"Berries in champagne?" I asked.

What on Earth was she making me do here?

We made something called *bløtkake*. Contrary to what I first believed, *bløtkake* does not translate to "blood cake" although that is really what it sounds like. *Bløt* means soft, and *bløtkake* is therefore a sponge cake which Norwegians layer with cream.

For this special occasion, berries of different colors (blueberries, raspberries, strawberries) are laid in the shape of the Norwegian flag on top of the cake. In another variation, a thin layer of marzipan (mix of egg white and almonds) covered the entire cake. That one is called *marsipankake* and has just as much sponge cake and cream inside.

That evening she got out a bottle and a box full of small pieces of silver.

"Now I have to polish the silver for my *bunad* and polish my shoes." she said.

That lasted a while, and we ended up going to bed late.

The next day, we woke up early in order to make sure her home was clean, and that the rest of the food was ready: salmon wraps, scrambled eggs, potato salad, and many other appetizers. I ran to the closest open shop in the morning because we needed more eggs. By the time the guests arrived, we were nicely dressed, Kaia in her *bunad* and shiny silver, me in my nicest dress. We had a traditional 17th of May breakfast with many of Kaia and Pål's friends. Pål was now officially her boyfriend.

After eating, we watched television with Norwegians all over the country and all over the world celebrating their national holiday. There were people skiing on Norway's highest mountain. They were in a snowstorm answering the questions of the Norwegian Broadcasting Corporation (NRK) journalist. A snowstorm on the 17th of May, and skiing to such a place willingly! Unbelievable.

I did not know anyone in the group except for my hosts as well as Ante, whom I had met at the taco dinner Kaia hosted. I asked him about the reindeer race at Easter which was held in his hometown, and he told me everything about it as he had just returned a few weeks ago. He asked me about France since he had never traveled outside of Norway except to go over the border to Sweden. He was as handsome and funny as the first time we met, maybe even more. His hair was not as blond as other Norwegians I had seen. His eyes were light blue and almond shaped. His laugh was very charming.

We continued drinking Cava and strawberries while slowly moving towards the city. The Oslo parks were completely packed with people sitting on the grass in their many different *bunads*, and there were small Norwegian flags everywhere on the ground. Ante was always somehow close to me, sometimes looking at me. He tried to make conversation. Think, I thought. This guy is interested, you need to make your intentions clear! The conversation I had with Kaia was vivid in my mind, as well as the sad story with Nils. I smiled back and touched his arm. Maybe this was clear enough?

We all walked to Karl Johan boulevard and saw the King and Queen waving at us. I had never seen so many people in the streets of Oslo, nor had I ever seen Norwegians so openly and collectively happy. Kids around had a sausage in one hand and ice cream in the other. Others were vomiting. Too much sausage or too much ice cream? I wondered. Was it the strawberries and the champagne?

Kaia and Pål and their friends decided to play a game called Kubb. They tried to explain the rules to me, something about knocking down wood pallets, but the mix of being slightly drunk and understanding the rules of a game I had never heard before made it hard to comprehend. I started running, thinking it was like baseball, and twisted my ankle in a hole. I was in a lot of pain and could not walk. I stayed on the side for a while, watching the game in silence, until Ante came and sat next to me.

"I have crutches at home from when I broke my leg a few months ago," said Ante. "If you come to my place, you can get them and walk almost normally after that," he added.

"Okay, but how will I get there? Do you live far away?" I asked.

"I am a strong man from the North. I will carry you," he said with a smile.

It took a split second for me to decide. This charming man was offering to carry me to his humble home. Maybe he would even have food in his fridge that did not involve the cold potato pancakes called *lompe* I had been eating all day with those salty Norwegian sausages and ketchup.

"Do you have food there?" I asked.

"Yes, and something way better than Taco Friday," he whispered, hoping not to be heard by Pål.

"Kaia, I'm leaving. See ya!" I said quickly before anyone would judge me.

"Have fun!" she replied with a wink.

Ante carried me on his back to his place in a street around Majorstuen and put me on his sofa. With ice on my foot, we decided to stay in for the evening. We got hungry again, and he told me he could prepare a great homemade dinner of duck, sweet potato purée, and red wine. The man was not joking earlier. He did have something in store that was much better than tacos.

He put on an apron and poured me a glass of red wine and smiled. Finally, a man who knew the way to my heart!

"Now, let's get to work," he said, while sharpening his knives. He put some music on.

"This is nice! What is the band called?" I asked.

"Valkyrien Allstars, they have good music," he answered.

They played an instrument I had never heard before: *hardingfele*, a Norwegian version of a violin. Unless violins are a non-Norwegian version of a *hardingfele*. In any case, the band had a very interesting sound, it made me realize I never listened to typical Norwegian music.

"Are there many singers or bands singing in Norwegian?" I asked Ante.

"Of course, so many. Do you know Vamp? And Kaizer Orchestra, a famous Norwegian band but they don't always sing in Norwegian, mostly in English. There is Dumdum Boys in another genre. All the heavy metal bands. Did you know that Norway has one of the highest proportions of black metal bands per capita in the world, after Finland and Sweden?" he said. I wondered whether the black metal bands had lyrics in Norwegian or in English.

I remembered debates in Danish newspapers saying Danes were afraid that their language would disappear because it is so hard to learn, and English is taking over the world.

Norwegians did not seem afraid that their language would disappear. The language was alive and kicking, with plays in theatres, bands playing concerts, movies in Norwegian and numerous books being written in this language.

We had dinner once it was all ready, and it tasted at least as good as it smelled in the kitchen while Ante was cooking it. When we were done, we sat on his sofa and listened to more interesting music from Norway. Ingebjørg Bratland, a beautiful voice. We got closer. I was trying to flirt with a Norwegian but I was struggling. What was it exactly? Eventually, he leaned in, and as our lips were about to touch, the soft and deep voice of Ingebjørg Bratland turned into a Celine Dion classic from the movie Titanic, with the horrifyingly out of tune voice of a man, "Neeaaarr, faaarr, whereeveerr you aarreee."

"What the…" said Ante when standing up suddenly. "Ken Tore, stop that horrible music," he added while throwing a pillow at his flat mate. I was less surprised by the music than by the name. Ken Tore? Really?

"Yes, people call me KT," he said, bringing forward an arm to say hello. In Norway everyone shakes hands when they meet, not like in France where women kiss both men and women on both cheeks, even when meeting for the first time. Here it is a handshake the first time, and then mostly a shy wave from a distance when one meets again. Unless you get to know the person really well or have not met for a long time, and then it is a Norwegian hug, a *klem*.

"Ken Tore is a Celine Dion fan, especially on karaoke," said Ante.

Ken Tore sang more. I was not used to this scene: seeing a grown man, almost two meters tall, with a beard and big metal earrings singing Celine Dion songs. A woman came in and said "Ken Tore is a sensitive type," with a smile. Inga was his girlfriend apparently, and she kissed him lovingly. I liked that about Norway: men can be sensitive, it's okay. They can like Celine Dion. I even heard some men join feminist groups. Amazing.

"It is getting crowded in here," said Ante, hinting towards a door which I imagined was his bedroom. He helped me to his room, and we kissed while listening to more Norwegian music. We got hungry after a few hours and I told him I had to head home.

"Stay, please," he said with a cheeky smile.

What should I do? My whole upbringing was clashing with the norms of this country which were completely different.

I decided to loosen up and spend the night there. I remembered what Kaia said: I had to show obvious signs of interest, or else Norwegian men would find another who is more interested. I recalled what my grandmother said: "Don't forget to have sex every now and then. It's good for personal hygiene."

Plus, I really liked Ante. Being a prude was something of the past, of my French life. It seemed like here women could be a bit freer as to whom they loved and when.

When I woke up the next day, Ante was on the phone. I tried to recognize which Norwegian dialect he spoke. It wasn't Swedish, I was pretty sure. It wasn't Danish either.

And it certainly did not sound like Norwegian. Maybe it was Finnish.

"Which language was that?" I asked when he hung up the phone.

"It's Sami language," he answered, smiling.

"I didn't know you were Sami!"

"Ante is actually a pretty common Sami name for boys, Norwegians know right away that I'm Sami. You want breakfast?" he asked casually.

I had many questions. What was it like to be a Sami in Norway? Did Norway have a violent history of oppression of indigenous peoples like Australia and the United States?

Unfortunately, the discussion seemed closed, and I would have to wait for another occasion to ask him, or do some research on my own. I worked with indigenous peoples' issues in Asia, and it was interesting to talk to someone who knew about those issues in Norway.

After breakfast, I felt like it was time to go home. Sleep in my bed, get over my hangover. Ante was in good shape, but then again, my liver was not a Norwegian one, used to weekend binge-drinking from the age of 13. In my country, women are not supposed to serve alcohol because "a bottle of wine is ugly in the hand of a woman." My ankle was better. I borrowed the crutches and asked Ante for a little help to reach the metro station.

On the way, I tried to figure out how I could meet this wonderful man again. He liked to cook, was kind and funny. His skin smelt like the sun. He listened to cool music and was pretty handsome. As we were about to part in front of the metro station, I kissed him on the lips. He avoided my kiss.

"Isn't it a bit early for that?" he said.

Wait a second – did we not just spend the night together? I was confused again by a Norwegian man's reaction.

"We don't know each other well enough yet to kiss in public. Then people will think we are in a relationship," he added.

Who cares what people think? I wondered.

We exchanged numbers, and I went home.

"*Vi snakkes*," he said, waving goodbye. What on Earth did that mean in Norwegian boy code?

*Note to self:* rule 865 of meeting Norwegian men: sex means nothing. It is absolutely not the beginning of a relationship, even when the man carries you, cooks for you, and replies to all your messages. It reminded me of this French guy I met at a party who told me this story which I found very funny at that time. A Norwegian girl came up to him and said "My place or your place?" He left with her for the night, and the next day she kicked him out at 7am because "I'm going kayaking at 8am." On a Sunday, really? Now that it was happening to me, it was not funny anymore. I remember my friend had told me that he met the girl by coincidence in the street a few days later and she ignored him. No wonder Norway had one of the highest rates of one-night stands, if sleeping with someone was as easy as taking them home and kicking them out a few hours later and never talking to them again.

I waited many days for him to call me back, which he did not do. Eventually Kaia told me to call him myself.

"Gender equality means it's not always up to men to do all the work," she said. So I called him back.

"Yes let's meet, that would be cool!" he answered. "Let's go hiking," he said.

Okay, I had other things in mind for a first "date," like maybe a restaurant, but fair enough. When in Norway do as the Norwegians.

At the end of this first date, I said, "You know, I'd like to see you again."

"Sure, he said, that would be nice," he answered.

We met again in town, at a bar to drink wine and beer. Every time was nicer than the previous time, and every time I ended up at his place. His breakfasts the next day were getting more and more grand, with waffles and homemade jam, or English breakfast with reindeer sausages from his mother. I was falling in love with him.

Then slowly but surely, despite answering all my messages, he never managed to meet me. He always had good excuses : "I would love to, but my cat is sick/I have to go back home for a wedding/my brother is coming over. Smiley face."

I told Kaia that I did not understand why he bothered answering all my messages if he was not interested.

"Go to his place with a pizza and a video game, he would like that!" she told me.

Are you kidding me? He should be the one coming to my home with chocolates and flowers. Were gender roles that much reversed in this country? When I said there was no way I was doing that, she added,

"Well, he might not be that into you anymore. Maybe he is seeing other girls at the same time? Many guys are con-flict-shy, they don't want to tell you right away that they don't want to meet you, so they reply something vague to your messages hoping you will get the hint."

Fantastic. Just what I wanted to hear...

I was tired of the game that I left it where it was, which is nowhere. He was Pål's friend so I hoped to meet him again by coincidence, and we would see what happens from there. One evening I went to a Valkyrien Allstars concert, and saw him speaking closely with a woman, holding her by the waist. I tried all I could to avoid him, and left the concert feeling sad. Our relationship was so insignificant to him that he did not even bother breaking up with me.

# HOW TO SEDUCE A NORWEGIAN

I was succeeding in most if not all parts of my Norwegian life. I was learning Norwegian language at the speed of light. Okay maybe not the speed of light, but I was understanding more and more. I was participating in meetings in Norwegian and my conversation skills were improving dramatically thanks to Kaia, with whom I only spoke Norwegian. At work, everything was great. I had good relationships with my colleagues and my job was even more interesting than I anticipated. I was even getting used to the Norwegian food, as I figured out which *pålegg* were my favorite. Although it was hard, I was also managing to build friendships. They were few, but they were getting stronger by the day.

The one code I just did not seem to crack was the dating one. What was so complicated, or different, about dating in Norway? The dynamics of flirting and relationships seemed to be so different from what I was used to everywhere else I'd lived. I had theories about why this was not working out for me.

Maybe Norwegian men were not interested in me because I was too loud and too different. Maybe they had such beautiful women from their own country, tall and blond, that they didn't care about a short dark-haired woman with curves Or maybe they'd been stuck in their fjords and cabins for so long that they didn't know how to approach women. Or maybe feminism and equality came so far here that women approached men, not the opposite, like Kaia told me that day.

I had one important question for myself: Did living in Norway mean I would be single forever? And if that was the price to pay, was I ready to stay in Norway?

"Just stop thinking of Ante, make a dating profile online," Kaia advised me one day.

I decided to try it all, in order to discover the Norwegian art of seduction and prove myself wrong about being single forever – and forget about Ante.

I observed that the general Norwegian art of seduction is based on three basic principles. The first one is eye contact. In any setting (on the metro, at a party, in a bar) a man or a woman will look you directly in the eyes for several seconds. You might think, like me, that this guy is looking at you in a strange way. Is he stalking you? No. He is trying to seduce you with his hypnotizing long eye-contact.

Scandinavian women look back if they are interested (it seems), with a wink (?) or some kind of long smile. And that is the start of something, I guess.

I wasn't not sure what happened after people had looked at each other for many long seconds. I assumed men would rarely do more than that in their part of the Norwegian seduction process. The rest seemed to be the woman's job (see principle number 2: inversion of roles).

The issue here is that such subtle signs of interest from men are completely invisible to foreign women's eyes as we are used to heavy flirting and seeing big signs made by men especially for us. Here, it's a little Post-It hidden in the guy's pocket. No wonder we can't read it.

It is only after some years in Norway that I realized men do flirt in their own peculiar way in order not to do anything that might invade your private space. They do come and talk to women they don't know, but only if alcohol is involved and if they have received obvious signs that she is interested, thus decreasing the risk of being rejected.

So conclusion number one: men won't do anything more than just look at you for a few seconds to show interest because they are shy and/or scared and/or very respectful of women. Sometimes they are even too shy to do that. If so, go directly to principle number three: alcohol.

The second basic principle is logically linked to the effect of the first principle. As men are not very brave and need a lot of moral support and encouragement to talk to women, I observed that there is an inversion of roles in what we southerners, see as the usual suspects: man chasing woman, woman playing hard to get, man trying to convince woman anyway by telling her that her eyes reflect all the stars of this universe, that she is beautiful, that no, she doesn't look fat in that dress. Patriarchal, probably. More romantic, definitely.

Scandinavian women work for it, whereas we sit there and bat our eyelashes. They get active and invite men to dance and flirt openly whereas Southern European women are taught to do these things subtly and discretely. You know, with a little style and dignity, not drunk with your fake tan melting off your face like I often saw in Great Britain.

In Copenhagen, every Friday and Saturday evening you'd see some kind of meat market going on in town, people looked at each other for minutes and hours across the room (party, bar) until one of them came up to the other and said "my place or your place?" Or women just come up to a guy in a café, handing their number and saying "I like you, call me."

Although I saw the benefits of women being like that, it was so foreign that I could only weep for all the Latin girls who would never dare to do such things. I talked to a few French men who had been offered, "My place or your place?" at the end of an evening in a bar or a party, and some had refused (some had accepted too). "There was no chase!" was the common answer from those who had refused.

Apparently when told "no", Scandinavian women get quite angry (of course this is second-hand information, I never experienced it myself). They are not accustomed to hear "No thank you, I am not interested in having sex with strangers with whom I haven't had a conversation.". Foreign men like the chase too, it's what we call seduction.

In more macho societies like France or Italy, such open flirting from a woman will be seen as an invitation for all the men in the neighborhood. Some men (not all, of course) already flirt heavily when uninvited, so imagine if you actively seek attention. To avoid being harassed as well as not to be considered as "easy" or worse, Southern European women smile a little, ignore a little, and let the guy suffer and try hard to seduce them. What happens to women who grew up in such a setting when they end up in Norway? Are you used to being seduced for weeks and months by men, with flowers and travels and dreams come true? Well, too bad for you, wink back and get over it.

So my second conclusion: Norwegian women are fearless. Which is good, I guess, when you think in terms of gender balance, feminist battles, and so on, but very bad for those others who were not raised in the North and who try to adapt to these foreign codes of equality even on their way to the bedroom.

The third basic principle, which is the most important of all, is the link between all the principles, the foundation of Norwegian seduction. Yes, I am talking about alcohol. Most would say that the French also drink alcohol. But Norwegians and other Northern peoples like Brits, Danes, Swedes, Finns, and Russians really drink a lot. So this is not about drinking a few glasses, this is about getting smashed, so drunk that you don't remember what happened, that you feel so uninhibited that you were not even yourself anymore and that it was great. At that point, just before you pass out, vomit, or get alcohol poisoning, you are brave enough to make a move on that girl sitting next to you in the bar. It is 3am and everyone needs to leave because the bar is closing. This is the moment for Norwegian couples in the making.

What comes next is the infamous party-trilogy: after-party, sex, and hangover (and sometimes a bonus like vomiting and the morning-after pill). Most of the time it ends there, with an awkward morning-after-moment: Who is this person? Why am I naked in their bed? Is this a real moose head hanging on the wall staring at me?

In some cases, you have breakfast with your one-night-love and end up realizing that you share real-life experiences (oh my God, it's so amazing, I've also been to the Roskilde Festival) and you exchange numbers. What happens next is out of anyone's control. "Are they interested?" seems to be a question no one, absolutely no one can answer. Then follow days, sometimes weeks of exchanging messages with more smileys than anyone can stand. People may hit it off and get together, and after many complicated commitments decide to call each other a couple. They might have kids, but rarely do they get married.

To all of those who spread the information that there are no codes of seduction in Norway, you are wrong. There are more than codes, there are scenarios that unfold over and over again every Friday and Saturday evening in the streets of Norwegian cities.

All these conclusions were based on my observations, and I was very conscious they might be wrong all together, considering that 1) I did not speak Norwegian well enough to communicate with the subjects of my studies (men) and 2) I was rarely so drunk that I did not know what I was doing, therefore decreasing my chances of going home with a Norwegian man by about one million. 3) I was very strange, in a sense that even a very attractive and interesting man lost many points on my scale of attractiveness once he was dead drunk, falling on me and saying in a *snus*-filled breath, "*Duu eerr søøtt duuu fransk dammeee.*" ("You are sweet you French lady").

Then I would always rather go home and read a comic book and wake up free and alone in my bed rather than facing a stuffed elk head in someone else's bedroom. Strangely enough, the few men I met in bars and eventually woke up next to the following day ended up never texting me back and pretended not to recognize me when meeting me on the street a few days or weeks later. My ego was not strong enough to bear the rules of one-night stands, so I tried dating online.

I created a profile on Tinder. I thought, naively, that online dating is like regular seduction. It is about seeing if there is attraction in a simple way (HA!) and being honest (HAHA!). Seduction in Norway is not simple at all for foreigners. So, as you can imagine, neither is online dating. I would say it follows rules which are even more obscure than regular flirting in a bar, all in a language that I didn't understand. In a bar you can get away with speaking English, not on Tinder where most small talk is in Norwegian. Sure, all you need at first is to swipe right or left, but things quickly become more complicated.

The first thing you need to know about Norwegian online dating is that there are passions you absolutely need to have if you want men/women to be interested in you. You need to love something called "*friluftsliv.*" It means "the life in fresh air," a Norwegian concept which is hard to translate to English, which basically means that you need to be "outdoorsy." To illustrate your love of being outdoors, you absolutely need one or several pictures of you in a magnificent, wild landscape. It can show you swimming in a majestic fjord or standing on top of a mountain, showing that you had to hike a pretty steep and narrow path to get there. Ideally, one needs to be doing these things without too many people around. You must show you are so outdoorsy that you boldly went where no man (or woman) has gone before.

Second important interest: you need to be sporty. You thought it would be enough to like being outside having a nice little walk. No no no. You need to like extreme stuff like going to the gym every day. Don't put pictures of you sweating in spinning class (unclassy) but do put a picture of you rafting down a crazy river in Thailand or cycling up some road in the south of France with a beautiful view of the sea behind you (a nice tan is a must have). I was swiping left and right, seeing the profile pictures of all these men. I realized I was totally unprepared for dating a Norwegian. I also needed pictures of me fishing, or shooting an animal, or riding a horse – I had none of those.

*Note to self:* It's important to be the same as everybody else but a bit different. Different, yet not too different. Confident yet not showing off. It gets tricky here. I don't know whether it's because of the "you are not better than anyone else" rule, but everyone writes the same things over and over again. I don't think it's because people are boring, just that they don't want to seem too eccentric or too confident. Okay, some *are* boring.

The will to follow the norm is painfully strong in Norway and is reflected on dating websites. You end up having to read this kind of sentence so many times your eyes hurt: "I like to stay at home, but sometimes I go out with friends. I also like going to cafés." Oh wow, just like the rest of the 500 000 people living in this city.

Roughly 99 percent of men's profiles I saw included that they like to "*gå på tur*," "*gå på ski*," and "*på hyttetur*" (hiking, skiing, and going on cabin trips – choosing to take week-long trips to some place in the middle of nowhere with no electricity or hot water.)

On one of those profiles where the guy had made the effort to write actual words and not just emojis, he wrote that the girl should be the "type" that pees in a bush without complaining. Seriously? Is that the criteria? It seems to me that all Norwegian girls have been raised to pee in the dark behind a *hytte* by -20 °C with reindeer and polar bears watching, so I am sure it's not a hard criterion to meet (for other foreign girls, it may be a bit different). Oh, and she also has to be the type who can put on high heels and look awesome and sexy to impress his friends, oh, and also confident and sweet. Man, what a job to be a girl.

How could I pull this off with dignity? I didn't have a cabin, didn't know how to ski, I had never entered a gym before moving to Norway because I am lazy, and I had no pictures of me sitting on the top of a mountain, or rowing a boat in the Lofoten Islands. In addition, I didn't speak Norwegian and I had no friends in this country. This did not sound confident, or sexy, or even slightly attractive. Conclusion: I had nothing to sell on the Norwegian market of love.

So I thought! I was wrong. Having a vagina opens a lot of doors while online dating in many countries of this world, including in Norway. I did get attention, mostly from men who were old and bald and living in Finnmark. They didn't seem to have met or talked to a woman in a long, long time. On the bright side, they are very dedicated to writing to you every single day and have a profession that can come in handy, like plumber or electrician

You would think young, hip, urban men would be easier to connect with, but some get very specific looking for a life companion, or should I say, a female person to appear in the pictures of the perfect family life they have imagined for themselves. "So, do you want children soon?" asked Per-Christian the second time we met. "Because, you know, I'm 35, and need to build a family and stuff. So if you're not in, I don't want to waste my time." "Hmm, can I give you my answer after dessert or will I have wasted too much of your time already?" I was tempted to ask him. I think I preferred the guy who dressed his dog in a pink tutu asking me out. At least he was being a gentleman. When I met them after matching online, others made me feel like I was at a job interview. It felt as if they had a check list where you gain or lose points each time you open your mouth. Watch out! If you are not sweet, sporty, and confident you might not get called for the second round. If you can't pee in the bushes with class and dignity, you're OUT!

I met boring men, surprising men (not in a good way), and others who were more interested in themselves than anything else. I knew I was bored if I looked at my watch and thought, "It's only been ten minutes? I thought I had been here for one hour at least." Others made a point in "educating me" on gender equality in Norway. They would tell me "You know why I am making you pay half the bill, right?" Kill me now.

Maybe living in Norway, enjoying the great things this country has to offer, means I have to sacrifice my love life and be single forever. *Uffa meg.*

III

# SUMMER

# UNDER THE MIDNIGHT SUN

A very exotic aspect of Norwegian life came by in summer: the midnight sun. During the month of June, I couldn't help but look at the sun all night. It was hard to believe the darkness did not fall on the horizon. Oslo is quite "south" (read south of the Arctic Circle, unlike Bodø, Tromsø or Vadsø), it does get darker during the night even on the shortest night of the year, the 21st of June. The Summer Solstice is also known as *Sankt Hans,* and Norwegians get really excited about this day. They build high lumber towers for weeks and set them on fire, like the memorable one in Ålesund which broke a world record for the largest Solstice fire, with an amazing 47-meter-high tower that was set on fire that night.

People drank and partied all night while cheering for the sun "turning" again. Afterwards it would only get "darker" until the 21st of December, with daylight getting scarcer every day.

Everyone at work had planned their summer holidays many

months in advance. I had no clear idea what I was going to do. My parents wanted me to return to France, but there was nothing new there, nothing exotic. On the contrary I was in a country I knew very little of, as I had spent most of my six months here in Oslo, which, guessing from my short Tromsø adventure, was probably not a representation of Norway.

I decided to explore Norway that summer. On my bicycle.

My office asked me to take a minimum of three weeks of holidays in what Norwegians call *fellesferie*. "The common holidays", which cover the school holidays from the last week of June to mid-August.

I planned to be at an indigenous festival in mid-July in a small village on the border between Troms and Finnmark, but other than that I was free to do whatever and go wherever I wanted.

I decided to stay in Norway and explore this country. I planned to visit the Lofoten Islands and Southern Norway to discover two very opposite areas in terms of geographical location in Norway.

Kristiansand is almost 2000 km away from Tromsø. This is why Norwegians like to say that if you turn Norway on its Southern tip its other tip will reach Rome.

Planning my trip was taking time. I bought a solid bicycle and a waterproof tent. Meanwhile the summer was wonderful, and I was enjoying everything Oslo had to offer on weekends and after work.

Kaia and Pål often invited me to picnics in Oslo's many parks. One could have written a PhD in anthropology on Norwegians just by sitting in those parks. Some would arrive early because they knew exactly where in the park the sun would disappear last.

Most Norwegians were half-naked, some women were in their underwear sun tanning, and the main activity was grilling sausages. It's as if the whole country became obsessed with grilling things just because the sun was out.

I have nothing against grilling, but these mini grills everyone used in Oslo were disposable and could only be used once, and cost surprisingly very little money. One lights them with a fuel impregnated paper on top, and then the coal burns in an aluminum box. The bins of the Oslo parks were cemeteries of *engangsgrill* (single-use grill), with apparently as many as 3000 of them dumped there every single weekend. They were so cheap compared to how much they cost to nature.

I did not understand how these super environmentally friendly Norwegians who love their forest and cherish their fjords could turn a blind eye to how environmentally unwise this was. And especially very avoidable since one could just buy a portable grill or find another way to heat those sausages that were pre-cooked anyway. All this waste to heat sausages.

Towards mid-June the weather was so warm Kaia and I wanted to bathe. On a Saturday, we took a boat from Aker Brygge in the center to one of the islands in the fjord, Hovedøya. It was unbelievable. We were in a European capital city, just a boat hop away from the center. Kaia and I talked about our summer plans.

"I want to cycle in the Lofoten Islands," I told her. "And Dagny's son lives in Telemark, so I'll be going to Porsgrunn by train to cycle from there to Kristiansand across Southern Norway."

"Alone?" she asked.

"Yes, why not?" I replied. "I want to discover Norway," I added.

I had traveled alone before, in Indonesia and in the Philippines, and it had always been the best way to meet people.

"You know what, I will be in Trøndelag with my family this summer. Why don't you come and visit us, and we can go on a cabin trip to our family *hytte*?" said Kaia.

"Oh, that would be amazing," I said. "But it has to be at the end of July or beginning of August because I also need to go to the indigenous Riddu Riđđu Festival for a conference for work," I added.

"No worries, I am there all summer. Just let me know."

Pål had joined us. He was more skeptical about Southern Norway. He came from Harstad, in the North, after all.

"Why would you go to Southern Norway on holidays? I would rather go abroad than go there. Do you know people are very stuck up there? You cannot even swear. Did you know that? A simple expression like *Satan i helvete* (Satan in hell – Norwegian swear words are often linked to religion) will make people blush and maybe put you in jail," he said, horrified.

"In jail? Are you not exaggerating a bit here?" I asked skeptically.

"Well, I am a sane person, and I never travel south of Sandefjord," he said.

"And alone, on a bike? Seriously, it always rains there. You are making a big mistake. You should spend your holidays north of Trondheim," he added.

Others at work were more concerned about the fact that I was planning on spending my summer in Norway.

"Are you seriously staying in Norway all summer? Don't you want to have a real summer? You're supposed to go South in the summer, not North!" said Ylva.

But I was not Norwegian: I lived south of the Arctic Circle all my life. Everything from the midnight sun to seeing wild seals and puffins was just amazing to me. I tried to convey this idea to Ylva, without much success.

"I have spent many summers in Provence, I know what they feel like. The Lofoten Islands, however, are unknown to me. It will be exciting!" I answered.

"You mean excitingly cold?" answered Ylva skeptically.

"See, we Norwegians go to *Syden* for all of our holidays where we don't expect to ski. You will regret it, I hope you have a ticket for the South of France just in case" she added.

Where was *Syden*? I heard it before. Was it a country? Was it France? Spain? Norwegians seemed to use the term for many different places.

*Syden*, it turns out, means "the South" and is a huge area consisting of all countries less than 12 hours from Oslo where it is over 18 °C in the winter and where alcohol is cheaper than in Norway. There needs to be direct charter flights taking you to a beach. That is a lot of places.

***Note to self:*** Norwegians are so strange. All they dream of all year long is for the summer to come, and then when it is there, they leave the country. Such a waste when one knows how beautiful Norway can be in the summer.

I did not care about their internal conflicts between Norwegian regions, or about the Norwegian fear of getting rained on during their summer holidays. I was going to cycle to Southern and Northern Norway no matter what.

# MY FIRST SEAL SAFARI

I bought a beautiful red bicycle for my first trip of the summer. The plan was to put it on the plane from Oslo to Bodø, take a ferry boat from Bodø to an island called Røst and cycle around the island for a few days.

I would take another ferry to Moskenes and cycle my way up the islands. I had addresses of a few youth hostels, and fishermen's houses on rental, locally called *rorbu*, as well as the address of Nina's sister, Ane's aunt, who lived in a small village along my route.

I bought a one-way ticket from Oslo to Bodø and no return ticket. I planned to return to Oslo when the Northern Norwegian weather forecast said the weather would no longer be cycling friendly.

A stress-free Norwegian holiday far from the city crowd, full of wild nature, *matpakke* and delicious fish meals made with the catch-from-the-day. I could not wait.

Røst is a small archipelago south of Værøy. Also part of the traditional district of Lofoten but much less touristy. It was a good place to start this stress-free vacation.

The Oslo-Bodø flight was a completely empty flight in July (the Norwegians were on a beach getting skin cancer). I then enjoyed the ferry ride to Røst with a very nice view of a fat Dutch family vomiting all their hot dogs.

All the tourists, including myself, were admiring the midnight sun: seeing the sun going round in circles above your head all night is pretty cool.

As we arrived in Røst's harbour, I realized how remote this place actually was. I couldn't imagine what a winter-storm would look like there. It looked quite flat and dangerously exposed in case of wild winds. I was thankful to myself for not being crazy enough to have come here in the winter.

As the ferry opened its huge mouth to let the few "Røst passengers" out, I hopped on my bicycle and started my search for the *Kårøy Rorbucamping*, or the Kår Island Fishermen Camping. It followed a unique concept of "indoor camping", and it also happened to be the cheapest accommodation in town. Well… calling it a "town" is maybe an overstatement.

I had no idea where this indoor camp was, but I wasn't too worried, I had a bicycle to go around and this place was tiny. Strangely enough, I couldn't find it. I started asking around, and everyone pointed to the sea. They probably didn't understand my question, I thought.

Eventually I saw a little lady waving at me from another island and calling Louulloouuloouu (that's me). She was the owner of the indoor camp and she was planning on taking me there… by boat.

What I misunderstood is that this fisherman's camp is on a small island next to Røst called Kårøy. Whenever someone wanted to leave the hostel they needed to row a boat for 10 to 15 minutes between the islands. There you go, free training for my back. When the wind was not in your favor it could take ages as I found out later.

The little lady even had to come and save me once when I had been rowing for at least 20 minutes against the wind without getting any closer to the hostel. Oh well, this is part of the adventure, right? It's not like I had many other things to do during the holiday than rowing a boat to get to my hostel.

I arrived on the small island of Kårøy and realized that the whole hostel was covered in seagulls, the big and noisy type. They were sitting on their nests on every parcel of this place (roof, windows, tables), screaming in a big choir of seagull chants.

"Do they get tired at some point?" I asked the old lady.

She started laughing and replied,

"Of course not! There is daylight all the time, so they never sleep."

Oh God, I thought. I came here for peace and quiet and I'll end up sleeping with hundreds of screaming seagulls over my head. After thinking about it, I realized it seemed a bit strange: seagulls can't stay awake for four months in a row just because it's never nighttime. They do look like stupid animals, but still...

After asking myself why the hell I went there in the first place, I went with the flow (and earplugs) and got all busy cycling on the island, sending a few postcards and chatting with the old lady who owned the indoor camping.

I was invited into their home after her husband saw me row back and forth to Røst. He told me, full of respect, that it had been years since he'd seen someone row like that. Wow, some kind of acknowledgement coming from an old Norwegian fisherman. I was so glad to see that my rowing talents were not going to waste. I might look like a penguin when I cross country ski, but at least growing up by the sea has taught me how to row with dignity!

There weren't a million things to do on Røst, and that's why it was such a good place to be on a vacation. I realized while being there that Røst is an "internationally recognized" bird-watching spot. I seized this opportunity to go on a bird-safari. A fisherman took me and a few other tourists on a tour in the boat he uses for regular fishing.

I saw many amazing things, such as puffins: a miniature flying penguin with a yellow and red parrot-like beak that the fisherman steering the boat described as a "very tasty little animal that we aren't allowed to eat anymore."

I had to wait in complete silence for hours before I could see some other birds fly and eat. I also saw seals, lying lazily on the rocks.

Besides cycling, watching birds, and rowing, I also spent time trying to communicate with the Røst locals – not that easy, and there weren't many tourists around either. However, the scenery of this place was breathtaking, with mountains coming out of the sea and nature reserves where one must stay silent so as to not disturb the birds. Little restaurants were scattered all over the islands, serving exceptional meals made of fresh fish and bacon and carrot puree.

I must say it was almost hard to leave. "Almost" because there came a point when I needed to have a human interaction with more than two persons per day, and the few fishermen on Røst were not very chatty.

After a few days, I took the only ferry to Moskenes to discover the rest of the Lofoten Islands with my bicycle, planning to see Arctic white sand beaches and Viking ships.

# CYCLING IN THE LOFOTEN ISLANDS

The ferryboat from Røst arrived at 2am in what seemed to be the middle of nowhere – but was in fact in a place called Moskenes. I needed to go to my youth hostel which was in Å. I looked around and asked a man for directions.

"Hi! Do you know which direction is Å?" I asked.

"Å? Never heard of that place," said the guy with a thick French accent. I traveled thousands of kilometers out of my country and the first guy I met on this island in the middle of nowhere is French. I continued in French.

"Are you sure? I thought Å was just a few kilometers away" I asked.

"Oooh, you mean A. You are saying it wrong, that's why I misunderstood. A is down this road, but there is no place called Å around here," he corrected me.

I wanted to hang around to explain that the little dot on the A means that the letter is pronounced Å (Oh) and not A (Ah) in Norwegian, but never mind.

The midnight sun made my five-kilometer bicycle trip to Å much easier. Such a unique experience to cycle under the midnight sun, in broad daylight yet technically in the middle of the night.

As I got closer to Å, the scene that appeared before me was completely magical. From the road, I saw a set of red houses sitting on wooden poles on the rocks. In the background, there were tall triangle-shaped wooden structures from which thousands of cods were hanged out to dry in March. The whole area was surrounded by a blue and pink sunrise mist.

Å was much nicer in the middle of the night, because to be honest the rest of the time there were too many people there. Mainly tourist vans coming in and out of the "typical fisherman's village." I didn't stick around too long and cycled north to my next stop: the house of Ane's aunt who lived in Ramberg and would host me.

I was not like some Norwegians that worked out like maniacs, which means I was not in especially good shape to cycle 80 kilometers a day on hilly roads such as in the Lofoten Islands.

While I cycled to Ramberg through what seemed to be the four seasons in one hour, I was thinking to myself: I am hungry, I am tired, I have crazy wind blowing against me, rain pouring down on my head followed by sun, which makes me shiver and then feel too warm. Why did I decide to do this with a bicycle instead of being in one of these warm and dry cars that drive fast in front of me?

The answer was obvious to me every five minutes when I looked at the view. It was as if I needed a camera to take pictures every five seconds. Everything was mesmerizing: the sky, the bridges, the view of the villages, the clouds. I had no words to describe the beauty and the pristineness of it all. It was all so pure. I felt the need to come back during the spring, around March, when they hang the cod out to dry.

"The air smells like money," said a local man I met who helped me change a tire.

When I arrived in Ramberg it was even more extraordinary. The view was breathtaking. The white sand beach and the pure blue sea and the mountains ahead made all the bad thoughts disappear. I knew that all the effort to get here was worth it.

When Nina's sister put a plate of spaghetti bolognese in front of me once I got to her house, there were almost tears in my eyes. I had been eating Svolvær paté and *knekkebrød* for the past week. I was so thankful for a warm meal.

I was not supposed to stay too long, but Annukka and Knut were so welcoming it was hard to leave. I was also having an intensive Norwegian course as they only spoke Norwegian to me, no English at all. Needless to say, my level was too low to be thrown into a Norwegian family from *Nord-Norge* discussing politics and making jokes. I managed to have "conversations," especially because Knut made extra effort to teach me some swear words and also teach me how to drink cognac.

I felt like my Norwegian was getting much better the drunker I got. Or was it that I was more self-confident, who knows? He taught me first and foremost to swear on the devil and hell.

"No, no, don't say 'what are you doing here?' you have to say '*Søkki helvete! Førrbainande jævelskap! Helvete satan!*'"

(These swear words and expressions are hard to translate but they involve Hell and the Devil). "'Don't say 'I don't agree with you.' Say '*Dra til helvete!*'" said Knut. (Go to hell!)

So I would repeat. "*Souki heulveute, fourbainneude jeuveulsquape.*"

"No, all wrong, you sound too French. Repeat after me. Try with the right intonation from Northern Norway: '*Helvete satan! Hæsskuk!*' By the way," he added, "*Hæsskuk* is not an insult in Northern Norway, you know that right? You can say that to a policeman and it's okay. A court even ruled it so after a man called a police officer a *hæsskuk* and it was decided that if a Northern Norwegian says it, it's considered regular vocabulary," said Knut while smoking a cigarette. He really liked to smoke.

Which context would I place the word *hæsskuk* in anyway? Maybe when a supermarket cashier asked me whether I wanted a bag or not with those groceries, I could say "*Gjerne, herr hæsskuk*" (Sure, Mister horse genitalia). No, that sounded rude, even with the "Mister." Or maybe I could use it at my office?

With this I could show my Norwegian boss and colleagues that my Norwegian was getting better. Instead of saying "*ikke sant*" every third word like they did, I would say "*Det regnet så mye i går jævla hæsskuk*" (It rained so much yesterday, bloody horse genitalia). I preferred not to try. I had to make many friends first to afford making enemies later.

We practiced like this every day. After the third day I was getting quite good, and he was so proud of me that he opened the cupboard after dinner and opened a bottle of his best cognac. "Smell this!" he said. "You deserve it. You worked hard. Now I will teach you one more. If you are in Østlandet with all those puritans and you think you cannot swear that much before they freak out, then a milder version is to say '*Dæven han smell bacon.*' My son says it all the time when he doesn't want to offend anyone down south. We call the devil but it's with bacon so it's okay."

I spent several days in their home, each morning thinking I should leave in order not to abuse my hosts' kindness. I had to cycle up north, according to my plan. Every day it was harder and harder to leave. I would leave for day trips with my bicycle to neighboring sites like the very charming Nusfjord with its dried fish and fishing boats.

I would eat ice cream sitting on the deck, feeling the sun on my face. Cycling there I would pass by a kind of lake, from which I could see mountains with white snowy tops and pink flowers. It looked almost like Switzerland. On top of that, I was so lucky that I only got sun for over two weeks. I took a picture of myself in my bikini to send to my colleagues.

"So, never any good weather in Northern Norway, huh?" I captioned the picture, knowing that Oslo had really bad weather at that time.

There was always something to do, something to see, pictures to take and peaceful moments to enjoy in this dramatic nature. My hosts were amazingly entertaining, and despite being far from home and familiar faces, I was never ever bored.

When I was with them in the evenings, I would bake them cakes. They would teach me swear words and dirty jokes. Some days the weather was so good we would sit outside on their terrace with the view on the white sand beach.

How can a place be so beautiful and so peaceful? I don't know. Why do Norwegians go on holidays to Las Palmas instead of coming here? Norwegians are so strange. What a waste! When one can access the beaches of Northern Norway, among the most beautiful I've seen in my life, why would anyone want to go to another country? I found out it had something to do with the temperature of the water, and that in Las Palmas it rarely goes below zero degrees in July.

I went on a hike behind Ramberg. After quite a short time I was on a peak, with the purest view.

The mountains dramatically coming out of the sea and the white sand beach would make anyone believe the picture was taken on some Caribbean island (except that the water was freezing cold). The surroundings were wild, and the spaces were huge. Looking at the view from the mountaintop behind Anukka and Knut's house made me think that this is the definition of peacefulness.

I never wanted to leave this place. I just wanted to become one with this beautiful nature. I ate a few blueberries and slept in the grass. What more could one need? There wasn't even another hiker to disturb me. In other words, paradise.

After almost a week at Knut and Annukka's home, I decided that if I did not leave, I would end up spending all my vacation here. That was a nice idea. But I decided to follow a saying from my neighborhood in Marseille: guests are like fish, after three days they stink.

Better leave while they still liked me, not after they got tired of having me around. I took my red bicycle again with my two side bags and left, promising them we would meet again.

My next stop was Stamsund. Stamsund is a little place which is connected to the world by the Hurtigruten. The famous Norwegian coastal route passes through Stamsund on its way to Bergen, signaling its presence by a deep boat sound.

On my way, I stopped on a beach and decided to camp. I was woken up by the sound of the waves. The great thing about cycling is that one has time to enjoy the view.

The next day I got very hungry and had no Svolvær paté left. I needed something warm. There were very few supermarkets in Lofoten, so I was very happy when I saw a Coop far on the road ahead of me. When I got to the shop, a sign was hung on the door: "*Ut å drekk. Sees i morra.*" (Out drinking, see you tomorrow). You have to be kidding me. It was 3pm!

In Stamsund, I slept in fishermen houses which had been transformed into a youth hostel. The beds in the dorms were cheap for Norwegian standards, but the foreign tourists had trouble getting used to the Norwegian prices.

"The owner is a grumpy Norwegian," said Claire, a French lady who was cycling from North Cape to Bretagne with nothing else than four kilograms of stuff with her.

She slept in barns and asked for peoples' hospitality every night when she was tired of cycling. She only ate when she had time, mainly bread, and admitted that she wanted to eat every animal she saw on the road, especially the sheep.

Compared to her cycling trip, mine was a spa. I was eating well, sleeping in real beds or at least in my tent. I did not cycle with my luggage every day, as I was stopping in places for several days, exploring the area, and leaving again.

The grumpy old Norwegian turned out to be very cheerful when I spoke Norwegian to him. He was just tired of foreigners. How could I blame him? The few German tourists sitting on the deck thought they owned the place because they'd spent three summers in his *rorbu*.

Without them he would be out of business. It was the only youth hostel around, and the cheapest bed in the whole Lofoten Islands.

He was named Jan and he mumbled all the time, often looking angry but without yelling. With me, he was as soft as a lamb, and even invited me to his home to eat a fish he had caught the same day. He told me he liked it a lot that I spoke some Norwegian. It showed I made an effort.

At his place I met his wife Herbjørg. She offered me a cup of coffee.

"You are a brave girl to come all the way to this area of Norway coming from the South of France. It's far," she said.

"Not really. I did not come all the way up here on my bicycle, I took a plane to Bodø," I answered with a smile.

We chatted for a bit, and I told her I loved writing and that Northern Norway was very interesting.

"You think Northern Norway is interesting? Why is that?" she asked.

"Before coming to Norway, I believed that it was a very homogeneous society. I am discovering now that I was wrong. I am discovering the cultural differences inside this society. There are definitely differences between Oslo people and those from Northern Norway," I replied.

"This is despite a small population of only five million people. I also find that Northern Norwegians are much closer to my own culture. It is easier to relate to them. They don't get offended when I get angry or swear or speak passionately about something," I added.

Herbjørg told me a great deal about the differences between Northern Norway and the southern parts of the country.

"It is not just the culture which is different, it is also the history. I will tell you what happened during the war," she told me.

"Maybe you can get another perspective on the people and the history of this country? Many think we are rich because of the oil, and we end up forgetting who we were, and what happened to us just a few decades ago. I was a child, I remember. The Germans came, they wanted the north because of the nickel mines. I come from a place called Nordreisa in Nord Troms, while Jan comes from here.

In Troms people were hiding under boats, in small huts. We were afraid of being discovered by the Nazis. The King had left for England, we were on our own. I was a child and all I remember was being hungry. So hungry. And seeing fear in my parents' eyes," she paused and drank a sip of her coffee.

The years had made her face look like crumpled paper which has been touched and read many times, with lines that moved every time she smiled or drank her coffee. She continued.

"They occupied us, and by the time they left, the whole

of Finnmark and Nord Troms was burned to the ground. Nothing was left. We had no homes, but we were free. We were sent to the Southern parts of Norway while our homes were being rebuilt.

When those who had lived through the war in much less harsh conditions saw us come, all they saw were hungry, dirty, scared families. We spoke strangely to them. We were less educated than them. Some of us were Samis. My family and I lived there for two years after the war. It was so rough. Not scary like during the war, but we felt shame down south. It wasn't nice. When the government rebuilt our towns, we moved back North." She stopped there. She was too tired to continue so Jan took over.

"And we kept an image of southerners as those who did not welcome us and looked down on us. And they remembered the poor and hungry northerners with their strange dialect," said Jan with a sigh.

Ah, it all made sense now, what the lady on the plane to Tromsø had told me.

"That is why Northern Norwegians were not welcome in Oslo until the 1970s." said Jan.

I could see they were tired, so I thanked them and left their home. I went back to the dorm where I rented a bed from them.

Some Italian girls were chatting all night, and I was tired from cycling.

"Can you please go to sleep?" I asked.

"It's impossible. It's so light outside. We decided to stay up until our bus tomorrow at 6am," one of them said with a thick Italian accent. Oh no. I left the room to look out at the sea. Nothing bad could come of that.

It was on the deck that I met a man called Tor, who was silently fishing. We exchanged a total of ten words and spent the evening next to each in total silence. I had too much respect for the fish to disturb them with my small talk, even though that meant them being hung dry and eaten later.

I didn't meet Tor the next day. I cycled around and later that evening went back to Herbjørg's house, where more coffee, and more stories awaited.

"All this was before the oil, you know," continued Herbjørg as if we had never left the previous day's conversation.

"At that time, we were so poor. Over a million Norwegians left the country from the mid-1850s until the early 1900s. Most of them settled down in Minnesota and Dakota between Canada and the United States. My grandfather told me, 'If you can leave this land, leave. There is nothing good here, only cold, death, and starvation.' All we ate as kids were fish and potatoes. I got so tired of eating them, but at the same time it is the food I was used to eating all my life. There was not as much meat as there is now. It was so expensive back then. Now the *ribbe* (pork belly) at Christmas time is so cheap people give it to their dogs. We had it only on Sundays or special occasions."

I was fascinated by these stories. The fact that Norway is seen as a country with a homogenous society, while it isn't. That it was occupied, poor and isolated then became one of the richest countries in the world almost overnight. It was mind boggling.

I told Herbjørg about my own family. My father was also from a very poor family. He was born in the 1950s in very conservative Québec, where priests had more power than the state. The priests would go around to houses, pushing couples to have more children. Increasing the French-Canadian population was seen as their only way to outbalance the economical superiority of the Canadian English.

That night I went out on the deck again, and Tor was there

with a bag.

"I'm leaving tonight. Going back to Oslo. Here is my number. Call me," he said, leaving with a smile.

Oh my. Was this Norwegian man hitting on me? Did he actually like me?

I stayed longer than planned in Stamsund. Something about this place, this house, this couple, the Hurtigruten coming in and out, was very special.

I cycled around the area, went fishing, slept on the warm rocks on the nearby "beaches". One day I woke up and realized my train was leaving for Oslo the next morning, so I gave a *klem* to Herbjørg and Jan and took a ferry to Bodø.

*Note to self:* I would highly recommend anyone to travel in the Lofoten Islands by bicycle. Many perks: you will actually enjoy the scenery instead of driving by really fast in your car. You will embrace the weathers (yes, a variety of weather): sun, rain, wind, clouds, beautiful rays of sunlight in the deep blue sea etc. You will also meet a lot of people (e.g. those who will help you fix your bike in the middle of nowhere, because stupid you took all the tools but have no idea how to change a tire).

See, a lot of new adventures are coming your way!

# CRYING IN SOUTHERN NORWAY

Now was the time to discover Southern Norway. This time, I took a train from Bodø to Oslo. Bodø was the furthest north a passenger train would take you in Norway. I rested for a few days in Oslo and took another train from Oslo to a place called Porsgrunn in Telemark to meet Dagny's son, Roar.

I would spend a night there and then cycle to Kristiansand.

I had an evening in Porsgrunn with Roar, who was the illustrator of Telemark county's biggest newspaper *Varden*.

He had also worked in several state institutions like NAV and the child protection services and was now the head of the "White Busses," or *Hvitebusser*, a well-known organization that took Norwegian teenagers on trips to Nazi concentration camps to learn about history.

Roar was a tall blond man in his 50s. His children were over for dinner, so I cooked for them to thank them for their hospitality. I learned many things that night, especially about

Vikings. Roar talked about a Viking ruler named Harald Hårfarge who was King in the 9th century. He explained to me how difficult it was for missionaries to Christianize the Vikings.

"You can imagine how a people who was used to raiding, stealing, raping, and waging war reacted to Christians telling them to show their left cheek if slapped on the right." said Roar as we were having dinner with his children.

"I never thought of that," I answered.

"I wonder how Norwegians, whose ancestors were Vikings, are now so peaceful and so respectful of women. That couldn't have come from Christianity, as Christians are not known for particularly giving a voice to women," I asked.

"The roots of gender equality go way back, actually. Women were very much respected during Viking times. Unless they were slaves. But the free women had the right to divorce, and some were fighting and raiding alongside men," he said.

"Christianity was pushed onto us through violence. But then it really took off, especially in the south of the country that some call the Bible Belt. The north was always less religious and conservative, and it was the last part they managed to convert," he said.

Great, that's where I was going, the Bible Belt. I was already imagining big signs like in the south of the United States: "Go to church, or the devil will get you," or "I kissed a girl and I liked it, and then I went to hell."

How conservative could this place be? I had traveled alone in Indonesia and the Philippines and everything had gone great. How hard could this be, really?

The next day Roar left me at the outskirts of the city for me to start cycling towards the coast. He gave me a lot of advice, including to stop at an island called Jomfruland if I had the chance, and a coastal town called Kragerø. The weather was sunny and warm, and he helped me strap my bags on the bike.

"Are you sure you're going to be okay?" he asked me, slightly worried to see me leave on my own to the great unknown.

"Of course I will be okay! What can happen to me? This is Norway, right?" I answered, waving goodbye.

After three hours of cycling happily, the sky started becoming gray, and then completely dark. It started raining. "No worries," I thought, "It's just a little rain. It will go away soon."

Then it started hailing. And then pouring buckets of rain. It was cold. When I understood that this would last for more than five minutes, I stopped under a tree and looked for my waterproof pants and jacket. I had not organized my bicycle bags properly, so I could not find them. By the time I found them and put them on, the rain had stopped, and all my clothes were wet.

Following Roar's advice, I did not follow the highway – in Norway most highways have cycling paths next to them. I took the old road called Villaveien and then Fossingveien to Kragerø. I passed a small place called Helle and thought it aptly represented the beginning of my trip.

From there, I cycled very fast as I was about to miss the boat to Jomfruland, an island whose name means either "the country of the virgins" or "virgin land." Not sure.

The boat trip from Kragerø made me forget all my miseries. It was so picturesque, sliding between all these small islands, some with a little Norwegian flag somewhere on them. The sea was dark blue and mesmerizing.

I overheard a woman next to me speaking on the phone telling her friend, "We took the wrong boat. We are heading to Jomfruland, not Skåtøy. Do you think we can take a taxi-boat from there?" A taxi-boat... never heard of that before.

When we got to Jomfruland, I thought of going camping on the other side of the island, where there were rocks and beaches, but the camping lady said that was illegal.

"It's a nature reserve. The fine is very high for those who camp in it," she added.

I set up camp in the camping area. What is the point of traveling to a virgin island only to sleep so close to other tents that one can hear the neighbor snoring?" I wondered.

I explored the island by bicycle; it felt so light without all my luggage. As I was peacefully cycling, I passed by this huge cow enjoying the view. I almost jumped in surprise. This island should be called "The island of the cows," not "The island of the virgins," as there were far more cows than virgins.

I dreamed of owning one of the romantic houses with a view of the horizon, the sunset, and the sea. It just looked so perfect. But strangely enough they all seemed empty. Why weren't the owners here enjoying their summer holidays? Were they also in *Syden* like my Oslo colleagues?

The rocky beaches were also very nice: so open, and with unusual colors like green and blue. It got cold as soon as the sun came down, and the wind was merciless. As I got back to the camp I thought that, like in France, there would be a big fire and people would chat away the evening with jokes and songs. Nope, all were with their own friends and families, not talking to any strangers like me.

I went to bed early, after a warm shower. I had already paid for the right to set my tent on this camping ground, but I found out when reaching the shower spot that warm water also had to be paid for. In small coins. Collecting change to pay for the shower took longer than the five minutes of warm water that would wash away the day's sweat and rain from cycling from Porsgrunn.

*Note to self:* in Norway, paying for a camping site may or may not include access to warm water. So one has to pay for showers by the minute…

Screams can be heard from campers who have run out of hot water but are still with soap in their eyes.

And that is when you've managed to find enough change to pay for all the minutes of hot water you need. It turns out an island in the middle of nowhere with nobody looking friendly isn't the best place to get change.

The next day I woke up to the sound of tents being disassembled. As I peeked out of my tent everyone had finished putting their things away. What on earth is happening here? Why are they all leaving at the same time? I wondered.

When in Rome, do as the Romans do. If all the locals were leaving at the same time there must be a good reason, I thought. I decided to do the same. First I had to fight with my tent to get it back in the bag and get water for my trip. I went to fetch water, and when I got back a guy was looking at my tent.

"Can you fit in there? Never seen such a small tent in my life," he said, laughing and pointing his finger at my little one-person-tent, which was light enough to put on a bicycle.

"Yes, I happen to be very short. It has some advantages," I answered with a smile.

We all took the boat back to the mainland, after one night and zero social interaction with the local population, except for the one man who laughed at my tent. I ate a waffle on the boat to give me some energy for cycling as I was expecting a tough day.

I checked *yr.no* and understood why everybody wanted to leave Jomfruland: the forecast was heavy rain for the next six days. The sunny weather would come back the day I planned on stopping to cycle. *Så hyggelig!* I decided to stick to my plan and cycle west to my next stop: Risør. Whatever the weather.

In a normal country with normal predictable weather, knowing that 1) it was summer time, 2) it had been so warm and sunny in the Lofoten Islands, located north of the Arctic Circle, 3) as a general rule in the Northern Hemisphere, it is warmer the closer one gets to the Equator. Based on these elements, I predicted warm and sunny weather during my trip in the South of Norway.

Predictable weather is a concept Norwegians laugh at. It does not exist. Freyr does not give a damn about the rules that apply in the Northern Hemisphere about the south being warmer than the north. In Norway, as I was going to find out, a violent storm can hit the most southern tip of the country while the Cape North gets sun and heat.

Unlike my departure from Porsgrunn, this time around I was prepared for the bad weather, or what they call *uvær* in Norwegian, literally translated as "unweather," i.e. bad weather.

I had my rain gear on me from the moment I started cycling from Kragerø. The rain was violently hitting my face as I cycled up and down, making its way through the small openings of my gear. On top of that, the gear I bought was of bad quality. It was waterproof but not breathable.

After two hours, I was as wet inside as outside my clothes, as I was sweating like a pig in there. Plastic was my downfall. At least I did not have to listen to the cars on the highway, as I was still on the old road, this time called Riksvei.

I needed to eat but it was raining so much, and there were no restaurants or even a shelter in sight. I stopped and sought shelter under a tree. Its leaves were dripping on me as I ate a piece of *knekkebrød* and a banana.

Why did I come here? I should have listened to Pål and stayed in the north, I thought to myself. I checked the weather forecast on *yr.no* again and saw it was sunny in Tromsø. Of course it was.

I took the road again. At some point, I was so bitter about being so wet and feeling so uncomfortable that I started repeating the swear words learned in northern Norway: *helvete i satan* and *forbanna selskap,* or whatever Knut had taught me. It made me feel better somehow.

Suddenly, as if it fell from heaven, I saw a sign "to the left, boat to Risør." According to my GPS Risør was still many kilometers away by road, but this was certainly a shortcut by the sea.

I turned left and arrived at a small place where a boat could indeed fit. There was no schedule. Just a small house, so I rang the bell. Three times. Until someone came to the door.

"Hello, I am hoping to catch the boat, do you know what time it is coming in today?" I asked the old man at the door.

"It is Sunday today," said the middle-aged man, closing the door in my face before

No explanation, no goodbye, or anything regular people say when they talk to each other.

I rang the bell again. I was probably being rude, but at this point I really didn't care. I put on my brightest smile when he opened the door again, with drops of water dripping from my hair onto my face.

"I understand it is Sunday. But there is no schedule. Is there a boat coming today?"

"There is no boat on the regular schedule today. But you might be lucky, as there was a wedding and he might come in after all," said the man. Okay, this was better.

He could have offered me shelter under his carport, with the buckets falling on me and my bicycle. But he did not, he just closed his door very quickly after giving me this piece of information. I stayed in the rain, under a ten-centimeter "almost roof" which kind of protected me. So much for Christian hospitality.

The small boat came, full of people in very nice wedding clothes. When they all got off, I asked the driver with the sweetest voice I had in my register whether I could come back to Risør with him.

"Wait on the side. I will see what I can do," said the man.

He came out after a while.

"Come on, I will take you, but there is almost no shelter on the boat. You will have to choose between covering your bicycle or yourself," he added.

That was the least of my worries. I was closer to getting to a place where it was dry, namely any building in Risør. I decided to protect my only dry clothes from the rain; those that were in my bags.

When I opened them I felt that the man from the Oslo sports shop who had sold me these "waterproof cycle bags" deserved to be hanged. I was so angry. My clothes were too waterproof, and my bags weren't at all. And all my supposedly dry clothes were soaking wet in my bicycle bags. How would I sleep in dry clothes tonight if everything in my bags was also wet?

Risør was described in my tourist guide as: "Snaking around the base of cliffs and hills overlooking a moody ocean, the ice-cream-white town of Risør is one of southern Norway's prettiest."

I looked closer as I entered the harbor with the boat. Moody ocean, I could understand. Southern Norway's prettiest, I didn't think so. Then again, the fog was hiding the whiteness of the town. I had seen much prettier places in the north in any case. Maybe I didn't have my glasses on? Maybe it was pretty only when the sun was shining?

I found the strength to ride my bicycle up a long road that would take me to Moen Camping site where I had booked a small cabin. It cost way more than my budget, but I could not handle sleeping in my tiny tent in wet clothes during the storm *yr.no* had predicted for tonight.

"The weather is usually very nice here. People swim there," said the lady at the reception of the camping site, showing me the waterfront.

From where I stood, I could see the storm coming, with violent winds lifting all that had been left outside.

"Right. Do you have a small heater for me to dry my clothes?" I asked.

She did not, neither did any of the people I met. When I asked them for a dryer it seemed like I was asking them to sell their soul. Had they never helped a stranger in distress? The only ones who helped me were Swiss tourists. We chatted and laughed at my wet clothes, which were taking a long time to dry.

I slept like a baby that night and hopped on my bike the next day. For another day of rain. This time I had all my newly dried clothes in plastic bags. I headed off to Arendal.

After around 30 kilometers I entered another coastal town called Tvedestrand. A ray of light illuminated the beauty of this small place and I was hopeful for good cycling weather again. I stopped and ate a pizza by the harbor, gazing at the swans and the white houses.

The town was filled with Oslo people wearing blue and white striped shirts, and leather "boat" shoes. They ate ice cream and spoke the way my neighbors in Holmenkollen spoke. It was probably the same people who used water scooters and made the crazy noise in the harbor. This was apparently where the richest people of Oslo took their summer holidays.

I still had some kilometers to reach Arendal so I left after my well-deserved pizza. A friend of a friend lived in Tromøya, an island in front of Arendal, and I had to get there somehow.

I was still taking the small roads, number 411 and 410, and most of the landscape was flat. I arrived at Arendal, only to realize I did not have the exact address of Kristina, who was hosting me. As I thought of finding her address online, the battery on my phone died. I had been checking the weather forecast on *yr.no* too much, as well as my GPS to find the fastest route to my destinations. Never really understood why the weather forecast site is called "yr.no" (fine annoying rain) rather than "solaskinner.no" (the sun shines). In any case, I needed to call and let her know I was close, and find the way to her place on the map.

This turned out to be mission impossible, as every time I walked towards people in the street to ask for their help they walked away from me. Not by coincidence. They saw me and actually walked backwards. One saw me walk towards him with a map and my phone and hurried into his car. I looked at myself. I wore a bicycle helmet and had big bags on my bike. I was wet and hungry.

In their eyes, I could see the way they looked at me. As if I were begging in the streets, dirty and alone. As if I had the plague or something. I had never felt more unwelcome in my life than in the parking lot of that local supermarket close to the bridge between Tromøya and Arendal.

Eventually, a tall man with another blue and white striped T-shirt took pity on me and let me borrow his phone. Kristina gave me her address and I gave back the phone to its owner. He looked it up for me on Google Maps.

"This is very close to where we are going. Let me give you a ride!" he said.

I could not thank him enough. He put my bike on the back of his car and drove me to Kristina's place. We chatted in the car, the man was from Ålesund. No kidding! I was pretty sure nobody from Arendal would have lent their phone to a stranger, let alone driven them somewhere. Think of all the things that could happen. They might have to talk to me; they might even have to trust me.

I learned that day that Arendal was the first city in Norway to make begging illegal. Somehow that did not surprise me. Was asking for help also considered begging in this area?

I got to Kristina's place and was so grateful for her hospitality.

"Thank you so much! I am so glad to finally meet someone from southern Norway who is kind and welcoming. I was starting to think people here are really not that nice," I told her.

She laughed.

"Well, I know my name sounds Norwegian, and I am blond, but I am not from here. I am from Belgium, the Flemish part," she answered.

Her and her Catalan husband spent that evening telling me how rough it was to live in Arendal.

"It is so difficult to make friends, even after the 10 years we've been here. And sexual and maternal healthcare is very weak here. It is the weight of the religion. Some of my friends have had trouble getting an abortion in southern Norway despite it being legal up to a certain number of weeks nation-wide. It is still taboo here." said Kristina.

"Jeez. But you have friends after all these years, right?" I asked them.

"We do, in a way. But it is a hard shell to crack. Even with the kids, you would think it would be easier to be invited into peoples' homes and accepted, but it's not," said her husband.

"And I was complaining about Oslo people being cold!" I said. They all laughed.

"If you think they are cold, never come to Sørlandet," said Kristina.

No problem, I had no plans on moving here. The signs on the road, which read "Welcome to the Bible Belt," with a picture of a white man and his son, were not screaming "Welcome!" to me. Neither were the studies saying that Sørlandet (reaching out to parts around Stavanger) had the lowest gender equality in the country. And the highest rate of vote for the far-right party who is not so immigrant-friendly. What's the point of moving from France to a place which is more conservative than my own society? No thanks.

I stayed for two days, exploring Tromøya and its beautiful coast, despite the rain and the gray sky. Kristina said to me "There are only three reasons to come to Sørlandet: June, July, and August." She forgot to add "on good years."

I looked at the weather forecast again for the coming days: more and more rain. I couldn't take it anymore. Especially not if the people were going to be so unwelcoming. I could handle bad weather in Tromsø, as it was easier to talk to people. But with this mistrust I felt here from locals it was no fun continuing my trip to Kristiansand. Pål was right after all. I could not wait to go back north after this disastrous southern Norwegian adventure.

*Note to self:* there are around 2000 kilometers between the north and the south of Norway, and that is about the distance separating the cultures of northern and southern Norwegians. If cultural, religious and social differences were so strong already in the only two places I visited in Norway, what other surprises were awaiting in the new towns and fjords I would visit? I could not wait to find out.

# THE SAMI FESTIVAL

I went to the Riddu Riđđu festival at a perfect time. It was the middle of my holidays. I was so glad to fly back to Tromsø in summertime. The organizers of the festival picked me up directly at the airport. I sent a message to Nina, hoping I could visit her in Tromsø on my way back from the festival.

I would help organize a conference on land grabbing and deforestation and how it affects indigenous peoples in Indonesia. I negotiated with my employer that after my job was done I could enjoy the festival as a regular guest.

The festival took place every July in Manndalen in Troms. It was primarily a music festival, with indigenous musicians from all over the world invited to perform on stage. It also included conferences and talks on political, linguistic, and other issues. After working on indigenous rights for many years, it seemed indeed almost impossible to talk about indigenous issues without talking about politics.

The struggle of indigenous peoples all over the world is sadly similar, fighting for their right to keep their cultures, languages and right to their ancestral lands after centuries of oppression. Despite living in one of the world's richest countries, Samis are no exception.

A few interesting people were gathered in the car taking us to Manndalen. One was from Majavatn and herded reindeer, another one was a singer who was Norwegian but lived in Sweden, and the third one, the driver, was working in measuring seismic activity for a company digging tunnels. Or something like that.

All spoke Norwegian, and I could tell I was a bit of an outsider when they started asking each other who they knew from which village and do you know Ola Andreasson? He is my aunt's cousin. And do you know Sigrunn? She was my father's neighbor from when he lived in Alta.

This went on for a long while, and as they were trying to figure out how they were all related. I had all the time in the world to look out the window. No matter how much small talk I was able to make, I could hardly be part of this conversation. Nobody cared where my grandmother was raised and whose cousin she was because there was no chance any of them were related to the passengers of this car.

This all seemed very different from the last time I was in Tromsø in the winter. The rivers were so rich with water that there were waterfalls coming from every mountain around. The snow melted down these mountains, even in July. Was this why the air was so cold? I looked at the temperature by peeking over the driver's shoulder and realized that he had put the air conditioning on: it was 17 °C inside the car and 20 °C outside. But...why?

After a while they switched the topic to reindeer. I sensed

that the two who weren't from Majavatn had questions I would have never thought of asking.

"Did your reindeer go north alright?" asked the lady who lived in Sweden.

The other one answered something I didn't quite understand. To be polite and be part of this conversation I asked the Norwegian lady living in Sweden:

"What about your reindeer, did they go north alright?" but she just laughed.

"I am not a reindeer herder, my family has never done that as long as I can remember at least," she answered.

"There are actually fewer reindeer herders among Samis than people imagine," she added.

I took that opportunity to ask about reindeer herding. Let me tell you, this did not not look easy. They told me there are eight seasons and many threats for reindeer such as roads and hydroelectric dams and even cabins. I could have never imagined cabins could be a problem for anyone or anything.

"But there is an office we report to, it's called Reindeer Management Office," she added.

Of course, I thought. Like everything else in Norway, even reindeer drifting is regulated by the state.

By the time we arrived it was 10:30pm, and still broad daylight. The view from the road on the Lyngen Alps was so beautiful I asked the driver to stop so that I could take a picture.

"What is there to take a picture of? There is nothing special here," he said.

I looked again. There was a fjord with a man fishing with his son from a small wooden boat. In the background one could see almost the whole chain of mountains, with a blue sky and the rays of the sun peeking from behind the mountains, giving an orange shimmer to everything. Some snow on the mountain tops, and the incredible proportion of the man and his boy against the immensity of nature around them.

The water was bluish, reflecting the image of the mountains. It was just breathtaking. It looked like one of those photoshopped postcards of Norway that we see in tourism magazines.

"For you maybe. How many times have you driven on this road?" I asked.

"All my life," he answered.

"For me this is very exotic and beautiful," I answered, and took as many pictures as I could.

"Yeah, I can understand why," he said, looking at the scene almost with new eyes.

"But then again, I have been driving guests back and forth from the airport all day. I think I am tired," he added.

We got to the festival area, located next to a river, and I was taken to the *lavvu* (the Sami tent) that I would be sleeping in with my two colleagues. There were several reindeer furs on the floor over some branches, and a fire was burning in the middle. The hole at the top of the *lavvu* made it possible for us to be warm without suffocating from the smoke. How will I get any sleep with so much light outside all the time? I thought.

After two nights, this *lavvu* was just like home. I woke up and looked at the sky through that hole for long minutes, smelling the birch branches and the fire. I wondered how it felt for generations of children waking up in such a *lavvu* in the middle of the winter. This warm place from which one could see the snow falling. It was always warm and comfortable, while there could be meters of snow outside, or even a snowstorm.

Riddu Riđđu, which means "small storm on the coast," was the name of this festival where people come for the music but also for art exhibitions, film screenings, courses in handcrafting and indigenous languages, and, of course, partying.

The director of the festival, a Sami woman who was raised

in Manndalen, told me that the most important in this festival was for different indigenous communities from around the world: Greenland, Russia, Democratic Republic of Congo, New Zealand, Taïwan, China, Honduras, and more, to share experiences, seeing where others live and understand what they all have in common.

I used this opportunity to join one of the Sami language classes, which was in a very peculiar hut dug in the ground on the side of a hill. It made it into an almost invisible house with walls made of soil. And from the outside, it looked just like a bump in the Earth, with grass all over it. The only thing that showed there was human activity in it was some smoke coming out of its top.

In this little hut, I learned Sami. Well, as much as one and half hours of learning can teach you, so not much, but I learned the essentials for these few days in the festival: ordering drinks and flirting in Sami.

"*Oaččun go vuola?*" which means "Can I have a beer?"

"*Boađat go mielde ruoktot?*" which means "Do you want to go home with me tonight?"

"*Manna eret*" which means "Go away."

"Samis can be very direct in love and seduction matters," said our teacher.

"What do you mean?" I asked.

"Men can be quite frank about what they want, and women are equally clear if they are not interested," she answered.

We asked a little about the language, and to my greatest surprise the person sitting there who asked the most questions was not the Taiwanese man, or the Russian tourist. It was a woman from Bærum, a municipality next to Oslo. She seemed to know as little about Sami history and people as the rest of us.

"We don't learn anything about Samis at school in Oslo,"

she said. "The only image we have of Samis in our books is a Sami man in traditional clothes next to a reindeer," she added.

"Since the Norwegianization policy after World War II, it has been hard to identify publicly as a Sami. Many are still ashamed. Many never learned their parents' language because Norwegian state policies forbid us to speak Sami formally between 1850 and the 1950s. And now there is an exoticization of Samis and their culture," said the teacher, a tall 27-year-old woman with dark hair and trendy outdoor pants. Yes, there was such a thing as outdoorsy fashion in Norway.

"How is it to be Sami in Norway today?" I asked her.

"It is both easy and complicated. I feel both Sami and Norwegian and it is simple for me to live with a dual cultural identity. But many Norwegians seem to have problems with it and always seem to be assessing how Sami we really are. So we get questions like, 'What percent Sami are you?' as if I have to justify my right to claim that I am Sami," she answered.

"I usually stay quiet, but I want to ask them 'How Norwegian are *you*, really? If your mother is Swedish and your grandfather was German? Do you have the right to wear a *bunad* more than I have the right to claim that I am Sami?' And of course, there are all the stereotypes we have to fight against every day," she added.

"Like what, for example?" I asked.

"Samis get discriminated against four times more than other Norwegians. We have to endure hate speech and discrimination in our daily lives. There is also prejudice about us, for example that all Samis herd reindeer, when actually a very small percentage of us do. That all of us speak Sami language. Which we don't, thanks to Norwegianization policies.

It does not help that kids in Norwegian schools do not learn about the history of Samis in Norway. Which leads to a reproduction of stereotypes based on ignorance," she answered.

"Which Norwegian political party is pro-Sami?" I asked.

"None of them are pro-Sami, but FrP is definitely anti-Sami," she answered.

Also known as the Progress Party, FrP was considered the most right-wing Norwegian party that was sitting in the parliament.

"They want to take down the Sami parliament, and some Samis are on their side. It's very sad. We have reached one of the highest levels of political recognition in the world and it is still under threat" she added.

The conference I helped organize took place that day. I carried stuff around, answered questions and translated what some of the speakers were saying in French and Indonesian.

That night, my colleagues and I stayed outside to enjoy the many concerts. When I say night, I must say the most disturbing fact about this festival was the non-stop sunlight and blue sky, 24 hours a day.

Where else than at the Riddu Riđđu festival can one listen to reggae music performed by a band from New Zealand, with hundreds of people of all ages dancing to the Maori swag, under the midnight sun and looking at the beautiful Lyngen Alps? It was surreal.

Yann Tiersen, a famous French musician who composed, among other things, the soundtrack for the film *Amélie from Montmartre*, performed that night. He was cycling around Northern Norway with his crew and asked to stop by to perform at the festival. I even got to talk to him and was starstruck.

The next day, the Indonesian team was taken back to the airport. They had a plane to catch to continue their tour in Sweden at one of our sister organizations working on environment and human rights, Naturskyddsföreningen or the Swedish Society for Nature Conservation.

After four days of festival, I lost track of time. I did not know whether it was night or day. I slept in our *lavvu* whenever I needed a little nap. I bought a *lukka* (a poncho made of felted wool or *wadmal/vadmål*) and was therefore able to be outside in the cold and wind, day and night. Yes, it got cold. What did you expect, it's Northern Norway and there was snow on the mountaintops! I spent the last night partying in a big *lavvu*.

We drank lots of Mack *øl* (beer from Northern Norway) and ate reindeer sausages. There was whale stew from the festival's restaurant which was worth a try. What I would remember most were the children, running all over the place, and the feeling of freedom and pride one could sense from the crowd.

On my last day, while waiting in line for food, I felt a tap on my shoulder "Hey Loreloloolo," said a familiar voice. Ante was standing in front of me, in traditional Sami dress and red hat with four spikes. It crossed my mind that I might meet him here, but did not know whether I wanted to see him again.

"Wow, you look fresh," I said with a smile.

We sat and ate together on a bench outside. I was not too resentful about how things never really ended with him. Though I could feel a little pinch in my heart when I thought about it.

We talked about the different bands, the atmosphere and our holidays. He laughed at my stories of travels throughout Norway.

"You've seen more of this country than most Norwegians," he told me. People would come up to him regularly to say hi in Sami.

"So, how are we going to spend this last day of the festival?" asked Ante with a smile.

"I don't know, you tell me. This is your hood," I answered lightly.

That last evening was beyond expectation. Ante came here since he was a child and he knew every corner of the festival ground.

We first attended a concert of Mongolian throat singers. I closed my eyes to hear the different voices coming out of their throats. I wanted to soak in every minute of this last evening under the midnight sun at Riddu Riđđu. When I opened my eyes again Ante was looking at me, smiling.

We had a beer at the bar area of the festival, and a few friends of his joined us. Another concert was on, a singer I loved called Ella Marie Hætta Isaksen, a young Sami woman who had won the Norwegian Idol song contest. She led a band called Isák and mixed traditional *joik* (Sami singing technique) with pop music.

We were lucky enough to see Mari Boine on stage, the most internationally famous Sami Norwegian singer. The quality of the music that evening was better than the other nights. As Mari Boine's electrifying voice resonated in the whole valley, Ante took me in his arms. I pushed him back.

"Are you kidding me?" I asked him.

"What do you mean?" he looked at me, not understanding where that came from.

"You left me! You have a girlfriend. I saw you two in the concert," I said.

"What? She was not my girlfriend, and neither were you. We were not in a relationship. I could do whatever I wanted, I never gave you any expectations of exclusivity," he added. "And we never had the talk," he said.

"Which talk?" I asked.

"The one where we decide whether we are girlfriend and boyfriend."

I was not aware there was a specific talk. It just felt to me like we were together. In France meeting so many times and sleeping together did mean something in terms of relationship.

Apparently, things were different in Norway. Here you have a specific talk, when sober, about the status of the relationship. Why was it all so formal?

"Stop taking everything so seriously. We are at the world's best festival. We are single and the night will not come tonight. You need to relax," he added with a smile, brushing my cheek with his hand.

Maybe he was right? I had to relax. Take things casually like Kaia said, instead of always imagining relationships. Maybe enjoying this moment right there and then with him was enough, and having no expectations was fine too?

I went to buy a beer and when I came back, I kissed him on the cheek.

"Okay then," I said.

I was in Ante's arms, humming and dancing slowly to the music. As Mari Boine sang her last song, Ante leaned over and kissed me.

"I like you a lot," he said. "We just need to take it slow and figure out where this takes us, okay?" he added.

When the concerts were over, he took me to a party *lavvu*. We laughed and drank all night with his friends. It was the most magical night since I had moved to Norway.

The festival camp was in an otherworldly setting, and even a pee break outside the *lavvu* that night allowed me to admire the mountains and the river with the colors of the Northern Norwegian sky. A dimmed sun, some pink lights and the promise that the night would never come.

Around 7am, or was it 9am, I fell asleep behind Ante, on a woolen blanket covering the birch branches of the *lavvu*. I am not sure how long I slept but awoke to the smell of coffee cooking in the middle of the *lavvu*, hanging over the fire. Ante's hat was next to me, but I was alone in the *lavvu*. He appeared again with his amazing smile, "Ready for breakfast?"

I had planned to take the bus to Tromsø that day, as it was the end of the festival. Ante was staying to help dismantle the tents and the scene.

"Stay with me. I borrowed a car, I can drive you back to Tromsø tomorrow, or the next day," he said.

I stayed hidden in the *lavvu* most of the morning, sleeping and daydreaming in the warmth of the tent. I left my cocoon to find some food. Ante was running around lifting stuff, and I felt bad for being so lazy so I offered to help. We ate together with the other volunteers and continued working until late. The festival camp was emptying itself and soon there was almost nobody left but us.

That night, when we went back to Ante's *lavvu*, it felt like it was the last one standing. As if we had been camping alone for days or weeks, there was almost no sign left from the festival, the music, the 3000 people. That night we made love in the *lavvu* and, for once, I did not overthink it.

The next day I took a walk alone in the area. I left the festival feeling whole. The soul of this place was something I had never felt before in my life.

Ante drove me to Tromsø and wanted me to stay with him at his cousin's place, but I had a good friend waiting for me. I did not want to miss out on spending time with her. He dropped me off by the Arctic Cathedral.

Nina opened the door to her house. I was so happy to see her again.

"*Takk for sist!*" I said, hugging her.

*Takk for sist*, that funny expression Norwegians use to greet a person. "Thanks for the last time" and not "Takk fascist" as Ramu believed it meant for a while. To be honest, it did sound like the latter.

"*Takk for sist*, Lorelou! What would you like to do this time in Tromsø? There is so much light now, and you are lucky it's such nice weather," she said.

"All I want to do is sleep," I answered.

And so I did, for many hours, catching up on the sleepless nights I spent meeting people and listening to music, running in the fields and bathing in the freezing river.

When I woke up, I opened my backpack and realized every single piece of clothing I had smelt like reindeer and campfire. The smell of Riddu Riđđu.

# TAKE ME TO YOUR *HYTTE*

My first Norwegian summer holiday was coming to an end. I had one last stop: Trøndelag. I would go on my first ever cabin trip, or *hyttetur*, with a Norwegian family. More importantly, I would reunite with my dear friend Kaia.

There is one thing that foreigners must experience to have a feel of the Norwegian culture, that is to live in a *hytte*, or Norwegian cabin, for a few days (or as long as one can survive without a shower, electricity, or mobile coverage).

Despite their very high level of income and their super modern society, Norwegians appreciate going back to simpler things and cutting themselves off from "the modern world" for a return to nature…

Note that if you are willing to live the true cabin or *hytte* experience, the one your Norwegian peers and colleagues will acknowledge as such, you better do it the rough way. Not in those cabins from the rich guys from Stavanger that have a washing machine and floor heating (Haha, floor heating! And they call it a *hytte*!). A "real" *hytte* should be made of wood, with a cold lake for a shower spot and a hole outside as a toilet (it does have a small roof and walls, to protect from snow in the winter).

When my friend invited me to her family *hytte* close to her hometown, I was thrilled. I would know at last what hid behind this look Norwegians got on their faces when they talked about their holidays in a *hytte*. I could see their eyes getting moist as their thoughts wandered between emotionally charged memories and amazing adventures.

Kaia's hometown was called Haltdalen. One supermarket, a church, and a psychiatric hospital. The term "town" might be an overstatement. It may qualify as a village although Norwegian countryside is not that structured on the village model.

Even when living in the middle of nowhere, Norwegians wanted to be far from their closest neighbor. In the case of Kaia's family, as they did not feel alone enough where they lived, in the 1940s her grandfather left his village and walked for some kilometers in the wild to find a beautiful spot with a view on the lakes. He built a hut there with a friend. Since then, her family had been coming there as often as possible. This was the real thing, right?

I was so excited about this trip that I packed adequately for it before leaving Oslo: everything from a bikini to *ullundertøy* (the must-have woolen underwear one wears as a first layer under one's clothes). Or that's what I thought.

When my friend said "prepare for any weather" what I imagined was nothing like the broad range of what could fall on you up there. No panic, Kaia's mum, Carina, took me to their basement and I discovered the illustration of the saying "There is no bad weather, just bad clothing."

Having good clothing apparently required a 60-square

meter basement full of all the clothes and shoes one can imagine, and everything available in several sizes.

I went on a "shopping" spree, helped by Carina who hand-picked everything I needed for the trip. A woolen hat, really? Two raincoats? Hiking shoes AND rubber boots? Waterproof pants for warm AND cold weather? I didn't even know these things existed and felt like she was exaggerating a bit. In July in Trøndelag you might actually need woolen underwear, fleece and a woolen hat. *Slik er norsksommer.* Such is a Norwegian summer.

As we got in the car, I thought we were driving to the *hytte.* We made a last stop at the local Coop store to buy what seemed like enough food for a decade. Kaia's mum was very kind and made a real effort to speak to me slowly to ask me whether there was something I wanted to buy. What did I eat for breakfast? Did I prefer raspberry or strawberry jam?

People around were looking at us in a strange way. Maybe they've never seen a foreigner, I thought. I learned later that for me to understand her she changed her Trøndesk dialect to an Oslo dialect. Her friends and neighbors were wondering whether she had become a snob or gone crazy. Dear neighbors of Kaia's mum, she was neither of those: she was just trying to help a lost foreigner who was still learning Norwegian.

We drove to the furthest place possible and started walking the few kilometers that lead us to the *hytte.* We got there after a few stops because the bags were so heavy with all the food. When we finally arrived, the place was stunning. The small hut, the lakes, the snowy mountains and our neighbors: the sheep and reindeer.

As soon as we arrived, everyone seemed to know what they needed to do. Except for me, the useless person hang-ing around. They didn't ask me to light the fire... for a reason. Where I come from, the only fires we make are on beaches to sit around and play guitar. Plus, Norwegians seem to have a huge fear of fires and they prefer to do it themselves.

I walked around, looking at the wooden construction, and finally someone gave me a non-dangerous thing to do: fetch some water. No way could I set the house on fire with that. Kaia's dad, Egil, asked me three times in his Trøndesk dialect before I understood what he wanted from me (*vatten* = *vann* = water).

I knew complicated words such as nature resource management (*naturressursforvaltning*) from work but I had never heard simple words such as pan, bucket, and shovel. I was in an everyday situation with a family and I was unable to communicate. I have to admit the dialect didn't help.

Off I went to the lake, trying to find the place where to fetch the water for us to drink and clean the dishes. I found a small pipe coming out of a side of the river, it should be there. I filled in all the buckets and dared to ask, "Can we drink this?"

The look on Egil's face seemed to say, "Shut up you city girl, this water is cleaner than any water you've ever drank."

Okay, mountain man, I will try to keep quiet unless there is an emergency, like an attack by a herd of reindeer.

I put my sleeping bag on the bunk beds I would share with Kaia. Her mum came to put real fur under my mattress.

"Is it going to be that cold? We have a fireplace, right?" I asked.

"Oh yes, she said, but Kaia is used to sleeping with the windows wide open since she was a child. She cannot sleep without fresh air on her face, so better you have this to keep warm," answered Carina.

What was it with Norwegians and cold bedrooms, I wondered? And what if it got really cold, below 0 °C (32 °F), I thought, should the window still be open? It's July, it cannot possibly happen, I reassured myself.

I was wrong, as we were close to 0 °C during the few days I stayed there. The bedroom window stayed wide open the whole time. Meanwhile, I dreamed that reindeer managed to put their heads through the open window and came to nibble on my feet.

When I woke up to Kaia's father's snores, I looked out the window. Luckily there was no reindeer there. I discreetly tried to close the window a little bit without anyone noticing.

The first evening in the *hytte* was wonderful: the sky was clear, and we stayed outside for a while, drinking wine and chatting. The next morning, I looked outside and the sky decided to fall on us. Rainy and gray. It didn't matter, nothing could kill my enthusiasm. I promised to enjoy every part of this experience by taking part in absolutely everything my host family did, whatever the weather was.

Despite the rain, I saw Kaia leaving the *hytte* with a towel. Was she going to take... a shower? I followed her and saw her taking all her clothes off and throwing herself in the lake. Brrrr!

It was not that cold outside but still, around 12 °C (around 53 °F). Why would anyone willingly swim naked in a dark lake that probably has little crabs in it that will try to eat your toes? I tried to imagine what the Mediterranean Sea would feel like right now. Different I guess, at least 15 °C warmer than here.

"Do you want to join me?" she asked. "The water is refreshing."

"Really?" I answered. Who are we kidding here? I heard you scream when you got in because of the cold, I thought to myself. But I answered, "Tomorrow maybe," instead, knowing I would never bathe in that lake in such cold temperatures.

Kaia's dad asked us to go help him set some fishing nets in the lakes. That took forever because we needed to row on the lake to get to the strategic points to hang the nets, then carry the boat on to land to reach the next lake. We set six nets over three lakes. It took a lot of time, but then again what else was there to do?

The next day it kept raining, and the temperature dropped to 4 °C (39 °F). Winds were also really strong. 4 °C in the beginning of July! I suddenly understood why Norwegians went to *Syden* for some sun during Norwegian summer.

I wanted to spend the day reading my book close to the fire. My plan was to leave the house only to run to the little toilet-hut which did not have water either (it is called *utedass*, apparently). My plan failed, as Egil left the house in a hurry, yelling that we had no time to eat breakfast because he was afraid the fishing nets would be blown loose by the wind.

"Come NOW!" he yelled while running off in his rain suit.

Kaia and I wrapped ourselves in waterproof clothes plus wool, and two pairs of socks, and a hat to join him.

The first nets were easy to untie. My mission was to kill the fish that were not dead yet. No blood please, so I crashed their heads between two rocks. That might seem a little violent, but they needed to die quickly. They were so slippery I was afraid they would jump out of my hands and into the water again.

We moved on as the wind got stronger and the rain started to fall on us by buckets. There were many fish and we needed to get every single one untangled from the net without damaging the fish or the net. It was not that easy.

Three hours, 35 trout, and one lost net later, we were really wet and cold. I could not feel my fingers and I had fish blood all over my clothes, but I felt good (and tired). We ran happily to the *hytte* to find a glorious meal prepared by Carina. The fire made the *hytte* very warm and we had dry and (almost) clean clothes waiting for us. This felt like heaven. Kaia and I decided to go swimming in the lake. Yes, it was colder than the day before when I refused to join her, but this day of fish-killing changed my mind. A swim in clean, fresh water while rain was falling on my nose sounded very nice and indeed it was.

That night other members of the family arrived. I did wonder how all of us would sleep in this small space, but it worked out. We stayed in, played cards, and drank what I thought was the German Jägermeister because of the bottle, although the alcohol was very sweet and did not have the taste of the Jägermeister.

It turned out to be moonshine. I did dare to ask (again) whether it was safe to drink because I had heard one could get blind from drinking homemade alcohol. These annoying French girls ask way too many questions... but Kaia's father did answer and said that only alcohol made by idiots who can't do it right makes you blind. I was expecting more of a scientific answer... but fair enough.

This evening was very pleasant, although I didn't understand everything that was happening. We were a bit tipsy, and they dropped the dialect I understood. It was taking much longer for me to understand jokes and more importantly the rules of the card games we played.

Egil told this impossible story about a family of bears that broke into a *hytte* and ate all the food including dehydrated bags of soup and cans of beer. I imagined myself in front of a bear. Or even worse, a drunk bear. Carina saw my worried eyes and said that there was no way a bear could come inside this *hytte* because it was built by her father (and I have five Vikings to protect me here, I thought to myself, and that should be enough). "*Sånn er hyttelivet*" said Egil. Which can be translated to "This is how cabin life is."

I understood what this whole *hytte* thing is about. It's about being tired not because you sat in front of a computer all day, but from fishing and cooking and fetching water and running in the forest to see reindeer all day.

It was also about eating a homemade jam of *multer* (cloudberries), defined by Egil as "Orange berries that Oslo people are stupid enough to buy at a high price while we just pick them outside our house,". It's about grilling fish fresh out of the nearby lake.

Most important, it's about being together around a fire, sweating for days and days in our woolen underwear, not caring about how we look or how we smell.

To make things worse, some Norwegians wear something they call *grilldress. Grilldress* are clothes that are from the 1980s or 90s with many colors like orange, purple, and green. It suits men who have long hair on the back and short on the sides.

When it was time for us to leave, we walked across the forest and back to the car with much lighter bags (full of garbage and empty bottles). Returning to modern life made me realize what great inventions electricity and hot water are. This was fantastic, but more tiring than expected. I could not thank my new friends enough for taking me into their home and teaching me all these things. I now have a better understanding of *hytte* life!

When I got back from the land-with-no-coverage, I had many messages, including some from Ante.

Only one corner of the cabin had cell phone coverage. It was two meters above ground level, just below the roof, which meant we took turns holding our cellphones in the air to get one little bar of signal on our phones. I did not have that many friends in Norway who would message me, so I decided to just turn it off the whole time.

Ante wondered whether I survived my first *hyttetur* and wanted to know when I was in Oslo to meet him. I told him we could meet soon. I wanted to stay longer with Kaia to visit

Røros and I would take the train from there in two days.

*Note to self:* Spending a summer discovering Norway is a great idea, if one has a very broad understanding of the word "summer". Unlike in Marseille, the word "summer" in Norway only gives the hope of warmth and sun, not necessarily the reality of it.

Growing up by the Mediterranean Sea gave me this crazy idea that once spring starts in March, the heat and the sun remain until the fall, which starts around October or November.

So the key words to a Norwegian summer are preparation and "enjoy now". One needs a very wide range of clothing such as woolen underwear, waterproof clothes, sandals, hiking shoes, a bikini, a sleep mask to be able to sleep at night, and everything one needs to survive when one is alone in the woods for more than two days.

Why is it worth it to spend one's summers in Norway despite the unstable weather and strong headwind? Well, the Norwegian people are as diverse as their landscapes and their dialects. This country is among the most beautiful I have seen in my life, despite gray skies and pounding hail. Those few minutes or hours or days of sun, when the different colors of the fjords unravel and the mountains free themselves from the fog, are worth all the rain in the world.

Nothing compares to summer in Norway.

IV

# FALL AND
# WINTER AGAIN

# FALL AND *FÅRIKÅL*

Summer holidays and my discovery of Norwegian territory were sadly over. I had to return to work. Surprisingly, my office wanted us to be back from our summer holidays early August because that was the end of what they called *fellesferie* or the "common holidays", when the whole country was away at the same time.

Even more disturbing, Norwegians were already calling the month of August fall. How long did a Norwegian summer actually last? If it could snow on the 17th of May, and August was already fall, summer lasted four to six weeks.

I knew first-hand that a Norwegian summer did not even guarantee sun and heat. As I experienced in Trøndelag during my cabin trip, it could be rainy and down to 4 °C (39 °F) in the summer in Norway. It snowed in Finnmark in July.

I knew the fall was coming just by observing the changes around me. Not only the weather but the people and the shops.

Suddenly the colors in the stores were "warm" colors, and Norwegians seemed to be buying enough candles to heat the Royal Palace for winter.

By the end of August, I felt the Earth getting colder and the leaves on the trees becoming more red, orange, and yellow.

Conversations about where we went over the summer shifted to conversations about where to pick berries and chanterelles and where to buy the best rubber boots.

Norwegians were trying to keep their summer tan alive and booking Christmas holidays. I could not believe summer was over, and that some people were already talking about Christmas.

Meanwhile in the South of France, it was 30 °C (86 °F), August being the warmest month. My family would bathe in the sea at least until October. Oh well. I would have to figure out what to do here during this transition period between a short summer and a very long winter.

Fall became my favorite season, with its blue sky, crisp air, and red leaves. In Norway, fall is the season for finding *kantarell* (chanterelle mushrooms) in the forest and making things *koselig* so that you feel warm inside and combat the cold outside. There were many things to do, and so much good local food to eat. It was crab season, as well as lamb season, which meant enjoying wonderful meals such as *fårikål*, where one cooks lamb, cabbage and black pepper in a big pot for hours. This time of the year, pumpkins were in season and high-quality pumpkins could be bought at a low price.

I decided that this time around I would do everything in my power to avoid the winter depression trap. As Ane had advised, I started taking one spoon of cod liver oil every morning from the first of September. I started running in the woods. I was using woolen underwear like Kaia had taught me and kept my head warm. I bought spikes to put under my shoes to continue running in the nearby forest, Nordmarka, when the Earth got icy. They are locally called *brodder*. I was trying to be sharp at work, despite the wintertime which made workdays longer than in the summer – yes, Norwegians don't work the same number of hours in every season.

My Norwegian was progressing fast. I stopped going to the Norwegian classes as I leveled up. One day, Bjørn entered a meeting a few minutes before it started and said,

*"I dag skal Lorelou ta referat. På norsk."*

I got most of it: today I had to write down the meeting minutes in Norwegian. Oh no! Management decided that nothing would be in English anymore to accommodate me and my language-learning process. Now it was game on.

That day, I tried to get everything everyone was saying in their different dialects. Western Norway, Northern Norway, and Oslo. By the end of the meeting, I was exhausted. I still had to get my notes checked to avoid sending everyone a copy with all my mistakes and misunderstandings. Torbjørn had the honor of checking the document. He laughed several times and corrected everything.

"It's okay. This is how you learn. Listen, I see your integration in the Norwegian society is going well, as you're a fast and motivated learner. But there is one experience I bet you have never had," he said, mysteriously.

"Like what?" I asked, expecting to be taken to another cabin where I would have to gut live fish if I wanted dinner that night.

*"Harrytur!"* he said with joy. "We are going with my partner this weekend. We're going every weekend until our wedding in June. It gets boring for us, but with you there, I am sure we'll be entertained," he said.

I called Ante to see whether he was interested in coming.

"A *harrytur*? Why on Earth would I want to get on that ride?" he laughed. So unadventurous of him!

# SHOPPING IN SWEDEN

"If a *hyttetur* is a trip to a cabin, a *harrytur* is a trip to a place called Harry, which I presume is in Sweden?" I asked him.

"No. Not at all. Harry is a person, not a place. Just join us this weekend, it will be fun," he answered. That is how I went on my first *harrytur*.

Our trip started at 8:30am on a Saturday. My first question was: why do we need to leave so early? It was Saturday for heaven's sake – why can't we sleep in?

"No, no, we need to get there as early as possible to avoid queues," says Torbjørn.

His girlfriend Urine was joining us. Jorunn is how it was spelt, I learned, but it did really sound like Urine.

"Queues? We are going to the Swedish border, where will there be queues on a Saturday at 8.30 am?"

The answer was: at the entrance of the Swedish liquor store.

While we were on the road, I asked all sorts of questions:

who was this Harry guy we were visiting in Sweden next to the liquor store?

Torbjørn educated me. In Norway, Harry is not a person; it is a concept. In Norwegian qualifying something or someone of "*Harry*" means they are vulgar and tasteless. I am guessing a haircut can be harry, as well as an attitude, or a type of holiday. So "*Harry*" is the opposite of "cool".

Typically, a *harrytur* or *harryhandel* is a trip Norwegians take to Sweden, alternatively to Denmark, in order to buy cheaper alcohol, cigarettes, meat, and a lot of other basic necessities such as candy and sports shoes. Okay, so we were on a trip only vulgar and tasteless people take.

"Wait, don't ALL Norwegians go on *harrytur*?" I asked. Cheap alcohol and *snus* just a few hours away are too tempting for anyone here.

Suddenly they scream "Woohoo!," I looked around; what was there worth screaming "Woohoo!" for? The land had been flat ever since we left Oslo.

"Didn't you see? On this road we can drive at 110 km/h!" he said, smiling.

Wow, Norwegians don't need much to get excited.

After a one-and-a-half-hour drive, Torbjørn announced: "We are in Sweden!"

"How do you know that?" I asked. We didn't pass anything special that signified an international border. We did drive over a short bridge (that was the border), which was, by the way, much shorter than the one between Malmø and Copenhagen.

Two minutes later we parked at a shopping center, where many cars with a big "N" were parked: Norwegian cars. The store was called *Systembolaget*, the Swedish alcohol shop. Just like *Vinmonopolet*, but cheaper. We entered the place and I could not help but notice that it was bustling with people.

"Oh, this is nothing," said Jorunn, "Before Easter holidays, the queue to get in can be dozens of meters long. We only get in when so many people have left the shop, you know, for security."

Like a bouncer in front of a club? How much cheaper is it really for Norwegians to go crazy over this?

The answer to that question was provided to me five minutes later, when a foreigner in the shop said very loudly in English with a thick German accent:

"This is not cheap! In Germany, a beer is less than a euro," he screamed.

Exactly. I looked at the wine and found the same thing: it wasn't cheap, it was just cheaper compared to Norwegian prices. For French prices this was still expensive. In the land of the blind, the one-eyed man is king.

Most Norwegians won't mind spending two minutes sending an SMS to bid for an apartment 300 000 NOK over the initial price. Yet they will drive several hundred kilometers in a day to Sweden in order to buy a bottle of wine 50 NOK cheaper than what it would have cost in their own country. Norwegian logic.

We made our way out of the liquor store and counted all our bottles to make sure we were not over the authorized quota. Then we headed to another place called Nordby (The North City in English). Nordby is an enormous shopping mall full of Norwegians piling up stuff they buy in big shopping carts. There, I entered the biggest candy store I had ever seen in my life, with two-kilogram Toblerone chocolate bars and one-kilogram bags of candy. There was so much sugar in that shop that I felt like I was becoming diabetic just by looking at it. If I had been a kid, I would have tried to get myself locked in all night and overdosed on jelly crocodiles.

We ate lunch in a place called MAX, some kind of Swedish fast food, and drank lots of Ramlösa, the local fizzy water which they sell in five-liter bottles.

The supermarket was cool because it had a much wider range of products than the supermarkets in Norway. Sorry Norwegians, I know you don't like it when Swedes do something better than you do, but if everything was that great in Norway, why would you need to go to Sweden? More choice in vegetables, meat, frozen food, types of cheese, and of course, more variety in *knekkebrød*.

At the end of the day we had pain in our legs, "minus" many Swedish kroners on our accounts, and many liters of alcohol in the car. And of course, our quota of meat per person: 10 kg. Some stack up their car with friends and family on their way to the border so that they can head home with dozens of kilos of meat, alcohol, candy, sports equipment, and tobacco. When I got home with my heavy shopping bags, I had to take a nap, no one ever told me being *harry* was so tiring.

"We are going back next weekend if you care to join us! We go every Saturday to stock up on enough alcohol for our wedding next June," said Torbjørn and Jorunn. Every Saturday? That sounded exhausting.

"Oh well, I think I'll make it a once-in-awhile thing," I answered politely.

I had bought enough *knekkebrød* for six months, and the bag-in-box wine will last a while too.

"Should we maybe visit something else in Sweden next time than the border?" I added. "I am sure there are other things to see there than the inside of Systembolaget."

"Yeah," said Jorunn, half-convinced. "We can stop at this little town called Strömstad that we can visit after we've bought alcohol."

Some hope, then, that I will see more Swedes than Norwegians on my next trip to Sweden.

On that day I reached a new step in my mission to integrate

Norwegian society. I did what all Norwegians do: I drove four hours to save a few kroners on alcohol but spent much more on gas and Swedish burgers. Was it really worth it?

Norwegians went through a lot to save those few kroners in a cheaper currency or buy kilos of cancy.

***Note to self:*** I learned three important things in the eyes of Norwegians: alcohol, *fart* (speed, another funny Norwegian word in English), and the quality of their roads.

Are Norwegians really that cheap? They do love to buy stuff on sale, whether it is in Sweden or elsewhere, and then brag about it. Like the value of something is higher if you got it cheaper than the regular price. They are also able to pay for sports equipment and apartments at insane prices.

*Harrytur* is not necessarily a Norwegian specificity: Norwegians go to Sweden, Swedes go to Denmark, Danes go to Germany, Germans go to Poland, Finns go to Russia, and so on. Local populations cross different borders in the world and go home the same day. The destination changes, but the motives are the same: cheap booze.

# JOINING A CHOIR

I was keeping my social life busy. I had a total of two close friends. Ane and Kaia. I managed to make two good friends in Oslo and many more in Northern Norway in less than a year. As far as I was concerned, I was doing amazingly well (self-pity does not help in times of Scandinavian winter).

I also had a boy who was a friend, whom I was not allowed to call my boyfriend, Ante. Yes, he had flatmates and many friends, but the last thing I wanted was to depend on him for my social life. I needed my own friends.

I knew Ane and Kaia would get busy with their lives, friends, travels, and families. I could not rely entirely on them to keep me entertained during the whole winter. Therefore, I decided to join some kind of activity which I could do on a regular basis and force myself out of the house at least one evening per week after work.

One evening, as I was having dinner at Ante's place, his

flatmate Ken Tore told me,

"You know what, I know an all-women choir, with very cool people. You should join. I can give you their contact details."

The Saint Halvard's Girls' Choir was exactly what I needed. I called one of the women there, and they asked me to join. I had a bad combination going for me: a mediocre singing voice and average Norwegian communication skills. I was aware of these weaknesses but I accepted.

Rule number 564 of making friends in Norway: don't say no to something social, especially if it's an invitation for dinner, a holiday at a family cabin, or a group activity.

Since we had been back from the festival, things were not exactly as I had imagined with Ante. On some days, he was very eager to meet me, and on others he seemed distant. He had to introduce me to some of his friends and did not say I was his girlfriend. What am I, then? I wondered. Almost a year in this country taught me that whatever happens in a Norwegian man's mind is not something that should influence my life, unless it is for the best.

The first choir meeting was rough. I was not expected to follow conversations about work but sing in rhythm to songs every other girl in the room knew. I did not understand all the words in the songs. Some were songs from their childhood such as "Bæ bæ lillelam" (Bah Bah Little Lamb) which repeated the word "Bah" so many times that I got completely lost.

"Let's start again at Bah," said Frida, the choir leader. "Which one?" I wondered.

Another one was from a children's television program called Ronja Røverdatter, which I never heard of.

"Did you not watch Swedish kids' television as a child?" asked Frida.

Other songs were in New Norwegian or *nynorsk*, because

Frida came from an island close to Ålesund, in Western Norway where people use *nynorsk* a.k.a. New Norwegian.

I was in contact with it almost daily since my colleague Ylva wrote in *nynorsk*, but we did not learn any of it in Norwegian classes, and to sing it was a whole other project. The sentences did not always make sense to me, so I just learned them by heart.

Why does Norway, with such a small population, have two official languages? Because Norway used to be under Danish occupation, Danish was the written language of Norway until 1814. When Norway became independent, many Norwegians needed to have their own written language that represented their national identity. *Bokmål*, or the "book tongue" if literally translated, is a written language inherited from Danish.

It is a Norwegianized version of Danish. Nynorsk or New Norwegian is the other written standard of the Norwegian language. Contrary to what many believe, it is not an oral version of Norwegian or even a dialect of Norwegian, *nynorsk* is indeed a written language at the same level as *bokmål*.

Ivar Aasen is a Norwegian linguist who traveled all over Norway in the mid-19th century to gather the vocabulary and grammar of Norwegian language which was little affected by Danish. This was the basis for a language which was said to be more Norwegian and from the people from the countryside rather than the city elite, than *bokmål*.

Today there is still a disagreement in Norwegian society as to whether *nynorsk* should continue to be mandatory at school. Around 15 percent of the Norwegian population uses *nynorsk* as their official written language.

In my case, whether it was *bokmål* or *nynorsk*, they were all foreign languages to me. It was just that I was more familiar with *bokmål* due to my Norwegian classes. If it is an official language in Norway, why not teach newcomers *nynorsk* too?

Back to the choir. My singing voice was not that nice to listen to but the other girls did not seem to mind. We were there to have fun and be together, and it was actually very... how do they say again? *Koselig*!

These Tuesday evenings with the choir were wonderful. As the weeks went by, I knew them better and better. A connection was growing. We were around six to ten women depending on the week. A woman named Frida was leading us as she had more musical education than the rest. She was a very good choir leader as well as a very funny person.

The choir practices were so cozy. We would meet in one of the homes of someone who was practicing that evening. She lit many candles and always had a bowl with potato chips and chocolate on the table. We chatted a bit, sang, chatted more.

After singing sometimes we went for a beer at a nearby pub. I was part of a community, for the first time since I moved to Norway. One that had chosen me, not like my work colleagues. These girls had a choice, and they had chosen me! One evening Frida shared exciting news: she was getting married. Even more exciting, she was inviting all of us to her wedding. I could not believe it! I was invited to a Norwegian wedding. It would be a long wait until next summer, but I was ready.

These girls from the choir were sincere and sober. We shared our thoughts, laughed and built memories together. Some got pregnant, some became single, and we were all going through this together.

I was making real friends at last, which brought me one step closer to wanting to stay in Norway.

# FAMILY VISIT FROM PROVENCE

My parents were busy with work and other things all year, but now they had holidays and the opportunity to visit me. They wanted to come in November but I was afraid that was the best way for them to never ever come back to Norway. November was the worst month of the year, I felt. No snow, yet so much darkness and cold rain. It was the worst of winter and fall in the same month.

My father was prepared for the cold, at least mentally, since he grew up in Canada. But my mum was having a hard time imagining how cold and windy it could be here. In November there could be thick ice on the pavements of Oslo. It caused many accidents with people slipping and breaking bones. I tried to use this as an argument for them to come earlier in the fall, but she kept telling me,

"I understand November is a bad month. Just tell us then which week it will be warm and sunny, and we will come."

But nobody knows that it can snow even in the summer in Norway. How can anyone living south of the Arctic circle believe that? Norway will never be warm enough for them.

The first challenge was that I had traveled so much in the past years that it was getting confusing. I moved from Denmark less than a year ago, and they have never been north of Paris in their lives.

My father, originally from Québec, was quite skeptical about visiting since he left Canada due to the cold weather. He had no intention of taking holidays in a place colder than Provence. My mother was more enthusiastic about discovering Norway, but still seemed to think of Scandinavia as one big country with regions: Norway, Sweden, Denmark.

She kept talking to me on the phone about the son of her friend Noor who lived in the same city as I did.

"He moved to Stockholm like you, and he says it's very hard to learn Norwegian. Maybe I can put you two in touch," she had said.

"Wait a second, if he is in Stockholm then he is probably in Sweden, not Norway," I told her.

"Of course," she answered. "In any case, it is a really hard language to learn," she added.

"I am sure it is, especially if he is learning Norwegian in Sweden!" I answered laughing.

I clearly had to make sure they would book their flight to the right Scandinavian capital city.

They arrived in October for a long weekend, and I was just in luck as the weather suddenly shifted from rainy and gray to sunny and blue sky. The forest behind my home was still very colorful, although the leaves became a deeper shade of red and some were starting to fall.

I had to work, so they had to spend their first day in Oslo

alone. I would be free to visit the city with them on the weekend. Ante knew they were coming but it seemed he hid in his home to make sure we would not meet, or rather that he would not meet my parents. It was fair enough, I did not want to start a whole discussion with my family on the direction my love life was taking.

On their first day, they walked on Karl Johans *gate*, the main street of Oslo, and up to the King's castle. They made their way to Aker Brygge, the main harbor of Oslo, and continued to Astrup Fearnley Museum of Modern Art. It had an interesting architecture, and hosted a beach and the best views over the Oslo fjord. Since they still had some time until they met me, they took the boat from Aker Brygge to Nesodden and a bus around the peninsula.

They met me by my office at 4pm after I finished work. We had coffee by the Norwegian parliament, and I asked them

"So how is Oslo?"

"I loved the museum," said my mum. "We saw an amazing exhibition, and everything is so spacious. I loved the view from the bus on Nesodden. Why don't you move there, by the sea? It would be so nice," she added.

My dad seemed disturbed by something.

"So it's a public holiday today right?" he asked.

"No, it's a regular working day. Why?" I answered.

"Why are the streets so empty then?" he asked, astonished. It made me laugh.

"Actually, right now is rush hour in Oslo as everyone is getting home from work," I explained.

I was used to it, but it is true that Oslo is much less populated than capital cities around the world, from Paris to New Delhi.

It had around 500 000 people, the size of a smaller city in France. In comparison, the city I came from in France had over one million inhabitants and was not the most densely populated city in the country. I was in fact living in a very populated area by Norwegian standards. Maybe the key was to invite them to Oslo on the 17<sup>th</sup> of May? There would be lots of people in the streets just as on a regular day in a French city.

We went back to my apartment, and the next day I took them to the Frognerseteren café above my home, and around the woods of Nordmarka. In the evening we were invited to Kaia's place; she wanted to show my parents some Norwegian hospitality. We shopped at the supermarket to get beers for our hosts and my dad came back running from the counter.

"I saw the price, I thought it was for the pack of beers. Lorelou, you will never believe what happened," he said, white as a ghost.

"… it was the price for one bottle?" I asked.

"Exactly. The price for one bottle is the same as for a case of beer in France. I cannot believe it. How can a can of beer be so expensive?" he asked.

We traveled to Kaia's place by metro. As it was fall, the need for *koselighet* was sneaking in on Norwegians again, so Kaia lit small candles in the whole house for our dinner. My parents were confused.

"What is happening here? Is this a Satanist meeting?" asked my mum, half-joking.

"No, it's to give some warmth to the room," I answered.

"Ah yes, I remember poverty from Canada too. We did not have central heating either," said my dad. Oh God. Help me.

We ate quite quickly and started drinking beers. I realized that while for the French food is the alibi to socialize, for Norwegians it is definitely alcohol. We had a great evening, but when we left my dad told me, "I cannot believe how fast they drink these expensive beers. Shouldn't they save them, for a special occasion or something?" he asked. Yes, I forgot to mention, Norwegians drink lots of beers, but even more if they are free.

I was absolutely sure my parents would be amazed by how polite Norwegians are, with their tendency to not invade others' personal space. This is one of the things I love about Norway and Norwegians. Unlike in my hometown, people here mind their own business, which I found relaxing. I also enjoy that Norwegians are so humble and not so openly aggressive, compared to the cockiness of many French people.

On the contrary, my parents thought that Norwegians were rude. My mother was shocked to see that an old lady on the bus had to stand because no one would give up their seat.

"In all societies, the minimum requirement is to respect old people. Why not Norwegians?" she asked me.

I tried to find explanations to what they witnessed: Norwegians are very independent and most of them would refuse help if offered. If this lady had been offered a seat, she might have been offended and refused. The common understanding is that, if she needed help, she would ask for it. That did not convince either of them. My French colleague Marc had another explanation: Norwegians have only recently started living in cities and taking buses and trains. Because of that they don't have these reflexes like in Continental Europe, they never really know what to do.

My dad was bothered by something else. "They don't seem to say "please" at all. Almost as if that word did not exist for them!" he said in a cynical laugh.

"Well, believe it or not, it does not really exist. *Takk* means 'thank you,' but there are only indirect ways of saying 'please' in Norwegian such as *værsågod* but it does not really mean the same as "please" in all contexts," I explained. "For example, if someone says "Can I sit here?" you can answer "*værsågod*," which in this context means "please, go ahead." If you want to ask something like "Can I please get a coffee?" then it would be said *"Kan du være så snill å gi meg en kopp kaffe?"* or *"Kan jeg få en kopp kaffe?"* In English, that becomes a bit dry: "Can I get a cup of coffee?" so that is why it might come across as rude. But when translating from Norwegian they really don't have many options," I added.

My parents traveled the world, so they began to understand the cultural differences between the French and the Norwegians, despite coming both from Western Europe.

"Also, I never seem to be able to read their emotions. Are they sad, happy, depressed? When I look at their faces, I never know what they are feeling," she said. Yes, indeed. How Norwegians show emotions is a topic on its own.

On the last day, we wandered around town. Everything was closed because it was Sunday. We went to a restaurant in a park called Ekeberg, which was open, and ordered a three-course meal. The view was amazing, as well as the service. The food was delicious. We all had a first course of fish soup. My dad had reindeer, my mum had whale, and I had a vegetarian dish with seasonal mushrooms. For dessert we enjoyed home-made ice cream with rhubarb and licorice. I had a gift for them: woolen socks, the thin type in merino wool which holds your feet warm without making you sweat, and a poster of the exhibition they saw at the Astrup Fearnley Museum of Modern Art. I texted some pictures of our meal to Ante who said he was jealous of the wonderful dinner.

When we left the restaurant, there was a pram outside, standing alone. The parents were inside having a meal. The baby was peacefully sleeping, wrapped in lamb wool with his face in the open air.

My mum could not believe it. "Did someone forget their baby here?" she asked.

"Norwegians believe babies sleep better when sleeping outside. They become less sick and more resistant to the cold, apparently," I said, trying to find a plausible explanation to what appeared illogical to her.

"But aren't they afraid their children will die out here or be snatched by someone ill-intentioned?" she asked.

"No, this is just the way they do it. Even in kindergartens. They park all the prams outside for naptime."

"I guess they know what they are doing," said my dad. "I mean, there are a few million of them and they seem to survive despite sleeping in the snow as children," he said. "Sure, and to be fair they aren't cold at all as Norwegians have all sorts of special gear to keep them warm," I added.

My parents left Norway with a sweet and sour feeling about the country and its people. They were happy to return to their Provence. They called me later that day to tell me they had arrived home safely. "We hope to see you soon in Marseille for Christmas," said my mum. I wondered when they would come back to Norway.

This four-day-stay brought doubts to my mind: was I delusional? Did I see great things in Norway where there was nothing to see? Those great things I saw were the peacefulness of Norwegian life. The respect at work. The freedom of not being in an overpopulated place. The beauty and immensity of Norway's dramatic nature. People's ability to give everyone the personal space they need. In conclusion, my parents did not like this wonderful place.

*Note to self:* Unless your parents come from Siberia like Ayta's, Norway will feel cold for your visiting family. They will also most probably think that the cost of living is insanely high in Norway, and that alcohol prices are prohibitive. On the bright side, salmon is cheaper than elsewhere and the water and air are very clean. When they visit, get them to take pictures of the fjords to show the exoticism of Norway to their friends. Ideas of souvenirs to take home: a cheese slicer and a pack of *brunost*, licorice, cured reindeer meat, moose and blueberry sausage, cloudberry jam, flat bread, and thin merino wool socks.

As soon as they left, I called Ante.

"They are gone! Should we meet?" I asked.

He invited me to go to his place. The weather was getting dangerously cold. People were entering their houses earlier, staying in the streets as little as possible. The night was falling faster by the day. Candle lights were appearing in every window shop. Norwegians were starting to nest for the winter and preparing to make things *kjempekoselig* (extremely cosy).

I was staying put in Ante's flat, leaving just to go to work. November was my least favorite month of all in Norway. It was so depressing and gray. There was no snow, which illuminates everything and makes any place look magical. November was the month of cold rain and depression, as days just got shorter until the winter solstice on 21st of December.

Ante and I were getting along well, I felt. I was practically living in his flat and had made friends with Kent Tore who had such a great sense of humor and was so kind. After a couple of weeks at Ante's place, I decided it was time to go home for a while.

I looked at my flat. I needed to make it look more winter-friendly. I noticed Norwegians changed their interior decorating when a new season came along, and especially when fall and winter started. It seemed strange at first, but now that I lived here, I realized that one spends so much time indoors during all these winter months that you need to feel as comfortable as possible at home. To do so, I wanted to buy some *koselig* carpets, candles, and new plants to replace those which died. Ante had a car so I called him and asked whether he could drive me to IKEA.

"Yeah, I actually also need some things for my home," he answered.

Great! We would go there next Saturday, on a rainy day. A perfect day to be in a big cement block without windows, looking at furniture and eating Swedish meatballs and ice cream.

Saturday morning I was eating breakfast when I received an SMS from him.

"Lorelou, I am sorry I cannot come. IKEA seems like too much of a commitment. Everyone will believe we are in a relationship, and I am not sure I am ready for that step. I need time to think," wrote Ante in the SMS.

Excuse me? Commitment? Who will think we are a couple? The cashiers in IKEA? Do they care if we are in a relationship or not? They see people arguing every day over a SKÄNKA pan. They couldn't care less.

I tried to answer in a cool way, trying to make some jokes to clear the air and promise this did not mean anything at all. Despite that, he closed himself like an oyster, and it was downhill from there.

I went to IKEA alone and tried to meet him again. But something had changed.

During the next few weeks, I kept trying to meet him. He always had good excuses not to do so. "My sister is in town." "I have too much work." "Not this time, I am not feeling well."

Eventually I called and said I needed to talk to him in person. We met in a café, and he gave me the coldest hug in the history of Norwegian hugs. At least he showed up, I thought, probably not that easy for him.

He looked at me with sad eyes and waited for me to say the words. He then said the deadly sentence, "It is not you, it's me," followed by "I like you, but you know, I am not sure I want to be in a relationship right now. It went too fast, and now I am not sure anymore. Maybe we can continue to meet casually."

My heart sank. This was even worse. As I saw it, he was keeping me as a side gig he could call when he felt lonely, but did not love me enough to want to be in a relationship with me.

"Ante, I like you a lot too, too much to accept this. I need to be with someone who knows he wants to be with me. I will not see you casually while you see other women too. I know where I want this to go, I want to be in a relationship with you because I like so many things about you. But if you don't want the same then I have to let you go," I said.

"Maybe we can be friends?" he asked.

"No, we can't. Not for a while at least. I am sorry," I answered. "Bye." I left the table before tears came down my cheeks.

Damn it, for once I found a great one. But he didn't like me that much. I had to accept the fact that I still had much to learn from whichever rules applied to romantic relationships here. And that I was single again. In Norway. In winter. Here we go again.

*Note to self:* IKEA is a scary place. For some Norwegian men it has the same function as a wedding fair. It is a place where one cannot get drunk and pretend the flirting did not mean anything. It is a place where couples plan their bedroom furniture, their children's diaper changing area. It is a place where you share a meal made of boiled potatoes and salmon while thinking of the future. This is why you should always be very sure of the feelings of your better half when inviting them to IKEA. Otherwise you could end up breaking a fragile relationship.

# VOSS WINTER WONDERLAND

I was feeling sad and grim. No matter how much effort I put into it, winter was always hard for me to get through. Ylva saw that I was not my jolly self at work and asked me out for a beer on a Friday after work. I told her about Ante and that I had given myself one year to figure out whether I wanted to live in Norway, and that some days I loved this country and some days I wondered how I would survive here without friends, family and a love life.

"What are you talking about? You have friends, you have us!" she said. "I hope you stay. I think it is great having you around. You are funny and you show us a perspective on our own society and culture that we Norwegians don't see often," she added.

The next day I received an SMS from her.

"I talked to my parents. Come to Voss to my hometown next weekend," it said.

My answer was, of course, yes. A train ride to the west of Norway, a place I had never visited, to meet a kind Norwegian family, was exactly what I needed.

I asked for a Friday off, using their *avspasering* system, and we left on the evening train on Thursday. The train ride to Voss, in Western Norway, lasted five and half hours. We traveled with Ylva's two kids as her partner Brynjulf was working.

They had taken this route many times, so they kept telling me where we were and what the view was like. Oslo-Bergen was apparently one of the most beautiful train rides in all of Norway, passing through the Hardanger plateau as well as the mountainous Finse area. Unfortunately, it was already quite dark, and we could not see much. We were basically going north-west from Oslo, towards the fjords.

We arrived in Voss late, and Ylva's parents picked us up. When we arrived at their house, it looked like a winter wonderland. There was so much snow, much more than in Oslo. The layer on the roof of their house was so thick that it blended with the snow on the ground. Some kids had actually slid off the roof and landed on a huge pile of snow. We could still see the traces of their sleds.

There were small lights everywhere, probably because of upcoming Christmas celebrations and all the houses were wooden. Some were red, others were yellow. It looked like a fairytale. We had *kveldsmat* (evening food) and went to bed. The next day we walked around and sledded with the kids, and they told me about Voss.

Voss is famous for many things. I believed until then that the Voss water came from Voss, but I was mistaken. The water comes from a spring in Iveland in the south of Norway, close to Kristiansand. They probably chose the name Voss as it is catchier than Iveland. There are an unbelievable number of professional skiers who come from Voss, including many of the medalists in the Winter Olympics across the years.

Voss is strategically located between Flåm, Sognefjord, and Bergen and attracts a fair number of tourists every year, at least before the pandemic. The highlight of the town was sports, including cross-country skiing, paragliding, water sports, para-bungee (sounds scary), kayaking, rafting. Basically any sport that can be done on a mountain, in the air above a mountain, or in a river.

"There is even an extreme sports festival in June every year," said Ylva's mother.

"Thanks for the tip. I'm at the level where I am trying to ski without cracking my skull on a rock. So paragliding over a river in a closed parachute is not for me," I answered.

She laughed.

"You have to learn how to ski. You know that Norwegians are said to be born with skis on their feet."

The next day we woke up and ate an athlete's breakfast, with oatmeal, fruits, eggs, homemade bread, *leverpostei*, homemade jam and more. After that, they drove me to Bergen.

Norway's second largest city, in fact, looks almost like a fisherman's harbor lost in time. When on the famous docks of Bergen, locally called *Bryggen*, this series of Hanseatic buildings reminds us of the city's extraordinary commercial activities over the centuries. For example, it was through Bergen that the Black Death entered Norway in the 14th century, carried on a boat that docked for trading activities.

Today, the collection of iconic colored wooden houses is on the UNESCO list for World Cultural Heritage and, to be honest, filled with way too many tourists for my taste. I was not there for more than a few hours but did manage to buy a few postcards to send to my grandmother.

We returned to Voss, since we had a train to Oslo that evening. I decided I would have to come back to see more than the postcard scenery.

# FRILUFTSLIV

# AN OUTDOORS WAY OF LIFE

Ylva invited me to dinner the week after we got back from Voss. This was a great opportunity to get to know her and her family. Her partner, Brynjulf, was a journalist and their two sons were small and blond and running around like little elves. During the meal, we discussed what it meant to be Norwegian, about the pressure many Norwegians feel in their everyday life to pretend everything is perfect.

It only half surprised me to hear there was a social pressure, as everything *did* kind of seem perfect. People didn't openly complain in Norway as they would do in France. I often wondered how Norwegians dealt with frustration and anger when they all seem to be doing great all the time.

"They go skiing!" said Ylva laughing.

"Or hiking, or camping. Why do you think Norwegians are always outdoors? It is to enjoy *friluftsliv* but mainly to deal with everything in their life. Being in nature allows us to think, calm down and refresh ourselves."

"*Fri*-what?" I asked.

When she said it with her dialect it took me a while to understand, since the sound of that word in my head, with a French accent, was very different. *Friluftsliv*, that thing on every single Tinder profile.

"*Fri-lufts-liv* is quite important when living in Norway," said Ylva. "There is even a Norwegian law that was adopted to ensure the right of all to *friluftsliv*," she added.

"But what does it mean exactly?" I asked. "I know that *fri* means free, *luft* means air and *liv* means life. Is this the right to life in free air?" I added.

Ylva and Brynyulf laughed.

"Not exactly. It means you can access wild nature, the countryside and spend time there for recreation. With *allemannsretten*, the freedom to roam, you can even sleep on people's private property for up to a couple of nights if you don't disturb nature. Us Norwegians have a special connection with nature, we need to be outdoors as much as we can. That's why we go skiing as soon as we have the opportunity, even after work," she explained.

Many things suddenly made sense. The runners on Saturday mornings even when it snowed, the colleagues taking their skis to work, my colleagues camping in the mountains with their small children in the winter.

"It is important for us that our children inherit this love of nature, and we try to toughen them up by teaching them to ski at a young age; sometimes, before they can even walk, we put them on cross-country skis. We also take them to our cabins without electricity to make sure they can enjoy a simple life, or on hiking trips to mountains. Often they complain on these trips which they find too long and too tiring, so we promise them chocolate and waffles when they reach the cabin," she said, smiling.

"Why is *friluftsliv* important in your life?" I asked Brynjulf and Ylva.

"It is almost like meditation for me," said Brynjulf.

"I go skiing for hours alone, using a lot of energy cross-country skiing and taking in everything. The fresh air, the forest, the snow, the silence. It makes me feel good afterwards. Almost like every bad feeling I had has disappeared," he added.

"You know we cannot get angry in Norway. All our frustrations need to go somewhere," added Ylva. "So skiing, or hiking, or running, or ice bathing, or fishing, all those things allow us to be in nature and process our feelings. We do it alone or with friends, family, or even colleagues," said Ylva.

"I even go on trips with my girlfriends camping in the forest in hammocks. It's amazing to be away from our husbands and our kids. Under the sky filled with stars, by a lake, with our thermos by the fire. We bond and we relax."

Ylva had so much warmth in her voice when she talked about this trip. As if she would leave now if she could.

I imagined inviting my Parisian girlfriends on a four-hour hike in the mud before reaching a place infested with mosquitoes, and sleeping in an uncomfortable hammock or worse, in a tent on a badly insulated camping mat. Not sure that would be a hit.

Before living in Norway, I was a city girl and a workaholic. I lived in densely populated capital cities, like Paris and Jakarta. I worked long hours and believed my value was in the amount of work I put into my professional career. If you asked me whether I wanted to go to the countryside for a weekend it would have meant dying of boredom. Now if I had the choice between a nightclub and a walk to a cabin with a good friend, I would choose the cabin. My experiences in Trøndelag with

Kaia's family, cycling in the Lofoten, waking up by a lake surrounded by reindeer and drinking fresh water from the river taught me there are better things in life than perfect lattes and skyscrapers.

I realized how Norwegian I had become when I visited Kaia after she moved to Bøler in the east of Oslo. We walked across the frozen Nøklevann Lake and sat by a fire on the shore. I felt an intimate interior peace just by sitting there in silence close to my friend, with a cup of warm coffee in my hand, the snowy forest behind us and the open icy lake before us. I didn't want to leave this place. It felt like everything I needed in life was here.

*Note to self:* If I understand Norwegian dialects from Trøndelag and Voss, and enjoy *friluftsliv*, does that mean I am integrating in Norway and becoming one of them?

Not really. As long as I take sips from other peoples' wines at parties I am not a true Norwegian, I thought.

# A NORWEGIAN CHRISTMAS

I was invited to my first Christmas party outside of work. My fellow choir members organized the annual Saint Halvard's female choir *julebord*. Frida hosted the Christmas party. We all brought some food and cooked together at her place.

In France, Christmas is a time when we buy expensive and exclusive products which we don't normally eat during the rest of the year. In my home, during a typical Christmas dinner, the first course is usually oysters still alive in their shell, snails baked in a mix of butter and parsley, and *foie gras*, or goose liver. We eat this with Sauternes, a sweet white wine. Then as a main course we make scallops in white wine sauce and/or a capon baked for hours in wine. There is a cheese platter and an ice cream cake that looks like a log.

I wondered what kind of food Norwegians really loved to eat but could not afford the rest of the year? What exclusive meals do Norwegians cook for their Christmas meal?

I was in charge of dessert and drinks. I baked a flan which they called *karamellpudding* in Norway. I heard this was a Christmassy dessert. I made several liters of *gløgg*, a warm wine with almonds, raisins, honey, clove, cinnamon, and orange peel. I also baked *pepperkaker*, the Norwegian gingerbread. I went to Vinmonopolet and asked the expert what kind of alcohol Norwegians drink for Christmas.

He showed me something called *juleakevitt* or Christmas aquavit, which seemed appropriate. He also sold me something else, alcohol-free, called *julebrus*. It translates to "Christmas soda" which sounded very strange. What does a Christmas soda taste like, I wondered? Cinnamon and cloves? They already had *påskebrus* or Easter soda, and now this.

Norwegians had invented such strange drinks.

When the day of the *julebord* came, I was ready hours before the time the dinner would start. I had never been invited to a traditional Christmas dinner so I wanted to be part of every minute of preparation.

At the last minute I had bought some marzipan pigs which Kaia told me were things Norwegians liked around Christmas time. Where did that tradition come from? How did anyone think of shaping marzipan and chocolate in the shape of pigs, and turn it into a traditional sweet to eat for Christmas?

As I was packing everything to leave for Frida's house, I realized this was way too heavy for me to take in bags on the metro. I would have to take a taxi. I had more than ten kilos of food and drinks. The six liters of *gløgg* did not help. The flan had to be held upside down to make sure the caramel would not run out before I flipped it.

I arrived at Frida's place and some of the other girls were already there, chatting in the living room.

"Put all the stuff in the kitchen! We now have everything we need for a Norwegian Christmas!" said Frida enthusiastically when I passed the door.

I entered the kitchen to put all the food in the fridge and the *gløgg* on the stove. It had to be lukewarm. To my surprise all there was on the kitchen table was four kilos of potatoes, a few vegetables, and boxes of red cabbage. She opened one of the red cabbage boxes, and said:

"Smell! This is the smell of Christmas. The whole house has the smell of Christmas."

"Does this smell like Christmas?" I asked.

"No, no," said Frida. "We will warm it up. Then it will smell like Christmas. Add some clove in the *gløgg* as well, then when the other guests arrive they will be so happy."

I did as she said, as she was the expert, not me.

"We will also need *Tre nøtter til Askepott*," she added. "I guess that is called 'Three Nuts for Cinderella' in English. You know that movie, right?" she asked me.

"Three nuts for Cinderella? I've never heard of that movie," I replied.

"Whaaat? That is crazy. We watch it every year. It's the kick-off for a Norwegian Christmas. We can stream it while we cook so that we have the right atmosphere."

She put the movie on Youtube.

I was expecting a movie in Norwegian, but the title that showed up on the screen was *"Tři oříšky pro Popelku"*. Which language was this? Definitely not any of the Norwegian languages I was aware of. Turns out the movie was a Czechoslovakian-East German co-production released in 1973. Absolutely nothing Norwegian about it.

The movie was about a young blond woman who seemed frightened all the time. Everything was happening in the winter, with lots of snow everywhere, and some of them wore ridiculous costumes including one rich lady who looked like a giant bat. I think the most shocking aspect of it all was that the original voices in Czech or German were on a low volume, but definitely audible, and a male voice was speaking on top of their voices in Norwegian. The guy was dubbing all the voices, the children, the men, the women, the elderly.

So at this moment I had to focus on four different layers of sounds: the original dialogues of the movie, with different male, female, children voices; the male Norwegian voice speaking over everyone, my choir friends cooking, and my choir friends chatting. I was getting a headache, so I decided to drink more *gløgg*.

I was trying to figure the movie out while Frida and the other girls boiled at least three kilos of potatoes in one pot. In another pot, they cut more potatoes with rutabaga in small chunks. When all of it was cooked, they mashed them together with salt, pepper and butter for a side dish called *kålrabbistappe*. It took me about two months to remember this word.

They kept some more boiled potatoes as a side dish. And, as if there weren't enough potatoes, they baked more potatoes to make a mixture of cooked rice, mashed potatoes, onions, ginger and cauliflower, which were then fried. They called it *vegisterkaker*, a vegetarian version of *medisterkaker*.

*Medisterkaker* are meatballs made with minced pork meat and nutmeg. That was for the vegetarian side of the dinner. Then came the preparation of the meat dishes.

One guest had something called *pinnekjøtt* or lamb ribs; another one brought pork belly locally called *ribbe*.

"Regular Norwegian families choose one or the other. We never eat both of these for Christmas, but since you are a foreigner, we wanted to show you all the diversity," said Frida.

I really wanted to help, but these ingredients were so foreign to me that I was useless in this kitchen.

"Should I fry the *pinnekjøtt*? Boil the *ribbe*? Make fries out of the potatoes?" I asked.

"No! No! Just sit and relax. Dress the table," they said.

I just watched them while sipping more *gløgg*. I was getting more and more drunk and wondered what the Christmas table would look like. I took a peek in the kitchen once in a while to see what they were doing. The lamb ribs were cooked already while the pork belly was put in the oven. The ribs had actually been in water for 36 hours (!) and cooked for three hours before landing on our table (!!). As it had been smoked, dried, and salted, one needs to get the salt out. The pork belly was cooking in the oven and looked like crisp dice laid on five layers of fat.

When all was done we sat at the table. The dinner was grandiose. Sure, it was not what I had imagined. It was better. At some point I asked

"Why is there only one man doing all the voices in Three Nuts for Cinderella? Was Norway so poor they could not afford more than one voice actor?"

They all laughed.

"No, don't say that. It is so *koselig* that he is alone doing the voices. We love it."

This was not helping my understanding of Norwegian culture. Even when something made no sense for the outside world, if Norwegians were used to it and it has become "tradition," then it may not be changed. It made people feel good.

We drank and laughed all night. I was grateful that Frida had not asked me to cook. It prevented me from seeing the disappointed faces of my choir girlfriends in front of a table filled with oysters, a small rooster in wine, scallops and smelly cheese. None of these smell like a Norwegian Christmas.

I still had the hope I would one day introduce some French dishes to the traditional Norwegian *julebord*. Maybe next year!

*Note to self:* the thing I understood that night is that what turns Norwegians on culturally is not luxury or novelty – it is tradition. They like to remember who they are, eat what they were used to eating, be with their old friends, and celebrate as they did last Christmas, as they will do next Christmas. Same with Easter, 17th of May and *hyttetur*. What they like is the comfort of doing the same things and knowing that despite all the changes around them, this does not change. There is a list of things that Norwegians need in order to feel like it is Christmas.

Later that night, we all went out on the town, and despite the cold and the darkness, the streets of Oslo were filled with people. As were the bars. We went to a place where we could drink a few beers with all of the boys' choir that was the counterpart to our girls' choir: Vox Grønland. They had their own choir *julebord*. We were meeting in town to celebrate together.

I was getting a beer and could not believe my eyes. Tor, the guy from the Lofoten, was there, also waiting to be served.

"*Hei, du!*" he said with a shy smile.

I was so surprised to see Tor. I invited him over to our table, but he said no since he did not know my friends.

He was looking at me right in the eyes, which I interpreted as a good sign from my extensive experience in dating Norwegian men. I invited myself to his table, with his friends, which seemed to be fine as they were all so drunk they would not remember me or avoid me if they met me again another day.

The next day he texted to thank me for a very pleasant evening. My experience with Norwegian men until now had been semi-disastrous. Was I ready to give Tor a chance, when I was still healing from the broken heart Ante had left in me?

He invited me for a drink – just the two of us. I had to think; I did not want to rush into things. In the meantime, I had a social life to attend to.

# WHAT DOES THE SHEEP SAY?

My second Christmas dinner or *julebord* was a new invitation from Ylva and Brynjulf, for a traditional Christmas dinner inspired by traditional Christmas food from Voss, Ylva's hometown.

"The head you will eat now is not a delicacy for those from Voss. In the fall we kill the sheep, and then we eat all of it, even its head, because we don't waste anything. I usually don't eat the skin or the eyes, but everything is edible. We have cut the tongue in two so that everyone gets a taste of the best part of the sheep's head. I also really like the muscles in the back of the neck," said Ylva.

Jesus, why did I accept this invitation for dinner? I asked myself while I listened to Ylva, who had ordered all these sheep heads for her friends to taste. I wanted to be adventurous and taste one of Norway's traditional meals: *smalahove* but, after staring at the full head of a sheep on my plate, I had second thoughts. I had only seen pictures of this meal and it looked even stranger on my plate. The head of a sheep, with its eyes, its ears, teeth, lips, everything was there.

On the table our hosts had given us everything needed for such a meal: *smalahove akevitt*, *lingonberry* jam, potatoes, mashed potatoes, Voss sausages. And beer of course, the famous Christmas beer or *juleøl*, which was quite dark and tasted like spices.

I looked in the eyes of this sheep, and it almost looked like it was alive.

"We salt and smoke the head, and therefore we can eat it until the last Sunday before Christmas," said Ylva.

We eat dead animals all the time, why is it so hard and slightly disgusting to eat it directly from its skull? Although this sheep died many weeks ago, it was still edible. I trusted the craftsmanship of Norwegian peasants who ate these sheep heads long before fridges and cold chain regulations.

The introductions of the sheep were over, so I attacked the beast. I started with the cheek, very nice in fact, and continued with the rest. It was salty, but actually very very good, melting in my mouth. A bit like a *confit de canard* except that I was eating from an actual head of a dead animal, delicately laid on my plate, with its tongue out and eyes closed. In other words, dead.

At one point I took out a piece of meat with my fork and it revealed the whole dentition of the sheep. One must have a tough stomach to eat this, as each piece of meat I detached showed more and more of the skull of the animal. The highlight was when I got to the tongue. Knowing this was supposed to be the best part of the meal, I needed to really appreciate this. I thought the best part was the cheek, unlike what Ylva said. As Norwegians say, *smaken er som baken, den er delt*. ("Taste is like the bum, it is divided and shared", which in English is "Different strokes for different folks").

Thankfully the *akevitt* was there to dissolve all of this in our stomach, no matter how much fat, salt or other unidentified things we ate that evening. At the end of the dinner I looked at the naked skull on my plate. Poor thing, at least I appreciated every piece of it.

I could not help thinking that the way I felt about seeing the head of this animal had something to do with the fact that our societies make sure we distance ourselves as much as possible from the actual animal we are eating.

My dad used to say that if you aren't able to see an animal being killed, or even kill it yourself, you should not be eating them. He was a vegan for 10 years and a vegetarian for 20.

In any case, I appreciated this kind of Norwegian food. This food is local enough, I thought. And it was so much tastier than Norwegian taco. At least this sheep and the way of cooking it was part of Norway's history. I would maybe not want to eat it every single day.

"Where did you buy them?" I asked Ylva as we had finished eating but were still drinking. "I would love my family to taste these someday."

"My parents ordered them locally and they were sent to us by post," she answered.

What if I did that and shipped it to France in my luggage or by post? What would the people at the airport who X-ray luggage say? "Six unidentified skulls in a suitcase. Potential animal trafficking. Arrest traveler immediately."

"My dad bought a house where we can smoke things, so the next *smalahove* will be one we will have smoked ourselves," said Ylva.

Oh, I thought, I would love to have such a house. Maybe then I could fish trout or salmon and smoke it myself. How wonderful would that be! Norway is really a perfect place for good food, I thought. In the kitchen, while we were cleaning, I told Brynjulf about my disastrous skiing course, and the fact I never took it up again.

"I can teach you how to ski," he said.

"Oh really? That would be amazing. But are you good at skiing?" I asked.

I knew for a fact that not all Norwegians were Petter Northug's child prodigy. He thought about my question for a little while.

"I can ski," he answered.

I interpreted his answer as insecurity. He must be in the high-mediocre level but still feels like he can teach me something, I thought. A good enough reason though, as I was a very low-mediocre skier.

# DATING TOR

I decided to accept Tor's invitation. We met again, this time around 9pm after I managed to sneak out of a *fredagspils* a.k.a. "Friday beer" with my colleagues without saying goodbye to anyone. It annoyed me in the beginning when Norwegians did that to me, but I found it to be a very practical way to leave without having to explain where I was going and who I was meeting. They called it an Irish goodbye, but it could also be called a Norwegian goodbye. I was becoming Norwegian at the speed of light.

Tor and I had many beers that night and decided to meet again the next day. That evening, he shyly offered to show me some paintings in his home. I politely declined. I couldn't make it too easy; I did that before and saw how that turned out for me. I wanted to know him better. We met a couple of times per week until one evening I agreed to follow him home. He was an artist, a poet, a painter. And a quite shy, sensitive man.

He was tall and very thin, the idea one has of artists that are so consumed by their art that they forget to eat. His blue eyes looked at you and beyond and his long curly brown hair was tied in a messy ponytail.

I got to his house in the dark, somewhere in the Tøyen area close to the Botanical Garden. The lights were very dim, and I could barely see the color of the bed, but we spent the night curled up in each other's arms, while he told me stories about a man who was the son of a mill owner who fell in love with the daughter of a landowner. He told me how beautiful she was, and how beautiful I was. I fell asleep, rocked by the sound of his voice.

The next morning I was woken up by the cold. He was already awake, trying to put a cardboard piece on a window. His flat, or rather his room, was really worn down. There were cracks in all the walls and it was cold. So cold. He was trying to fix a broken window.

"Shouldn't you call your landlord so he can fix this?" I asked.

"Well, I pay almost nothing for this room," he replied. "I can't really expect anything."

He did not say a single word during the rest of the morning. He looked at the wall, then at his book. A book called *Victoria* by Knut Hamsun. After two hours of this silence, I thought that he seemed much less talkative when sober. The only time he dropped his book was to drink his coffee. Then he said

"This is a great day to paint. *Vi snakkes?*"

He was kicking me out.

Kaia had warned me. If a Norwegian man said "*vi snakkes*" (we'll talk/let's talk someday) it was a very bad sign. It meant he would most likely never call me back and not answer my messages either. But there was still a slim chance, as he did not say "*vi sees plutselig*" which basically means "we'll probably bump into each other, someday, or maybe we won't, and I don't need to be sure that will happen because I don't care about you." So, this "*vi snakkes*" was not the worst news. Kind of. I wanted to see him again, but I was not going to put too much effort into it either.

Tor did call me back. It turned out he could be fascinating. And funny, and chatty after a few beers and glasses of whiskey. Every time he was sober, he was silent and depressing. Which part did I have to like? It was like two different people, and I never knew whether the silent and extremely shy person was as fond of me as the cool outgoing man who spent his nights telling me stories and painting imaginary pieces of art on my body.

A few weeks later, he invited me to his parents' cabin in Valdres. This is a make it or break it moment, I thought. If we can stand each other for three days in a house without a shower or neighbors, we can do this. I was looking forward to it because I loved getting away from the city, and I liked him, so a romantic weekend alone with him seemed like a great idea.

We drove north of Oslo, across flat lands which were among the only fertile lands of Norway, making it into the richest Viking kingdoms. We then took roads up in the mountains. The snow was getting thicker and thicker.

We arrived in the most freezing *hytte* I could imagine. It was literally colder inside than outside, and it was at least -8 °C (17 °F) outside. We lit a fire for about eight hours until it got warm, wearing our jackets inside until then. We were cold but it was so beautiful and romantic, as we cuddled against each other for warmth.

I imagined we would spend the weekend under covers laughing and drinking wine. But he had other plans which did not include me: he was reading his newspapers, one after the other, after waking up, not giving me a single look.

I remembered Ylva saying she could tell that a man was

the right one when they could read newspapers on Sundays without a word. Too bad she had a boyfriend already, or I could have found a new one for her.

I did not take any books with me as I thought I would be busy doing other things which did not involve reading glasses. Luckily the radio was broadcasting shows to entertain me. They interviewed a writer called Karl Ove Knausgård about a book he wrote. From what I understood, the author said that he didn't like people to know about his personal life.

The journalist said that was strange for a man who wrote hundreds of pages about his feelings towards his kids and details of his wife's psychiatric state in three volumes. That was a good point. As the program was going on about the details in the author's life, I got bored and switched channels. On the other channel, NRK P2, there was a show about survivors of gulags in Siberia. This was getting better and better.

I was stuck in a cabin in the middle of the woods with a radio broadcasting Norwegian shows I would love to not understand, a man who would have given me more attention had I been a package of *gamalost*, and no way out as there was only one car that we had to take to Oslo together. I decided to go for a walk, which he approved with a nod of the head.

After my long walk in the knee-high snow I returned. Tor was still reading his newspaper, maybe the fourth or fifth. I was about to commit suicide with anything available. A kitchen hose, a stone or by locking myself into a sauna for 15 hours. I went to bed and he joined me later without me noticing.

The next day he woke up and read the newspapers he had not read the day before, and a book by Knut Hamsun he had brought with him. Such a shame, had I known he would be reading I would have brought the phone book. At least I would have had people to call.

That night, he got some moonshine from his parents' alcohol cabinet. We played cards, with candles illuminating the *hytte*. He dropped his book by Knut Hamsun. I was tempted to throw it in the fire so that he would be all mine for the rest of the weekend. Just as I was winning the card game, he told me,

"Come with me, I want to show you something."

He heated the sauna some hours before. He took off his clothes and went into the sauna. After a few minutes ran outside and rolled himself in the snow laughing. I entered the sauna and did the same. The snow did not feel that cold, just very fresh. It was so silent outside. I could hear every snow-flake reach the bed of snow. We went back inside and he made us very strong coffee, because the alcohol got me completely drunk. Then he looked at me and said:

"I want to paint you. May I?"

Of course you may. As he was painting me, I was imagining myself as the next Mona Lisa. A painting of me done by a very broke but surely talented Norwegian artist. Who said you need to go to Paris when Valdres is just fine. We fell asleep and woke up slightly hungover the next day, having to clean the whole place because his parents would arrive soon. We drove back to Oslo. In silence. With the painting of me in the trunk of the car.

He drove me home and I didn't hear from him for a few days. Eventually he invited me over. As I sat in his room, feeling cold and looking at the cracks in the wall. I asked him where the painting of me was.

"Right over there behind the sofa," he answered.

I took it out. The painting was a bowl of fruits. Bananas and apples.

"This is not me," I said.

"Right. I didn't like the painting of you, so I painted over it. I have to reuse my canvases. They're expensive," he said.

Whaaat? My five minutes of glory were hidden behind a bowl of fruit? You had to be freaking kidding me. I swallowed my pride and pretended to not care. After all, he was the artist. It was not his fault if I was a lousy muse.

That day he asked me whether I wanted to be in a relationship with him. This was some improvement, as it meant commitment from his side, something many Norwegian men seem to have trouble with.

It reminded me of Ante who could not even face IKEA employees who might mistake me for his girlfriend. Tor knew what he wanted, but did I? I had trouble understanding what being in a relationship meant for Norwegian men.

Again, more unwritten rules. In Norway, saying publicly that one is girlfriend and boyfriend is a huge commitment. On the other hand, the rate of Norwegian couples, whether married or in civil partnerships, breaking up or divorcing is as high as elsewhere in European countries. If they can break up when they have kids, how big is a commitment to just say that we are officially in a relationship? It made little sense to me.

"I don't understand what it would change," I answered.

"Not much, I guess. Let's continue as we were doing until now," he said with a smile.

It made me think. Where was this relationship going? I could surely live with the fun guy he was when drunk, but the shy, introverted, extremely silent man he was all the other hours of the day made me doubt my will to commit.

I did not know who the real Tor was. I could not imagine introducing him to my family; the cultural gap would be too big. The more I thought about it and the less I called him. He was not that active in contacting me either, so eventually it became silent on both ends.

Some weeks after our last exchange, I received a book in the post: *Pan* by Knut Hamsun, a story where a lieutenant and a

woman called Edvarda from a small town feel strongly attract-
ed to each other, without understanding the other's love. I was
so proud of myself; I managed to read a book in Norwegian. I
had read books like "When the Robbers Came to Cardamom
Town" or "Karius and Baktus" in Norwegian, but they were
children's books. This time I managed to read a book for adults!

When I told Kaia he sent me *Pan* by mail, she marveled at
how romantic the story was.

"Oh my god! He just declared his love to you!" she said
excitedly.

"Did he?" I asked.

Why are Norwegian love declarations so subtle, I thought?
Where are the flowers and the trips to Prague and the home-
cooked meals?

*Note to self:* I know many French or other non-Scandinavian
men overdo it with the romance and the seduction game. But
I missed the exuberance of how men but also people in general
show emotions outside of Norway. Love, passion, anger,
irritation. I wanted to see movement and life, and here everything felt so even all the time. Was this the sacrifice I had to
make to fit in? Accept a slow and even life with a man who
would show me his love without me even noticing?

# THE LAND OF UNWRITTEN RULES

At first I thought Norwegians felt nothing, at least much less than us Latin people. They always looked so even, never really angry, never really happy. If I asked a friend back home whether she was fine, she could answer anything from "I am doing great!" with a smile to "Awful, you cannot imagine what happened to me." Both were the beginning of a conversation, which could be interesting, sad, funny. In any case, it was a conversation I looked forward to.

In Norway, on the other hand, whatever the question: how is the food? How are you? How was your holiday? The answer was always somewhere along the lines of "*bra*", "*greit nok*" or "*ikke så verst*". (Good, good enough, not too bad). God forbid one shows massive enthusiasm for anything, or major sadness or unhappiness. Even in the Norwegian way of saying "hello": either a wave from far away, or a handshake.

Rarely do Norwegian people get close enough to exchange

germs (like kissing each other on both cheeks for example), whereas French people kiss even those we meet for the first time. Maybe that is why the coronavirus pandemic hit France much harder than Norway? In Norway, keeping a one-meter distance is just called a Monday. Being asked not to touch is not really seen as a social sacrifice, more like a relief.

There were two options here: 1) Norwegians feel less emotions than we do, because alongside a liver made of steel to survive binge drinking they have a heart made of steel to survive long winters alone in a valley. 2) They feel just as much (maybe even more) but keep it all inside. As you have guessed, the second option is closer to reality. The question is why. What are they afraid will happen if they show their emotions?

This could be due to the history of the Norwegian people. Norwegians used to live in small communities scattered over the country with little communication between them. Even where there was transportation across mountains and fjords, communities could easily be cut from the world for weeks or months due to the snow, bad weather, and other issues.

Open conflicts with a neighbor for that matter were a major risk of social exclusion, and social exclusion meant loneliness and potentially poverty or death. Nobody would help you if you were in need of something, like food, building your house, or saving your boat from a storm. The idea is then that Norwegians don't show too much emotion to preserve social peace and ensure survival. They needed community, no matter how small it might have been.

Although this made sense, I didn't believe this was the full picture. Living in a lost valley with more sheep than humans is not a good enough reason to ignore foreigners or be scared of showing one's emotions of sadness or happiness.

Many populations in the world have lived scattered and with little resources, in a hostile environment. Greenland, Siberia or even Finnmark have much rougher weather and are even less populated than Southern Norway. Yet I had rarely met such cold and closed-off people as in that part of Norway. There had to be another reason.

I found that Protestantism and especially a vigorous pietistic movement that came along with its values of frugality, enterprise and personal diligence have influenced Norwegian society more than Norwegians themselves realize. When I brought this up, I was met with counter arguments such as "It's not possible, because Norwegians are not that religious." Sure, the churches might be empty in many areas of Norway, but it did not prevent these religious values from becoming so strong and mainstream that they turned into social values in the Norwegian society.

Think about how the Norwegian government decided to manage the oil money. At the end of the 1960s, Norway discovered substantial oil and gas fields in the North Sea. The booming oil revenue was nationalized, and until now there is a strict limit on how much of it can be spent by the government. The rest is saved to a pension fund for future generations, or for a time of crisis.

This way to manage money is very clearly influenced by Protestant values: sure, we got super rich, but let's continue working hard, let's keep saving taxes. The money will be saved and managed for the good of all, and no elite will benefit from this, but the whole population equally. Can you think of any other country who would have done this with such a tremendous amount of money? Mine would have definitely not managed it like that.

Another argument I have heard is "It cannot be true, remember how Vikings were, proud and unapologetic." I don't know which societal values Vikings had exactly, but what I do know is that today's Norwegians have very little in common with Vikings. Vikings are a people who lived in Scandinavia over 1200 years ago. Recent archeological findings show that "Viking" may have been a job description rather than a matter of heredity. More importantly, many things have happened since then in Scandinavia and in the whole world.

The image of Vikings has become part of a marketing strategy for Scandinavian countries. It doesn't reflect what the people in modern societies are like.

Protestant values and especially pietism put a moral value on emotions, encouraging the feeling of shame when one does not comply with what is expected of diligence, frugality, hard work, and high morals. This is the sign of a suppressed society. Not that Norway is a suppressed society today, but it definitely used to be, and from what I see heavy traces of that past are still there.

It can be very interesting to consider how Norwegians deal with their emotions when they use alcohol. A Norwegian saying goes, *"Sannheten kommer fra fulle menn og barn"* – the truth comes out of the mouths of drunk men and children. In French we just say truth comes out of children's mouths. We don't need to be drunk to speak our minds, but Norwegians do.

The rest of the time it is not acceptable to speak your mind. In a work meeting, one cannot just say, "I disagree with you, this is a bad idea" openly, because that would potentially be the beginning of a conflict. A conflict means risking exclusion, so it is to be avoided at all cost.

This is very challenging for foreigners trying to understand Norwegian people around them. Their partners, their parents-in-law, their colleagues, their bosses. As my neighbour Dagny once told me,

"Norwegians never tell you what you did wrong, and they never forget what you did."

Reading Norwegians' feelings about me, but also conveying my own intentions with accuracy, had been quite a challenge. The problem is that "accuracy" is a very subjective concept when it comes to how other people, whoever they might be, interpret what you mean and how you feel.

I realized that I could easily offend a Norwegian without even meaning to do so, or appear angry when I actually felt calm. Once, maybe one or two months after I started working in Norway, I had an informal meeting with Torbjørn. We had a nice and relaxed chat, without much disagreement. Ylva passed by and overheard our conversation.

"Why are you angry?" she asked.

I was speechless. I wanted to say, "I am not angry. Why would you think that?" I was so surprised by her interpretation of my intentions that I kept silent.

"She is not angry. She is just French," answered Torbjørn. Thank God someone understood me.

"I was being what I thought to be my peaceful self," I told Torbjørn later. "This is the lowest volume I have in store. Do I sound angry even then?" I asked him, very worried.

He just smiled.

"Don't worry, we know you are a foreigner, we don't expect you to follow all our codes," he said.

That was not very comforting.

I learned that even when I spoke calmly (according to my standards, that is) some Norwegians interpreted that as *engasjert*, i.e. you care about something and openly show it. In my world, being this way is not negative. In Norway it is, it means you are too direct, slightly aggressive. All of which can mean being hostile in Norwegian social interactions.

Others seem to confuse two things which are very different: debate and conflict. People not agreeing is seen as the beginning of a conflict, when for me and most French people, a disagreement is the start of an interesting conversation.

How boring would life be if we all agreed on everything, had no dissenting opinions, different taste in food or interior design? Conformity, looking at other people and seeing one-self in the mirror, never made life exciting.

How much of my personality would I have to shed to survive socially and professionally in Norway? I have a tendency to swear. I did not want to transform myself into a pink pony with a glittery tail because some people could not take my di-rectness. It made me reflect on the whole thing even more. From my experience of traveling in Norway, social codes are different depending on where one is in the country. South, north, city, countryside. The supposed culture of not showing emotions is actually quite conservative and what one finds in the south and the east, and the capital. That does not apply to people in the north.

I had not been much to Bergen and the west coast, but it seemed the culture there was also different from the south, and from Oslo. It felt like the place I really felt home was Northern Norway, where locals could stand my directness and laugh at my swearing. And not be offended if I raised my voice because I was *engasjert* in a topic that is important to me.

I put a lot of thought into negative emotions, such as anger, frustration, irritation. How did Norwegians show pos-itive emotions such as love, happiness, appreciation in friend-ship? There, too, it always seemed Norwegians were much more reserved than us southerners. It took me a long time to get used to shaking hands or never getting physically close to someone in Norway.

When I touched someone's arm when talking to them I felt right away I was invading their personal space. I kept it to the usual: shaking hands even with women, waving "*Hei*" from a few meters away. Giving a *klem* to someone I felt close to.

Norwegians showed their emotions in a subtle way. Like Tor. He was very fond of me, but I did not see it. People feeling lonely or depressed might not be so vocal about it, but people feeling happy might not either.

Unless they showed it on their social media, which they did. A lot. It was almost as if they had this urge to tell the world how perfect their life was. Meanwhile I came to work letting everyone know "I am in a bad mood today". Once Ylva laughed when I said that.

"You are funny, a Norwegian person would never do that. But at least you let us know, and we can tease you about it" she said.

"Please do!" I answered.

*Note to self:* Norwegians, especially in Oslo can seem cold and shy as they hide their feelings away. They can do very irritating things such as roll their eyes to the sky like a teenager during a meeting instead of saying out loud, "I don't agree with you. Let's talk about it and move on."

Many will avoid conflicts at all costs, which can become problematic for foreigners who did not even notice there was a conflict in the first place. It is also hard to notice if a Norwegian likes us, unless they are drunk and then the truth might come out. Like at Christmas parties, where it is socially allowed to tell your bosses how you feel about them after everyone has had at least five shots of *aquavit* and later pretend you never said anything. Otherwise the signs can be very subtle.

The key here is to learn Norwegian, I believe, as one starts to understand all the spoken codes, before getting the unspoken ones. Spoken codes: "*Vi sees plutselig*" means the person will not make an effort to meet you again. In a meeting when someone says "*Takk for innspillet, men…*" (Thank you for your input, but…) it means they disagree with you.

Unspoken codes: someone not speaking in a meeting,

crossing their arms and looking at their cup of coffee probably means they have a lot on their mind. A colleague smiling at you every day, asking you how you are, laughing at your jokes definitely appreciates you a lot.

# THE *BRUNOST* BOMB

$I$ had not been home in almost one year. I took ten days off to go visit my family in Marseille. Every other holiday, I wanted to explore Norway, but this time it was time to visit my family during what Norwegians call *romjul(a)*. *Romjula* is "the room/ space between Christmas and New Year's." Another time of the year when everything is closed in Norway as people rarely work.

I brought home lots of typical Norwegian food (at least, food I could travel with) to cook besides the usual Christmas dinner for my whole family. I found *rakfisk*, the trout that Norwegians put in barrels to ferment. *Lomper*, the potato pancakes, *rømme*, the Norwegian crème fraiche. Blueberry-infused *elg-pølse*, dried sausage from Valdres, smoked salmon, *gravlaks*, dried and smoked mackerel.

I had a long list and I ran around town to make sure I had all the food I wanted to bring back. I packed everything in my suitcase. In Gardermoen airport I stopped at the last tourist supermarket and realized I forgot to pack *brunost*. How could I forget to buy *brunost* to bring home?

There were no direct flights from Oslo to Marseille so I had a connecting flight in Frankfurt. I had very short transit time so when I arrived at the last security check in Frankfurt, I felt like I was almost there. But I was stopped by security. The lady made me open all my hand luggage and started shuffling around. "I have nothing that could be problematic here," I thought. "I packed everything in my checked-in luggage" She proudly got out the pack of *brunost* I bought in Oslo airport.

"What is this?" she asked me. So I start laughing – a very bad idea when talking to a German security officer.

"It's cheese!" I answered.

"No, what is this?" she asked again.

"Yes, it is cheese! Norwegian goat cheese," I said.

"Goat cheese?" she said, looking very skeptical. "It does not look like cheese," she added.

"Tell me about it!" As I was about to tell her all about the food misery I faced in Norway, she called the other security officers. A smiling security officer took the pack and asked me again what it was.

"This is Norwegian cheese. I bought it in Oslo. I have the receipt if you want to double check," I answered, laughing less, looking at my watch more. I had to board my flight.

"No, that won't be necessary. If this is cheese, then would you eat this?" he asked.

"Yes… but…" But it's a gift and I don't want to open it, I wanted to say. But that would have sounded suspicious.

At this stage there was no point in saying that I'd rather leave the *brunost* and run for my plane, because they had started pressing the pack and some brown paste oozed out. It was mushy after spending three hours in my bag, so it now qualified as an explosive according to German authorities.

They asked me again and again, and I kept explaining that it is sweet, and yes brown, look it's written on the package: in Norwegian *"ost"* means "cheese."

They brought me and my cheese to another guy with a big machine. He asked me one very last time, very seriously: "So you say this is cheese?" He put it in the machine and gave it back to me after some time, and let me go with a smile. "Have a nice flight." Yes, it was cheese. But I nearly missed my flight home.

I was so happy to be in Marseille. Provence, my home. The sun was shining, which was a considerable improvement for my quality of life. I could actually see the sun more than a few hours per day, and it was shining. And it was 16 °C (60 °F). In December.

"Why did I even leave this country?" is the question I asked myself during the first 24 hours of my stay. I did not need a winter jacket. I did not need gloves. Nobody was running or skiing outside like maniacs, making me feel bad about myself. I did not need to think before speaking, nobody was laughing at my strange way of pronouncing words.

French is my native language, and I could express everything I needed to say, even the nuances. I understood all the social and cultural cues of the people around me. I could disagree and engage in a debate and nobody would think I was angry unless I was. I could enter a shop and find 15 types of cheese, none of which were "mild." Wine was available in any tiny supermarket. I could buy it at almost any time of day and even at night.

After 24 hours, I ran into some complications. Norway had influenced me a little more than I thought.

"Why do we eat so late?" I asked my mum. "I'm so hungry."

"We will cook dinner later," she answered.

"Later? But it's 6pm. I will start cooking right now." I said.

"We will eat around 9pm when your dad comes back from work. Even if you start cooking now it won't make us eat earlier," she said.

After two days I got sick. I was eating so much cheese and hefty portions of everything because I missed food from home. The first evening I ate 40 snails. The second day at lunch I ate three slices of cake, after a beef bourguignon and a seafood *entrée*. I felt nauseous and had a continuous stomach ache, like a big stone was stuck in there. I had to stop eating for a few days.

I missed eating oatmeal and fruit for breakfast. I ate that every morning in Norway. Unlike Norway where oats are found in any supermarket, in France only organic shops sell it. To add to my misery, none of my friends from home (or my family) understood why I moved to Norway. I had to explain myself all the time.

"Soooo aren't Norwegians cold?" asked my aunt.

"No, I made some good friends," I answered.

"But it's freezing up there, right? And snowy all the time?" added my uncle.

"Yeah, we live in igloos, I have a pet reindeer. We go to work on skis. The usual stuff," is what I wanted to answer.

Instead I had to be polite and repeat the same thing I repeated to everyone.

I was not the only one to be surprised. My parents were quite shocked at my new attitude. I was lighting candles when night came, letting the tap water run for a long time to get cold water, and leaving all the lights on in rooms around the house.

"This is not the Versailles," said my dad. "When did you start wasting energy like that?"

"In Norway we like our drinking water really cold, and we leave the lights on because electricity is renewable and quite cheap."

I was infected by Norwegian norms relating to children's rights, the condemnation of arrogance, and gender equality. In France, those three ideas are unpopular, and I was the weird one for promoting them.

In Norway it is not an unwritten rule that children need to be protected from physical violence, it is embedded in the law. Hitting a child is a crime that can cause you to lose custody of your own child, and potentially go to jail.

When I saw my cousin slap her child and scream at her, I almost had a heart attack. I went up to her and told her this is not a way to treat children.

"Hey, this is called discipline. We need to tell him who is the boss, otherwise he will not function well in society. What do you know about raising children anyway? You don't have any of your own," she said.

"Well, yes, but in Norway... we don't hit children," I answered.

"Yes, but we're not in Norway. We're in France," she said. "Your mum told me that they keep babies outside alone in the cold. So isn't that worse than a slap on the bum?" said my cousin.

*Note to self:* going "home" can be harder than you think when living abroad. It can mean having to deal with conflicting values; those you were raised with and those of your new host country. My experience is that living abroad makes us cultural hybrids. I was myself becoming more and more Norwegian, yet always a foreigner in Norway with my French accent.

# JANTE'S LAW

There were so many issues where I disagreed on with my fellow Frenchmen. People feeling superior, making patronizing comments to others and saying things such as "*trop bon, trop con*" were offending me more and more (a French saying which translates to "nice people are idiots"). I could never stand arrogance, even when I was living here, but after one year in Norway it became unbearable. I just did not understand how making others feel inferior either in terms of intelligence, wealth or anything else made anyone's life better.

Last time you thought someone was smart, was it because the person told you or because you found out on your own? If one is so smart, one does not need to brag about it. Other people will notice.

The problem is that in French culture people can feel elevated by pushing other people down, pretending they are more intelligent, have more knowledge and culture and so on.

It is about winning a debate, usually by quoting a dead philosopher or showing off one's superficial knowledge in one way or another. Among friends and family I was seen as dumb if I answered "I don't know" to a question I was asked about something. In France, I should have made something up and looked at the person who asked as if they were the biggest idiot on the planet.

After one year in Norway, I was not going to do that. Sure, being humble or nice might make people think I am stupid, but it turns out I did not really care what people thought of me.

When I told friends in France that I was happy to pay taxes, which paid for schools and teachers and hospitals, and that I often called the Norwegian tax authorities to make sure I did not make a mistake in my declaration, people exploded in laughter. "

Are you kidding?"

"No, I am not kidding," I would reply. "I also get a refund from the tax authorities if I paid too much. Without having to ask for it."

"Suuuure," they would answer. "And I live in Disneyworld with you and the other teddy bears," one answered.

The mistrust in the ruling elite is so important in French culture that talking about such common things in Norway seems surreal.

In Norway, on the other hand, it is socially encouraged to be humble. Being humble and nice and honest gives you brownie points in society and gains you respect. If you are extremely intelligent, giving back to society is even more respected. If you are very rich, same thing: you need to give back. Olav Thon, the hotel mogul, is an exemplary citizen in Norway. Not because he is so rich, but because he pays every penny of his taxes (as far as I know), and continues to wear the same old red hat, drive the same old car, eat the same lunch made of bread and *makrell i tomat*, and is married to the same woman. He is a man of the people, despite his success.

On the other hand, a professional skier like Petter Northug who won a lot of competitions but is extremely arrogant (at least by Norwegian standards), annoys a lot of people with his behavior. Can you imagine that the King of Norway himself is not above that social rule of being humble? The current King's father, King Olav V, even took the tramway to Holmenkollen with his skis in 1973 in order to inspire the people.

At the time, there was an energy crisis, and the Norwegian people were advised not to use their cars, so he took public transportation, and a picture was taken of him trying to pay for his ticket. I imagine the political elite of my own country. Ministers don't even take the bus, so what would a French King do if we still had one? Maybe that's why we don't have one anymore?

I remember Danes saying that Norwegians are very naïve. Maybe they are, but isn't it relaxing to live in a country where people are humble and trusting? The answer from my side is yes. I learned that one of the worst things one can do in Norway is not to make a mistake. It is accepted that we are humans, and that we make mistakes, even big ones.

It is important to admit our mistakes, even publicly. Sometimes even before they are found out. The worst thing one can do is lie. To break the trust people and society has put on you is the worst thing one can do in Norway. This is probably also because of the Protestant values.

There is something much written and talked about in Scandinavia called *Janteloven* or the Law of Jante. It comes from a book by Aksel Sandemose called *A Fugitive Crosses His Tracks*, where one follows the story of a young boy living in the fictional town of Jante.

Danes and Norwegians fight over whether Jante is in fact in Denmark or in Norway, and whether Sandemose is from one country or the other, because when the novel was written Norway was under the Danish crown.

When people talk about *Janteloven* they usually refer to the ten "commandments" written in this book, which are often referred to in articles and books about Scandinavia:

1. You're not to think you are anything special.
2. You're not to think you are as good as we are.
3. You're not to think you are smarter than we are.
4. You're not to imagine yourself better than we are.
5. You're not to think you know more than we do.
6. You're not to think you are more important than we are.
7. You're not to think you are good at anything.
8. You're not to laugh at us.
9. You're not to think anyone cares about you.
10. You're not to think you can teach us anything.

There is in fact one more commandment in the Law of Jante, which appears a few chapters before this list:

11. You are not to drink alcohol, which is, according to the author, the most important commandment of the Law of Jante.

Many believe *Janteloven* reflects the importance of equality in Scandinavian societies; others say it explains the social pressure to be humble and never believe you are better than others. Or that it forces all to blend in.

I have heard stories of Norwegians waiting decades to paint their house, because as long as the neighbor has not done it, it was socially forbidden. On the day one person on that street paints it, all the neighbors would follow. The social pressure is real in the book and in the reality of modern Norway, but are Norwegians always defending equality, and fighting arrogance?

The reality is that Norwegians aren't always humble. They aren't always equal either. Sometimes they brag, but in their own way. Norwegians brag indirectly by saying where they went on holidays, how much they spent on their property, or how many miles one skied over the weekend. Many people show subtle signs of wealth and success such as an expensive car or a house in a posh area.

Since everyone has access to every other person's tax report and can see the price that properties were sold for, it is not hard to know how much your colleague earns. A super brag is to say that one has qualified for this or that skiing or cycling race. There is a ranking of those that will give you more social status points, especially in the Norwegian elite class, such as Birkebeiner and Marcialonga races.

If you live here long enough, you might realize that Norwegians can be arrogant when talking about their own culture compared to others. A study by the Pew Research Center in 2018 showed that Norwegians are those who most believe that their culture is superior over others.

As a foreigner, one can hear things like "Norwegian hospitals are the best in the world" or "the Norwegian school system is the best" until you wonder with irony how people survived and thrived outside of Norway, following a whole other set of rules and cultural norms.

A scandal a few years ago was quite representative of that, when a Norwegian skier tested positive for steroids and blamed a lip balm from an Italian pharmacy. The status quo was, of course, that Italian medicine does not indicate whether there are steroids in a cream, and how the opposite story – if an Italian skier blamed a Norwegian medicine – would have scandalized the whole of Norway. Of course, Norwegians do everything right, so that situation was impossible.

Do you remember Brynjulf? He told me he could ski, as if he had skied a bit in his life and could maybe teach me the few things he learned that one winter. After Googling him I realized he was in fact in the top 15 best skiers in Norway when he was in his 20s. A French person with this track record would brag about that early in a conversation, whereas he did not even mention it. Many Norwegians are, in fact, extremely humble.

In terms of equality, Oslo is a perfect example of an unequal world. The difference in life expectancy between the east and the west of Oslo is ten years. Reasons are differences in wealth, standard of living etc. Similar differences can be found between Oslo and the other regions such as Northern Norway.

*Note to self:* Whatever inequalities and arrogance could be found in Norway, it was nothing compared to what I was used to in France. Not all French people, of course, but enough to be quite irritating, especially when those arrogant people are your bosses.

I found that the worst cultural divide between Norway and France was about women's place in society.

The general discourse about women in France drove me crazy. I forgot how bad it was, and coming back home after living in Norway was a cultural shock.

I saw my own patriarchal society from the outside. The paroxysm of this misogyny came to life during a New Year's Eve party I attended at the home of my childhood friend, Natacha.

# BEING A WOMAN IN NORWAY

"This year my colleague did something really bitchy to us: she got pregnant," said the guy sitting across the dinner table.

I nearly choked on a slice of camembert. I had never heard such negative comments associated with pregnancy.

"She left for three months on maternity leave. I mean, seriously! And then you wonder why companies don't want to hire women in their 30s."

This did not seem to shock anyone around the dinner table, including a guy with his baby son in his arms and my friend who was eight months pregnant.

"She just leaves us like that, and then what are we supposed to do?" he asked everyone.

I suggested a shy, "Replace her until she comes back?" (I know, I have such revolutionary ideas sometimes). I added that in my Norwegian office, at least one person went on parental leave every year, and for much more than three months.

The person was replaced and came back after the leave and everything went quite smoothly.

As both women and men take parental leave in Norway, employers can't think while hiring someone that women are more likely to take leave as both parents will take one anyway. This sounded very foreign, and not at all a practical solution for him.

"But it takes time and resources to replace someone," the guy added. "She should have warned us that she was trying to get pregnant so we would have time to plan for this. It was quite unprofessional of her."

I could only imagine the solution to this "unprofessionalism": an update at staff meetings where women report on a monthly basis whether they are planning on getting pregnant, the date of their last periods, and an ultrasound picture if necessary. Now it was my turn to say… seriously?

At the time I moved to Norway, it seemed to me that the general assumption across the whole world was that men are sex addicts. They have "sexual needs" that women don't have. This was often used to justify men harassing and catcalling women in the streets, at least in most countries I had lived in. It also made it acceptable for male colleagues and leaders to make sexual and degrading comments about a female colleague's outfit, make-up (or lack of).

Strangely enough, in Norway no one seemed to accept such attitudes, whether it was in the street, at work, or in politics. Men actually respected women, and those who didn't faced social if not legal consequences.

Colleagues looked me in the eyes, not the breasts, and female co-workers were considered equals, not coffee-bringing photocopiers. On my first day at work at my Norwegian job, my boss Bjørn even asked for my opinion. As it was the first time in my working life that had happened, I looked around to make sure he was actually talking to me.

When I went out in Oslo, I didn't choose what to wear based on whether I would walk home alone. Sexism stopped colonizing my everyday thoughts.

Of course, most French or other non-Scandinavian men respect women, but sexism still seems socially accepted to the point where it can become unbearable. Women weren't always criticizing this situation. Like my friend who was eight months pregnant, at the same dinner, who thought it was a normal reaction for her employer not to renew her contract when learning about her pregnancy.

Anti-discrimination laws exist in France too, but are rarely followed, and sexist comments are "jokes" that women like me don't laugh at because we "lack a sense of humor".

I knew things weren't perfect here either. There was also sexism in Norway, as well as rape and domestic violence. I learned that the majority of business leaders in Norway were still men despite women reaching leadership positions.

The situation however seemed very different.

In Norway gender equality was a debate, something people and politicians talked about and tried to improve. While in France it was a non-issue.

"There are more pressing problems in France now than women's issues, like unemployment," I was often told.

No matter how much I loved my country, I realized I was not ready to leave the joys of being a woman in Norway for any lower equality standard. That probably meant I could never move back to my home country. I was not sure what happened here that turned Vikings into champions for equality, but it sounded good to me.

Even though Norway was still far from perfect equality, I was ready to settle for that, as it was the best one could find.

After a week in France, I was counting the days until my

return to Norway. I could not wait to go home. To Norway.

That day came, eventually. As I packed my bags, my dad brought me the *brunost*, almost untouched, and said:

"Lorelou, you might as well take this with you. No one here will eat it."

So much for risking my life to expose my family to Norwegian delicacies.

"And don't become too Norwegian," he added.

"Remember to drink red wine, swear at people in traffic, and eat proper dinners which don't involve too much of that crunchy bread you've gotten used to eating," he said while hugging me.

My dad was right.

I had no intention of liking the Norwegian way of life in the first place. But Norway became my home and, strangely enough, Norwegians became my people. I felt closer to them than to my fellow Frenchmen. How was that possible when my Norwegian language skills weren't perfect, and after only one year? Maybe it was destiny?

*Note to self:* equality is a funny game. Being a young woman I always imagined this was just how my life had to be. Fighting to speak in a room full of men.

Proving my experience, my expertise at work.

Thinking of what to wear and trying to avoid being noticed by men in the street.

Once you get a taste at gender equality, and respect, there is no going back. Even if winters are long and dark, it is worth it.

# HOME IS WHERE THE HEART IS

My last stop before going back to Norway was Paris. I visited my grandmother to grab some of the things I did not manage to take to Norway the first time. My grandmother had given up driving in Paris a long time ago, so I met her downstairs from her apartment. With much lighter luggage than the last time I saw her. The Norwegian goodies I had brought home to Marseille had been eaten and drunk. I did have a few things up my sleeves for her though.

She squeezed me in her arms and said

"You look pale. Are you sick? Have you been eating enough in Norway?"

"Yes *mamie*, I am well. I am probably pale because there isn't much sunlight these days up north," I answered warmly.

I sat comfortably in her living room while she fetched some tea and a cake she had baked for the occasion.

"Tell me everything, *chérie*."

I talked to her on the phone but she wanted more details.

"Have you met a man? You know I'd prefer you to meet a French man, so that you can come back to live here," she said.

"Everything's better when you are close to family."

Was it, though?

"No, no man worth talking about," I answered.

"But I have met wonderful friends. And I love my job. They treat me well, I get very interesting projects, I travel," I said.

"They even raised my salary."

My grandmother was thinking, with her cup in her hand. She knew her opinion was important to me, even though we came from such different generations. She was born in 1930 and was nine years old when World War II started. She remembered everything. She married at the age of 20, which was old for marriage at that time. By 28, she had five children. Needless to say, I was behind schedule. I was 28, childless, with no ring on my finger.

"You know what the most important thing is in a woman's life?" she asked.

I stayed silent. I was expecting a long speech about the importance of children, family, commitment, and traditions, but my grandmother surprised me.

"To earn your own money. To be independent. This way you will always have a choice," she said.

"My generation of women did not have a choice. We married a man we thought we liked, without really knowing them, and then if we argued or wanted to leave, we were stuck. You have an amazing chance here at living your life on your terms and deciding what is best for you."

I was astonished.

"But I don't understand why you have to do that in Norway. Is it that good there?" she asked.

I told her about the progressive labor law, gender equality

at work, flexible working hours and respect for young women.

"Sure, they eat strange things, and they can seem unfriendly when one does not know better, but it is a good place to live. It is peaceful," I said.

"I know how hard it is for your generation to get a decent job in France. I understand why you want to stay there" she answered.

"Just come back to visit me once in a while. I miss you."

"*Mamie*, one more thing. I think I am going to buy an apartment. Alone."

She was amazed. A woman alone, working, was able to buy a flat on her own.

"I am so proud of you," she said.

"Just make sure you are not too independent, otherwise you will scare men away. Just pretend sometimes that you need them, ok? Otherwise, you'll end up like Aunt Lydia with her five guinea pigs and her endless monologues about the colors of a modern living room according to the magazine *Femme Actuelle*."

Here we go, the enlightened feminist grandmother had disappeared.

She took my hand.

"Now tell me all about the food, and the men."

I told her everything. About the food, Norway has more than potatoes, I told her. They have sheep and trout and reindeer and really good cheese from a place called Røros. I told her about Taco Friday, the sheep's head, and the Grandiosa pizza. She laughed at my failed love stories and suffered with me when I told her about the sweat and the tears I shed while cycling to Southern Norway.

"Tell me about the northern lights. Did you know nobody in our family has ever been this far north?"

I was an adventurer in the eyes of this small woman who

loved me and wanted me close as much as she wanted me to succeed.

A week later, I left her, this time with all my belongings. The flight from Paris to Oslo was not that surprising anymore. I was accustomed to the tall people dressed in the same brands at the airport in the line for the Oslo flight. I didn't need anybody's help to lift my suitcase, and managed to chat with my neighbor in Norwegian about banalities Norwegians love to discuss. When we flew over Jutland beaches up to Oslo it was still light outside. I admired the beautiful virgin landscapes of snowy forests and lakes.

We landed in Oslo Gardermoen airport, it was 3pm and it was getting dark. The snow was wet, falling on the tarmac and illuminated by the airport's strong artificial lights. Although for most people this seemed uninviting, the one thing I felt is *I am home.*

I left the plane in silence and passed by the Norwegians from my flight throwing themselves at the duty-free wine as if it were their last chance to buy alcohol, my luggage filled with my uncle's wine. I wasn't that Norwegian yet.

# EPILOGUE

Not long after this first year in Norway, I started a blog called *A Frog in the Fjord*, www.afroginthefjord.com. My goal back then was to vent my frustrations and challenges in understanding Norwegian culture and learning Norwegian language.

To my great surprise, some of my blog posts went viral in Norway and the United States. I was writing my blog anonymously and I was afraid that revealing my name would affect my professional life. I was writing about my failed relationships and how weird Norwegians were, it could only make me look unprofessional in my day job, I thought.

I was wrong, and once I started writing using my real name, many opportunities came along. Norway's most popular newspapers and media outlets asked me to write articles for them, from Aftenposten and VG to NRK. I was offered to be a columnist in VG *(Verdens Gang)*, Norway's largest newspaper, and have been doing so since 2014. I write about Norwegian culture and society with a foreigner's perspective.

In 2017 I published a book with Norway's well-known publishing house, Cappelen Damm. It is called "En frosk i fjorden- Kunsten å være norsk" (A Frog in the Fjord, The Art of Being Norwegian). It was briefly one of the top ten bestselling books in Norway, and is still being sold, read, downloaded and listened to.

I was invited to talk shows and had to speak Norwegian live in front of hundreds of thousands of people and be that funny French girl. Those were some of the scariest moments. Now that Norway and Scandinavia have become trendier, I am interviewed by international media like CNN and Elle magazine about typical Norwegian concepts like *koselig* and *friluftsliv*. I am also holding courses for universities and companies to help their foreign employees understand the Norwegian working culture.

All these years I have kept my job in human rights and the environment and have worked for organisations such as WWF Norway and now for the Norwegian government.

Despite my initial plan to stay in Norway for only a couple of years, I never left it, not for France or any other country. I lived in Jahn Teigen's rehearsing studio for five years. I realized this temporary stay in Norway was looking more and more permanent, so I eventually bought an apartment.

I still live in Oslo, now with my husband and our baby. I am enjoying the perks of motherhood in Norway, which has given me the opportunity to discover a whole new aspect of the quirkiness of Norwegian culture.

I still cannot ski, but I have learned to like *brunost*, but only when served on warm Norwegian waffles.

Surprisingly, or maybe unsurprisingly, I married a foreigner, who has also been living in Norway for a while. He is from

Romania. I guess love with a local wasn't for me.

I am still friends with Kaia and the girls from Saint Halvard's Choir but have lost contact with Tor and Ante. I don't see Ramu much but we still have some contact. I still meet Nina every time I am in Tromsø, as well as Carina when I am in the Lofoten Islands. Roar, my contact in Porsgrunn, became a dear friend and we often spend holidays together.

At the time of this book's second revision I received the confirmation that the Norwegian authorities have granted me the Norwegian citizenship.

All I need now is a *bunad* to walk around the streets of my city on the 17th of May like a real Norwegian!

# THANK YOU

I would like to thank Ionuț Burchi for taking care of our home and family so that I could finish this book, and for his unfailing support when I doubted myself, Hans Petter Sjøli for giving me a chance in VG, Scott Remborg for his unfailing support in my art, David Nikel for his precious advice, Ampy Basa for her support and positivity, Ole Johnny Hansen for his sense of humor and talent that both inspire me, Sebastien Hogan for promising to be my driver once I make it, Kine Hilmo Dybdalsbakk for taking me on my first *hyttetur*, Sverre Bjørstad Graff for his humor and friendship, Annette Katherine Mohr for laughing at my jokes, Joakim Moen Tønseth for cooking French meals and teaching me Norwegian slang.

Ayesha Wolasmal for being who she is, Fritjof, Ellinor, Torbjørn, and Lotte Katborg Grønning for the warmth of their lovely *hjorteborgen*, Anja Veum and Brynjar Skjærli for sharing their insider's view on Norwegians, Sebastin Britto and his goat, Sankt Halvards *pikekor*, Kingsford Siayor for trusting me with pieces of his life story, Ariane Bouchardy Gauthier for her support all the way from Montréal, Tori Lind Kjellstad for her creativity and humor, Fosia Mohamed Hansen for her warmth, Øyvind Eggen for his support and his laughter, Lucie and Thomas Bassetto for being there through thick and thin, my uncle Pierre Mrejen, Rune Paulsen for his friendship full of humor, Unni Delgado for teaching me Norwegian, Lotte Havemann - my Danish nanny, Kajsa Kemi Gjerpe for showing me the Sami way, Carina, Egil, Joppe and Liuda for being my family in Tromsø.

A special thank you to Øyvind Bryde for his great taste in music, his parties, and his friendship which I will miss forever.

My colleagues and friends from Rainforest Foundation Norway who patiently explained the Norwegian way to me in the first years of my journey: Anja Lyngsmark, Geir Erichsrud, Vemund Olsen, Anja Lillegraven, Nils Hermann Ranum, Lionel Diss, Kamilla Berggrav, Ann-Kristin Berg, Britta Ødegaard, Lars Løvold and Yngve Kristiansen.

My parents Catherine and Denis, and my siblings Grégoire, Marielle, and Chani Desjardins.

My dearest grandmother Arlette Mrejen.

The three little Norwegian trolls in my life: Joan, Erik and Isak.

And all the readers of my blog afroginthefjord.com

Made in the USA
Monee, IL
24 December 2024

75337145R00177